P9-CRP-164

TOM MIX
DIED FOR
YOUR SINS

DARRYL PONICSAN

TOM MIX DIED FOR YOUR SINS

A NOVEL BASED ON HIS LIFE

DELACORTE PRESS/NEW YORK

Copyright © 1975 by Darryl Ponicsan

Library of Congress Cataloging in Publication Data

Ponicsan, Darryl.
Tom Mix died for your sins.

1. Mix, Tom, 1880–1940—Fiction.   I. Title.
PZ4.P797To [PS3566.o6]   813'.5'4   75–15555
ISBN 0–440–05969–0

TO DYLAN

Illustrations follow pages 91, 187, and 271.

When double pneumonia orphaned me in '99, near Bandera, Texas, the town that gave me my name, our little spread went into the hands of strangers. Ain't that always the way with poor folks? I set off on my own, never willing to stay one place for long. Like that, by the time I was twenty, in 1904, I hadn't missed a whole lot, but I never did see the equal to what led the Oklahoma Cavalry Band down the street to the opening of the St. Louis World's Fair.

Clean-shaven and dark he was, and his eyes deep as doom, a man so thoroughly convinced of himself he probably could of flew. He was five foot and ten inches tall, an inch over me, though we likely weighed in the same. He was narrow at the hips, and appeared to be fit. His smile, offered judiciously to the palpitating lovelies along the sidelines, brightened a day that was already a skull-splitting shadowless glare. The boys and me had been all night raising hell and pissing underneath it. We would have said thanks to a bushwhacker.

This feller strut like his daddy just bought him that 72-man band marching behind him as a birthday contraption. If it'd rained, he'd a'drowned. "Hey, your feet stink?" yelled Buck Matson, figuring that was the reason he carried his nose so high.

He wore a dark blue velvet coat with tails, trimmed with white lace and gold braid. On his head was a fuzz-covered hat a foot and a half high, with a glossy black visor and a strap like to pull his chin off. He wore black striped pants tucked into the gaudiest pair of boots I ever did see. He carried in his hand a silver stick as tall as he was, for to keep cadence with. There was a silver whistle clamped betwixt his teeth in case he needed to get somebody's attention, though seemed like he already had it.

I was there with Colonel Zack Mulhall's Wild West Show. We was to put on a show and rodeo that afternoon. We'd been wetting our noses most all the night and thought the thing we follied along the parade route was only one more vision conjured up by Old Tangleleg. There was Buck and me and Will Rogers and Terrence O'Hara and T. W. Brown, and we follied him right to the trickling away part, half expecting they would pack him up in straw and send him back to Oklahoma City. Needless to say, we got in a fair amount of verbal abuse along the way.

At parade's end, he took off his fancy coat and his outrageous hat and handed over his whistle and his stick to the bandmaster and drew his pay.

The bandmaster mentioned another date they had in three days and said he wanted him if he was free.

Seems this bird was a free-lance traveling drum major. Add that to your list of little-known ways to make a buck.

"Ain'tcha gonna take off the drawers?" yelled one of us. It was Terry O'Hara, he had the sense of humor. "We got us a bet going."

Well, that drum major put his pay in his pocket and walked over to us like we were on his way anyhow and the next thing I know Terry is asleep in the dust. I never seen the punch. I put in play all I knew about the manly art: that is, I lowered my head and charged him. I took one on the ear that started a ringing that ain't fully ceased even after seventy years. I can be sitting, perusing a newspaper maybe, and all of a sudden my left ear will start ringing like the sirens of hell, and I remember all over again the first time I met Tom Mix.

Most folks think the expression "seeing stars" is a figure of speech, but I can testify that's what was actually before my eyes, stars and Buck Matson flying through the air. T. W. Brown then stuck his hands in his pockets and started walking away, quick step, whistling a little tune. The drum major took the few steps toward Will, the only one of us left there on our feet. Terry and Buck was unconscious and I was being real hesitant about getting up. Will's turn, I thought. But he put on that embarrassed grin of his and stuck out his hand. "Will Rogers," he said.

The other studied it for a spell, cautious-like. "Tom Mix," he finally said, taking the offered hand.

"Any Indian in you, Tom?"

"Quarter-worth. Cherokee."

"I thought as much."

They had to shake hands all over again now that they was members of the same tribe.

"Where you from?" asked Will.

"El Paso."

Well, he might of been an Injun, but he sure wasn't a Texan. My guess was he wanted to be. I had run into other easterners who harbored the same desire.

It looked safe for us to get up, so we did, brushing ourselves off and trying to get together what dignity we could. We ambled over and Will said, "Meet Terry O'Hara and Buck Matson here, and this one we call Kid Bandera." Terry O'Hara stuck out his hand like it was a dead fish and said, "Chormed." Terry was one of those guys who don't learn from past mistakes. I shook his hand with the proper respect you give a feller who almost knocked your brains out your ear. "That was a dumb thing, what you did," said Tom Mix to me. I hated him, but I was in no mood to argue. "You shoulda kept your left up like

[3]

this," he said, dancing on the balls of his feet, "to ward off blows. Then feign a punch . . ." Which he did, sending me for cover. ". . . And let him have it with the right." Which he did, a playful slap on my face. I took it and made up my mind to have seconds of him someday, I didn't care if he had made a study of it. I reckoned he had.

He and Will, the two Cherokees, hit it off pretty good and he hung around with us right up to showtime. He was drifting along, he told us, taking odd jobs as a drum major, bartending, whatever he could get until he could sign on somewhere as a cowboy. The year before, he married up with a schoolteacher, and he taught physical fitness and sports to the boys in her school. As long as she had a job, so did he, but according to Tom her father talked her into annulling the marriage and going back home to Kentucky. He didn't want her married to no cowboy was Tom's story.

Far as I could see, the girl's father had no cause for complaint, for Tom Mix did not know horseshit from tennis balls. I pegged him for a dude first minute I laid eyes on him, confirmed as soon as he opened his mouth. He could have passed for an Okie, having almost mastered the drawl, but my guess was he hadn't been west for long.

There was a peculiar shiftiness in his eyes that made me think there might have been a poster out on him, but most of the crowd I knew, myself included, had a couple of jurisdictions to stay out of.

He leaned against the top rail with us, watching the events. Will was the rodeo clown and was out there in his baggy pants and derby hat and big round red nose. It was all old stuff to us but Tom was like a mule in mud and his excitement got kind of infectious. Then something happened that sure wasn't on the program.

During the steer roping event a steer shucked the lasso off one horn and jumped right over the fence like he was a trick pony instead of a ton of beef behind two horns. He took off up the aisle of the grandstand, tripping up the steps, amidst a fair amount of screaming from the spectators, who moved like two waves of water in opposite directions.

Good night, I thought, that steer's going to take out some ordinary folks. A cowboy's entitled to the risk of being gored or stepped upon, but a spectator is what you'd call an innocent party.

Will grabbed a rope, jumped the wall, and run after him. Now, Will was not a rodeo cowboy as such, for he was nothing if not sensible, but no man ever put a better hand to a rope than him. He lassoed the critter first try from a fair distance. We was across the ring and of no use, but other cowboys got to help him and in no time they had that steer hobbled. Will, playing the clown again, pulled him by the tail back to the ground.

"Willy," said the announcer, "whatcha doing with that animal?"

"He can't sit up here," answered Will, "he don't have a ticket."

Well, the crowd went wild. Will come running over to us and said, "Figure we can make this happen at Madison Square Garden? Those New Yorkers will wet their drawers."

A little girl of fourteen come hopping on the rail next to Tom. "Oh, Will," she cried, "I was scared to death." Then she looked at Tom and smiled, indicating the real purpose of her visit.

"Olive Stokes," said Will, "may I introduce Tom Mix."

"You certainly may," she said. "I saw you leading the band today, Mr. Mix."

Will ran back to his clowning chores, leaving Tom to deal with little Olive. He bored him a small hole with his heel and finally said, "That ain't my regular line of work, missy."

I knew Olive just as one of the kids that always hung around the cowboys. I'd seen her before at shows and rodeos and she was quite the little cowgirl in her own right. Her family had a ranch in Oklahoma.

"Well, you sure did a wonderful job of it," she said.

He commenced then to describe the action in the ring, as though she didn't know more about it than him. She went along with him and played little girl dumb, but I reckon she was the only one amongst us who had the glimmer of an idea that in four years' time she'd be married to Tom, and I don't believe even she could of guessed that a short spell after that she'd have him pinned down with her Winchester 30–30 hoping to put a bullet up his ass.

I grew a bit hot listening to his blather, for he was criticizing the rides. Cowboys don't have a critical nature, as I reckon one mountaineer finds it hard to criticize another once he's traveled the same rough trail, yet here was this bird, who as far as I knew spent his days courting nothing more dangerous than dressing up funny and blowing a silver whistle, setting in judgment on riders who when they pass blood are apt to say casually, "Looks like I'm pissin' red again."

My ride was coming up and I was so sure of what he'd be saying to Olive about it I had no stomach for my turn. Don't get me wrong, partner, I was twenty years old and eager for the best, but when you got a heckler on the sidelines it throws you off your game, I don't care what your game is or how good you are at it.

You're going to laugh, for the mount I drew was called Widder Maker, but the truth is that at practically every rodeo I ever rode there was always some bronc called Widder Maker, and this time he was mine. But I was not afraid of him. The cowboys have a saying: There ain't a horse that can't be rode or a man that can't be throwed. It keeps us both hopeful and humble.

I had been looking forward to riding old Widder Maker and collecting the fifty dollars prize money for best ride, but Tom had got so on my nerves I turned to him and said, "Look here, if you know so much about it, why don't you ride in my place? Nag called Widder Maker."

I was betting that the last leather on his ass was his daddy's belt.

[6]

He couldn't drop the bait without belittling himself in front of Olive and the guys. I had him where I wanted him.

He looked at me mystified and said, "You don't mind?"

"Sure I mind," I said, "but you talk like you know horses, so I thought I'd give you the chance to show us."

"I do know horses," he said, "if it's the only thing I know."

"Well, you can have Widder Maker."

Then he threw me off again just like he did when he feigned the punch, for I expected him to find a dozen excuses for not riding that day. I expected he might have a stomachache or a bad back or a pressing engagement in another city. Instead he broke into a wide smile and pumped my hand and said, "Gee, thanks, Kid."

We went and made the substitution and I went back to stand with Olive and some of the fellers. I was starting to feel pretty low, wondering whether the dude would come away from this a dead one.

The announcer said, "Riding in place of Kid Bandera, on Widder Maker, Mr. Tom Mix of Oklahoma City."

The gate opened and out come this black beast with a belly-ful of bedsprings. He put down his head and come straight up, twitching his rump eight feet off the ground. He changed ends and went up in the air again, this time reaching back for a bite out of his rider's leg. And that crazy drum major was fanning him with his hat and digging his spurs in him every time he hit the ground!

"Isn't he beautiful!" screamed little Olive, and naturally I figured she was talking about the horse.

Tom flew at seven seconds, and to be honest with you I'd have to give him two seconds over what I might have done on that outlaw.

"Lay flat, Tom!" I yelled, and he did, offering as small a target as he could. Only trouble was he stayed flat.

I ran out with a couple of others, thinking how bad I was going to feel if he was a goner. We slapped him to and his first words were, "How long?"

[7]

"Seven seconds," I said.

"I know I can do ten."

We helped him to his feet and I walked him off to a good round of applause. He looked behind him to the noise coming from the crowd. It warmed him considerable. I noticed his left arm was dangling at his side.

"Hurt your arm?" I asked.

"Broke it," he said, smiling.

2

Since I felt partly responsible for Tom's injurious arm, I went
with him to the bone cracker. He fortified himself with a few
hard drinks, and not to have him drink alone I had a few too.
I recollect the bone cracker having a few himself, so that by
the time that arm was set and cemented none of us was feeling
much pain. Afterwards, we had to go have some more drinks
to celebrate the success of the operation.

He had no voice, but, oh, how he loved to sing, and did so
long beyond when me and the bone cracker lost our tongues.
Though Tom was four years older than me, we parted like
close friends, wishing each other tall range grass and deep
watering holes.

I went on to Madison Square Garden with the show, where
they rigged a break in the fence and trained this old steer to
run through it and into the stands whenever they gave him a
kick in the ass. Will would rope it and say the line about the
steer's having no ticket and the audience would fall all over
themselves.

We took the show up the eastern seaboard and it was near
time to winter out anyway when I got fired from it. I got from
one town to another by putting on demonstrations of trick

[9]

shooting and roping, near my overturned hat, until I got far enough west to start riding the chuckline.

I reckon it's changed now, people have growed suspicious of one another, but in those days you could ride from ranch to ranch all across the land without having to buy so much as a can of sardines. If there was no job for you, you was free to stay as long as you wanted, though it was a sign of low character to linger longer than a week. For your grub you would muck out the bunkhouse and help the cook and do any little thing that popped up. I have lived happily that way for months at a time with no more in my Levi's than some traces of tobacco. Now you'd need a dozen credit cards.

You're talking to a graduate of Chuckline U., magna come, where you wear your report card on your belt, and proof of your degree is that you're alive and still in the saddle. I've held counsel with the best and the worst of its drifting faculty and learned what I could from both. It's an education you couldn't buy at any price, yet was there for the taking, and at fifteen there wasn't much I cared to miss. Not much I cared to miss five years later either.

In March of '05 I found myself in South Dakota where Seth Bullock was putting together what he called The Cowboy Brigade to travel the train to Washington, D.C., for to march in the parade at Teddy Roosevelt's second inauguration. Though I had seen some likenesses, I had never seen a president in the flesh, and I thought that would be something worth the doing.

There was ten or a dozen of us left from South Dakota and then along the way we stopped and others joined up with us. Well, we stopped near Omaha and it happened I looked out the window and saw this bird atop a fine blue-black cow pony, just sort of loafing around and watching the train. I jumped off for a closer look. It was Tom.

"Where'd you steal the horse, Major?" I yelled. I called him Major in jest, because of his drum majoring job.

"Belongs to a lady I know," he said, as though he talked to me just the other day.

The horse was called Old Blue. He wore a short saddle with a high straight cantle, which gave the rider a military bearing.

Tom broke into a smile and we pumped each other's hand.

"How's the arm?" I asked him.

He bent it a few times. "Better'n ever. When bones break they mend stronger than they was."

"Glad to hear it," said I.

"Where you headed, Kid?"

"Washington, D.C. Gonna see in Teddy for another term."

Well, it turns out that Teddy was second in line on Tom's all-time hero list, just a nose behind Buffalo Bill Cody. I never had any heroes myself, and I reckon that's saved me a heap of disappointments. I think of every other man being more or less like me, and I've never been far wrong. I went to Seth and got Tom invited along. We talked about holding the train so's we could get a ramp to the stock car, in order to load up Tom's mount.

"Ain't necessary," said Tom. "Only open up the door."

So I slid open the door. Tom backed him up a bit, spurred him on, and Old Blue just up and jumped in. I don't mean to give the idea that that old pony just flew in. He kind of flew halfway in and crawled the other half after. I reckon you seen him do that stunt in the movies. Well, that's where he got the idea for it.

We had a nice reunion on the way to Washington, filling each other in on the year previous. Tom went back to Oklahoma City after the fair, and the only job he could find there was tending bar, an occupation he disliked because it was indoors and he had to watch everybody else drink whiskey whilst all he was allowed was flavored bellywash. He met a girl named Kitty Perrine, whose father owned a hotel in town. Before long Tom took up residence in the Perrine Hotel, living there on the cuff.

"I kind of made a promise to marry her," said Tom, "soon as I find decent work. That's what I'm supposed to be lookin' for right now."

"On her horse?"

Tom smiled and said, "My days afoot are over, Kid."

"And here goes you and the horse both to Washington, D.C."

"Ain't it funny the way the trail turns?" said Tom, and we both laughed about it.

We got to Washington shortly after dawn on Inauguration Day. I had been there once before with the show and Tom said he had too, during the war, but we was like two kids, keyed up to see the President and the wonders of the capital. We got us breakfast there at the depot and rode together horseback to the gathering place for the parade. There was forty of us in the outfit and we must of been some sight for the eastern dudes, who watched us pop-eyed as we casually rode city streets. We was a rough-looking bunch and could of been took for marauders from the Wild West.

I was riding a good little sorrel quarterhorse I called Toby. I tied him up with Old Blue, and Tom and me thought we'd go off on foot for a while and try to see us some of the local color. We hadn't walked more than a couple of blocks when I felt something at my feet like you do a snake when you come upon him and he slithers away from you. Before I could jump or see what it was, Tom and me was both on the ground, our feet lassoed together neat as your momma's apron.

"What the hell!" yelled Tom, ready to deal some misery to whoever was at the other end.

I knew right away there was only one man could whisper a rope as slick as the ass on a brass monkey. Will Rogers. There he was, grinning full of mischief and letting out some slack. The big man laughing next to him was Zack Mulhall.

"Sorry, gents," said Will, "but you sure looked like mavericks to me."

Cowboys don't bear grudges very long. I was glad to see Zack though he had fired me, and he was glad to see me, even though I did miss a couple shows. Will, of course, was the kind of bird you were always happy to see and sorry to see go. And Tom, when he saw the culprit was Will, held no hard feelings.

Colonel Mulhall remembered Tom from his ride on Widder Maker at the fair. "I compliment you, Mr. Mix," he said, "on your riding . . ." and just as Tom was getting all rosy with pride, he added, ". . . though your falling lacks a certain grace."

Still smiling, Tom said, "Well, sir, I have had very little practice in the fallin' part."

The drinks were on the Colonel. We palled around with them and took in a few sights before the parade. The place was crowded with people come to the big event, and I felt a bit unsettled jostling with so many after spending the past months in a solitary sort of way. Tom loved the crowds. He liked it when folks looked and pointed at us because of our outfits. He swaggered tall, with his jaw out.

The Mulhall Show was in town to entertain the President and honored guests after the ceremony. Tom was all but overwhelmed to hear that Zack and Teddy were personal friends.

"It sure would be the honor of a lifetime to meet the man," said Tom. He had a way of being bashful and brassy simultaneous, and some found it endearing and some found it annoying.

Zack thought about it for a minute, probably trying to decide if we was apt to scratch our asses in view of the President or commit some other cowboy crudity, but finally he invited us backstage, so to speak.

The parade was a glorious thing. We rode down Pennsylvania Avenue, our outfit right behind Teddy himself, who rode standing up in a great open car. Tom was next to me on the outside and he waved and tipped his hat to the crowd like it was him and not Teddy they had elected to lead the country.

"This'll be somethin' to tell your grandchildren, Kid," he said.

Along the rest of the route he kept reminding me, "Make

[13]

sure you give him a strong handshake. He'd hate a soft hand."
A little later it was, "Smile when you're introduced. You have
a tendency to frown and if you frown he'll think you didn't
vote for him or you're not happy he won." A mite further along
he felt obliged to say, "Comb out your hair and your moustache before you meet him and wipe your mouth with your
bandana so's there's no loose grub hangin' on you."

Well, hell, I was all but ready to let him go alone and I would
tell my grandchildren about something else, but finally there
we was in the White House along with Geronimo, another of
the honored guests. What a sorry sight it is to see a man who's
lived thirty or forty years too long. The old chief had converted
to Christianity and was probably on a diet of cream-style corn.

Tom and me was wallflowers, holding our hats and waiting
for Zack to collect us. Before long, we found ourselves behind
him in a line of folks approaching the President. There was
Zack and me and Tom behind me. Teddy was small in height
but like a barrel full of bricks. "Mr. President," said Zack, "I'd
like to introduce two of our cowboys, Mr. Kid Bandera and Mr.
Tom Mix." Well, Teddy loved cowboys and Indians and to have
us and Geronimo there a-mingling with the heads of state just
purely tickled him, you could tell. "Delighted," he said, and we
locked a grip on each other. He smiled like he was biting
through a length of rawhide. I moved on and Tom come up to
hand wrestle with him for a minute. "Happy to have you," said
the President.

Tom's chest swole up with pride and he said, "You probably
don't remember me, Colonel, I was one of your Rough Riders."

Well, I about came out of my boots, and Zack did what
Buster Keaton used to call a double take. I knew Tom did
not meet Roosevelt before that day and I suspected that at
one time or another Teddy must have met each of his
Rough Riders. I'm reasonable sure Tom never even *seen*
Teddy before. A lesser man than the President might have
said, "Shovel it back in the bullpen, bub," but Teddy in his

[14]

understanding of the human animal only looked him over for a second and said, "Bully!" He even gave him a comrade's slap on the arm.

Tom's feet never touched the tile as he walked away. Zack, who really *was* a Rough Rider, whispered to me, "If everyone who claims to have been there with Roosevelt really was, Cuba would have sunk into the sea under the sheer weight of them all."

I asked about signing back on with the show, but there wasn't any openings, so I went outside with Tom to where our horses was tied. We'd have to hurry to catch our train. We was mounting up when we saw Will Rogers running toward the White House. We hailed him and he come over.

"We just met the President of the United States," said Tom dreamily. "You're a mite late."

Will had something on his mind, you could see. "I got tied up with a fella name of Willie Hammerstein," he said. "Seems he wants to put me on the stage."

"Doing what?" I asked.

"Well, he has the idea that if I come out on the stage and tell a few stories and do some simple passes with the rope, folks would buy tickets to see it."

Will was an awful entertaining feller, sitting on a fence just passing by the time, but both Tom and me doubted the wisdom of what Hammerstein proposed.

"Zack's against it," said Will. "He says I'd be out of my element. Well, I figure that a man kind of carries his element around with him wherever he goes."

We wished him the wind at his back whatever he decided and took our leave, for we had no time to spare if we was to catch our train. Will turned and walked toward the White House. Then the devil come out of Tom's dark eyes and he reached into his saddlebag for a .45. He drew a bead on Will and shot his hat clear off his head. Will hugged himself to the ground. This was Tom's way of repaying him for lassoing us

[15]

earlier. Tom laughed, reared up on Old Blue, and galloped away. I stayed long enough to see Will get up and look for his hat. When the President's guards started pouring outside, I rode away too. You should remember that McKinley's end was still fresh in everybody's mind.

Independence, Kansas, was as close as our train got to Oklahoma City, so Tom got off there. He saddled up Old Blue halfheartedly and tarried about before mounting up.

"Don't much feel like goin' back to Oklahoma," he said.

"Well, at least you didn't find a job," I said from between the cars, trying to cheer him up.

"It's a letdown to go back to pushin' drinks, after meetin' up with the President of the United States. I don't guess old Teddy ever wasted his time servin' to a bunch of elbow-benders. He wouldn't be our President today. He was out makin' a name for himself. C'mon, Kid, get off that train and team up with me. Let's strike out across this land and claim our birthright!"

I declined the invitation, but he didn't hear me.

"Let's ride out of here and find what's ours!"

He was standing in the stirrups and shaking his fist and painting us out like real musketeers. I guess I was getting to know him pretty good as you do when you ride with a man for a few days. It wasn't just adventure he wanted. He wanted to be President. Or something.

What the hell. I'd be looking for work wherever I got off. I unloaded Toby and we rode off together. He had a way of convincing a person there was something big waiting at the end of the trail. That was when we were too young to know that one trail only leads to another.

I've read many a time that Tom Mix was a marshal, a sheriff, and a Texas Ranger. It's been reported he brought the law to assorted counties in Texas, Arizona, New Mexico, Oklahoma, Kansas, and Tennessee. Hell, I wouldn't be at all surprised to read he was an agent of the FBI. The plain truth is that, with the exception of posse riding when there was nothing more exciting to do, Tom was a lawman, of sorts, only twice. I'll tell you about the first time right now.

We rode out of Independence looking for something, neither of us knew what. We didn't have far to go. In half a day we come on a tent city: a boom town in the making.

Now, I've seen gold boom towns and silver boom towns, coal boom towns and borax boom towns, and some towns that boomed just on the force of a secret desire to boom, but LeHunt, Kansas, was the first and only town I ever seen that boomed on *cement*.

To make cement in plentiful proportions, I learned, you need two things: limestone and the natural gas to process it with, and LeHunt was given by nature the lion's share of these two resources. In case you're thinking the place was named after some town in France where they also make cement, forget it, partner. It was named for Leigh Hunt, the bird who built the cement factory there, giving birth to the town that sprung up around it.

As I say, it was tents when we rode into it, a spanking new town not even on the maps. Tom pulled up Old Blue and looked at the place like we stepped on the Mother Lode. "Listen to it, Kid," he said, that damned dreamy and smiley look on his face. "Listen to the sound of America risin' up."

I listened, but all I heard was the Kansas wind rubbing its belly over the settlers' canvas.

"We got to pitch in, Kid," he said. "We got to become a part

[18]

of all this and grow with the land. Sure the ground may be your bed for a spell and your bent arm your pillow, but then you'll have your own tent and later you'll marry a daughter of fine pioneer stock and have you a house and children, and I'll send for Kitty and we'll all live here forever and . . ."

He waxed on like that, arranging my future. God, did he have the talk. A couple of years later he would say a thing in my presence that I never heard before and am slow to repeat even now. He said, "Git along, little dogie." You want the truth? Believe it or not.

On that chilly day in March, '05, we was to settle down forever and become . . . what? Tom never got that far, for when we seen the men walking back from the factory, all white and ghostly like, Tom's desire to grow with the place slackened considerable.

Howsoever, between us we could not finance the rolling of a cigarette, so we sought out Mr. Hunt to ask him for work other than that done by the men we had seen.

He sized us up and said, "A town like us draws more than its share of bullies and opportunists."

"We do not come in that category, sir," said Tom like a forthright diplomat, if that ain't a contradiction of terms. Must have been the influence of Teddy.

He sized us up some more. "Can you handle yourselves in a fight?" he asked.

Tom beamed. "I have passed many fine afternoons engaged in the gentlemanly art of boxin'," he said.

Ever since Washington I had the feeling that something had popped loose in Tom.

Mr. Hunt looked at me and I reckon I sort of grunted or something to get across the idea that no man's fists scared me much. I didn't indicate how many had inflicted damage.

"Either of you two boys ever serve the law before?"

"My friend here was a deputy in Deadwood, sir," said Tom, "and I myself was for a time a Texas Ranger."

Naturally he was impressed with our background in the law-enforcement trade. I was too, since the only star I was ever behind was the red one on the door of a working girl's crib in Nogales.

"What was your last job?" asked Mr. Hunt.

"Tendin' bar," said Tom. Occasionally he would stumble over the truth, but he'd get up and go right on as though nothing had happened. "Actually, you could say our last job was guards at the inauguration of President Roosevelt, who will speak very highly of us if you care to inquire."

Tom was not wedded to the truth. I think he found it a load easy enough to shuck off. He sometimes took advantage of women, too. (He was still riding Kitty's horse, after all, and her wondering whatever happened to them.) But when it came to other folks' money, he was scrupulously honest. You could ask him to hold a dime or a couple hundred thousand dollars for you, as a feller once did, and you could be sure that when you ran into him again he would have it to the penny.

What feller? Oh, that was during the Dempsey-Carpentier fight, in 1921, it was. Jersey City, I believe. Tom and Jack had become great pals. They used to spar together. I remember once Tom tried to take a Sunday punch at him and wound up with a beautiful shiner. Anyhow, Tom went to this title bout, which was a total sellout, and the promoters was worried about getting knocked off for the gate, over $200,000. They wanted to slip the money out of the place, inconspicuous like.

Tom walked into the arena wearing a great white hat, kid gloves, a black crushed velvet shirt with seventeen luminous buttons around three big embroidered long-stemmed mums. He carried a suitcase, which the usher took from him.

There was a round of applause for him as he walked down the aisle to his seats. I say seats 'cause at events like this he always bought a ticket for his Stetson. He sat down, put the Stetson on the seat next to him, and watched the fight.

Between the second and third rounds the usher brought his

suitcase down the aisle to him. Dempsey finished Carpentier in the fourth round and Tom, the most conspicuous bird there, next to the champ himself, got up and left, to another round of applause, carrying the night's receipts in his suitcase back to his hotel.

I reckon Mr. Hunt was a good judge of men in that respect. Lord only knows what he thought of me, but he made us the whole constabulary of his town and payroll guards for his factory. Every Friday we'd ride with him to Independence for the payroll and ride back with him to LeHunt. It usually ran $35,-000 to $40,000 and every Friday I was sorely tempted to tie Mr. Hunt to his horse and make off with it. Tom kept me honest. He had a holy respect for other people's money, though he seemed to have had no regard for his own once he come into a big bunch of it.

By summer the town had started to take on a permanent look. Houses of four rooms were built and flower gardens planted in front of them. Leigh Hunt and a few of his superintendents had themselves built houses of two stories. Electricity was supplied by the factory's generator and every two houses shared a well. In time there was a post office, a church, a school, a general store with a telegraph, a fire station, and a billiard parlor. There were two hotels, one for bleached hides and one for tanned.

It was like any other new town of the period, with one exception. We had sidewalks. Partner, did we have sidewalks. Up both sides of the street and all the way to the factory. Little sidewalks spurred off of the big ones, leading right to the door of every house in town. We had sidewalks didn't go anywhere, just round and about in case you wanted to take a walk, for the ground was always either mud or dust. There were some wanted to put one big sidewalk over the road itself, and they would have too except for fear the horses and wagons would have a hard time traversing it.

Cement's a funny item. Once you get fooling with it, you

can't hardly stop. One of the town's folks, a strange little man they called Winky, drunk a deep draught of cement and kilt himself. We built our jail out of it. It wasn't no Hilton, but we had two cells in it, each big enough for two men if they didn't move around too much. We seldom had a full house, though, because often in our duties we'd have to tag an hombre on the button just to get his attention, and we generally figured that was punishment enough for whatever he done. It wasn't a bad town. We never had any real desperadoes ride through, and no major crimes committed. Except for one.

The Shonts brothers, Bert and Ernie, was well above average in the category of miserable murdering cattle rustlers. Wanted from Texas to Manitoba, they was, for years on end, and the posses that pursued them might as well have been racing with the moon. I never saw a likeness of neither of them, nor heard two descriptions that matched. Ghostlike they were, committing their cowardly deeds and vanishing into the mountains of New Mexico.

The year was 1901, and into the midst of still another posse rode a tall silent Ranger named Tom Mix, age twenty-one. He was the Marshal of White Oaks, New Mexico, and he explained to the befuddled members of the posse that sometimes there ain't no strength in numbers. He would track down the Shontses alone, and bring them in alone.

"Damn youngster's gonna git himself kilt," said Gabby.

"Maybe he kin do it," said Luke. "He got a way about him. By God, I believe in him!"

Marshal Mix smiled and rode away, alone.

He tracked them to Fort Sumner, where Pat Garrett had kilt Billy the Kid. He asked a cowboy loafing in front of the Silver Slipper if the Shonts brothers had rode through with a herd of rustled cattle.

Displaying the good citizenship and respect for the law traditionally associated with out-of-work cowboys, he directed the Marshal to the White Mountains.

Tom come upon their hideout just at dawn. He hunkered back in the woods and watched them for two days, rationing out his canteen of water and eating nothing but an occasional lizard and a handful of small pebbles. He wanted to know their routine.

Dawn of the third day, he stole into the barn. When one of them walked in, Tom asked, "Bert Shonts?"

"Ernie," said the other, going for his iron. Tom drew his faster and dropped him where he stood.

"No grudge," Shonts promised before he expired.

The sound of the shot brought the other brother out of the house, and this one got off the first shot, shattering Tom's leg. But as Tom went down he put one right through the bandana knot.

Tom lay there bleeding for seven days, until the posse that never went out 'cause Tom wanted to go it alone found him and saved his life.

Now, what the hell a Texas Ranger was doing as marshal in New Mexico is something I don't know, but then I try to keep my nose out of government and politics. And why White Oaks? Which as far as I know ain't even been discovered yet, let alone settled. And in 1901 Tom was a first sergeant in the U.S. Army, stationed in New Jersey. Now, could of been he got the Shontses in Fort Hancock, but I'd find it not likely they'd go that far east to rustle steers, even if the army had some there for them. What's more, I never even *heard* of the Shonts brothers, and I spent a lot of time in that part of the country.

The truth is that history confused the Shonts brothers, rustlers, with "Chance" Brothers, tinhorn.

A professional gambler in those days was like a professional gambler these days. Whilst he was in the chips he was a full-time gambler; when he run out he was a bartender or a store-keep or a cowboy or whatever he could be 'til he pulled to-gether a stake. What we called a tinhorn was generally a professional gambler who had smooth hands and a change of shirts. But Chance Brothers was towards being that fancy item we now get to see in the movies. He wore a silk vest, sure enough, and on his shirt was stitched an ace of diamonds, a touch Tom found particularly fruity, this from a bird who in a few years would have his monogram on everything, including his underdrawers. Chance also had manicured nails and he submerged himself in water once a day, so it was said. Most important, to his image and this story, he carried a Derringer tucked away in his waistband. That little popper was his undo-ing.

Every man has his druthers. I'd ruther shoot than rope, Tom would ruther fight than dance, Chance would of ruther play cards than drink whiskey. But they all count for second best, for what we'd all ruther have is a woman than any of those things. So even though Chance was ahead of the game and the whiskey was out of another feller's bottle, he cashed in his chips and excused himself, claiming he had a bad case of diar-rhea.

Tuck Ferguson, sitting across the table from him, was on a hot winning streak. Earlier Chance had even thrown in a few winning hands just to feed Tuck's luck. With him so occupied, Chance felt free to avail himself of Tuck's pretty young wife, Alma, who evidently had no misgivings about the arrange-ment.

Poor Chance, who lived his life according to the odds, would not have bet that in rapid succession Tuck's straight would be sucking the hind teat to another man's flush, that his three queens would play second fiddle to a full house, that his kings over sevens, on which he had bet his whole stack, would be beat by aces over fours.

When everything was going well with Tuck he could just barely be tolerated. Things never got so good that he could actually be liked. And when things went wrong he could make a sidewinder look like mighty fine company. He went home that night looking forward to nothing more than kicking Alma around the house for an hour or so.

Once in the house he followed her loud moaning to the bedroom where damned if she and the tinhorn hadn't been finding a fair amount of pleasure in each other. Tuck stood and watched for a few seconds, like a man does when a horse steps on his foot or when he sees the tip of his finger on the block next to the turkey's head. Then he noticed the shirt with the embroidered ace of diamonds on the chair next to the bed and he let out a roar to stop the earth. He took three lumbering steps towards the bed, but by that time Chance had grabbed the Derringer and put a bullet into Tuck's forehead. There was a second or two before he folded over when he could have been a Catholic on Ash Wednesday, cataloging the surprises of a rotten day: first the aces and fours, then his wife and the tinhorn, and now this.

If life had followed the fair plan, as it sometimes does and sometimes don't, Tuck would have been the one to kill Chance and the rest of us would have sighed and understood. As it was, we didn't reach for a rope and ride away in a rage seeking after justice. Nobody liked Tuck anyway and we felt his wife Alma was wasted on him. Where Mrs. Ferguson was concerned, we was all tickled to know for sure, as men always are, exactly which women enjoy it enough to take a little risk. If Chance and Alma had hung old Tuck in the closet and rode out of town together on the morning stage, they would have stood a good shot at happily ever after, but Chance lit out of town on Tuck's horse and that was not allowed.

Somebody sent for us. We was in the office where I was teaching Tom how to twirl a six-shooter. We went and examined the *corpus delicti* and together rode out after Chance. We both knew the bird, thought him harmless, and kind of got a kick out of him, really; but adultery, murder (for Tuck was

TOM MIX DIED FOR YOUR SINS

unarmed 'less you count what the Lord gave him), and horse-thieving, all in the course of one night, might have turned him dangerous.

I reckon I've had the saddle on my shoulder for longer than Chance had his ass on the saddle, so we wasn't too surprised less than an hour out of town to meet Tuck's horse on the way back. We expected the tinhorn got throwed and was probably lying on the road in a state of severe pain.

Well, we found the spot where the horse throwed him and saw where he cut across the field on foot. We rode after him real slow for it was clouding up and the night getting dark. Off the road, amidst trees and growth, I begun to have some second thoughts.

"Tom," I said. "He can't be too far ahead of us. What about tying up and going after him on foot?"

Tom would ruther ride than walk.

"Kid, that Derringer got a range of about twelve feet."

Dark as it was, he could probably get that close to us. Then, of course, I remembered seeing the hole in Tuck's head and it was sure of a sufficiency.

"Didn't see Tuck's rifle in his saddle holster," said I.

"It was there," said Tom.

Which was a lie. Tuck didn't even have a saddle holster.

"The night we approached San Juan Hill was like this," said Tom. "We weren't on horseback then. Only Teddy himself had a mount." I let him go on. "There was snipers in the trees. They got these big tall trees down there. They'd let us go by them and take their good old time drawing a bead on us and then they'd plug us in the back." Sounded like the best fun in the world was being shot at. "You couldn't see the birds. All you could do was pepper the tops of the trees. Teddy just rode ramrod straight. He didn't give a damn, and, Kid, neither did I."

It's my opinion that the army's major function must be to turn boys into fools.

[27]

I finally convinced him to dismount, and sure enough five minutes later we spied Chance hiking up a shallow dry wash. We paralleled him and Tom said he would run up ahead and stand in his path. I was to ease closer to him at his side.

It's a known fact of science that in the dark a sound in front of you could just as easy be coming from behind you, and you don't know if something at your left ear is really there or at your right. So with Tom in front of Chance and me to the left of him, when we yelled reach for the stars, old Chance thought he was surrounded. He got off a shot, which we were willing to let him have, since the Derringer only had but one to give.

Quick as a rabbit, I circled behind him, expecting him more or less to come along peacefully now. But somewhere along the way he had picked himself up a six-shooter and he started blasting all points of the compass.

Tom and me had shotguns, not trusting to single pieces of lead whilst shooting at something with the wherewithal to return fire, so when we opened up on him, hell, those of my pellets that missed old Chance hit Tom and some of Tom's shot hit me, but most all the rest took root in Chance Brothers.

I got Tom in the right leg and he got me in the left shoulder, which ain't been right since. We all three went down. By the time I was ready to get up again Tom was already dragging his bloody leg behind him to inspect the damage done to Chance.

Right about now, you're probably feeling pretty sorry for old Chance, but remember that the loss of innocence is a powerful sad thing too.

"Tom, you must of seen lots of dead men in Cuba," said I.

"Nothin' like this," said Tom, his face turning white.

Now, I know you'll accuse me of debunking a great man, partner, but I was airing my paunch too, right there next to him, and I'm as great to me as he is to you.

"The onions, I reckon," said Tom, leaning on me for support.

"The turnips, could be," said I, leaning on him.

In a minute we felt better, enough to face again what used to be Chance.

"Well, Kid," said Tom, "you kilt 'im dead."

"Me?"

"You do have the best eye I ever seen. You know I couldn't hit a bull with a bass fiddle."

Tom wasn't exactly the best shot in the world, about which I'll have a lot more to say later, but he was far from the worst, which you'd had to be to miss Chance with a shotgun at that range. We commenced to argue our claims that it was the other man's shot that kilt him, but looking at Chance's poor old useless body it was hard to say whose round was kind and whose was cruel.

Tom laid down against the side of the arroyo and I went back to get the horses. My shoulder was on fire and later I was to spend most all the night getting the pellets picked out of it. I led the horses back and when Tom come into sight I saw him rub his leg and heard him to say, "Little *sis*ter." I didn't know what the hell he was talking about.

There was a flask in Tom's saddlebag that he had confiscated from some drummer stopping in town. We had a drink and Tom said, "Here's to my little sister."

I drank to her. "What's her name?" I asked.

"Pain," said Tom. He had a spooky streak in him, getting wider the longer I knew him.

"I believe you love her overmuch," said I.

We had to take Chance back to town, but neither of us wanted to touch him because anyone who touched Chance was sure to bring away some of him on their hands. We both had slickers tied behind our saddles so we laid one out on the ground and sort of kicked Chance over onto it. Then we put the other one over him and sandwiched him between. Then we rolled it all together like some kind of rubber burrito and tied it up.

We put him on Old Blue because he was closest at hand, and we rode back. At the edge of town I rode to the telegraph office. We knew Chance was St. Louis born and I was to wire there and try to tell the next of kin. So Tom rode in alone with

Chance draped over the horse's behind, and I don't pretend to know what transpired 'twixt him and the fancies of the townsfolk, but I'm sure that by the time Tom became a movie star Chance Brothers had become the Shonts brothers and Tom's bloody leg where some of my pellets landed had become a broken leg shot that way by Shonts elder or younger.

I'm reasonably sure that, besides Chance, Tom never kilt nobody, 'cept the feller he once was. Some say he never kilt that feller neither, he just sort of rearranged him. At the risk of sounding philosophical, I could say that's all we done to old Chance Brothers.

LeHunt had no government, other than the cement factory, and when Tom tried organizing one, with the suggestion that he'd make the best mayor, I thought it was time to move on. I've always hated politics, and, besides, any one place gets awful tiresome after a time. So one morning we wished each other dry leather and hot frijoles and I drifted out of town, not to return until some forty years later, after the war.

I had been on my way to the coast from New York and I stopped to take a sentimental side trip to LeHunt. It was a ghost town and had been since 1915, I was told, when cement dropped to forty cents a sack. So, all in all, it had been a town of only ten years' duration, about the lifespan of a beagle who never got to hunt.

The houses had all been transported to Independence. With the houses moved, the sidewalks seemed to start at nothing and go to nowhere. It looked like folks, sore at the new worthlessness of the cement they built their dreams on, took to throwing the stuff around and letting it harden where it lay. Ponds of cement held fast to rusting wheelbarrows, like some mason's nightmare. Pick handles and shovel handles stood up in dry cement like some workingman's kind of boot hill. Even the smokestack was filled, and recently some wag had gone back to it and painted across it: TOM MIX DIED FOR YOUR SINS.

Heroes do, I reckon.

Leaving Tom to his campaign, I rode on down to the Salt Fork, near Bliss, Oklahoma way, and signed on with the 101 Ranch, which was one of the biggest outfits of that or any day. In the Cherokee strip it was and went to a hundred and one thousand acres, so they say, but I believe it was considerably larger, and if you ever had to ride it looking for strays you'd believe it too. Didn't get its name from its size, though, as you might expect, for in truth it was named for a popular whorehouse near the start of the Chisholm Trail.

The 101 was a place like none other, being all in one a working ranch, a dude resort, and a traveling Wild West Show. Cattle, there was 25,000 of them, 100 head of horses, and 300 miles of fence. It had its own electric power plant, its own dairy and poultry farm, its own community store. It even boasted of its own little restaurant. And cowboys, my God, partner, nobody ever seen so many cowboys. There was over two hundred of us, and we did everything. We were seasoned hands and did the hard labor of bronc busting, roping, branding, and cutting, along with the less desirable jobs of shoeing, fence mending, and just plain shoveling shit. Then at night we'd sing a song for the dudes and dance them around a spell if they wanted to. In our spare time we practiced our shooting, fancy riding, and roping so that we'd be ready when the 101 Wild West Show took to the road, leaving the ranch work to those wranglers too old or lame to join us in the fun. And mostly it was fun. In addition to the rodeo and trick stuff, we'd do a stage holdup and a quadrille and a reenactment of some favorite massacre and . . . what all. The 101 turned out more movie cowboys, circus performers, and rodeo champions than any single outfit in the U.S.A.

It was run by the three Miller brothers, Joe, George, and Colonel Zack, not to be confused with Colonel Zack Mulhall, whose own spread was over near Guthrie way.

Until old itchy ass set in, it was as good a place as any to bide the time. Better than most, and to remember it's all gone now can move the smile off my face.

Two people showed up my first season at the 101, one as unlikely as the other. Bill Pickett was the first.

Black as the inside of your pocket he was, all lips and a nose that flared right across his face, and as he come riding alone toward the roping ring the bunch of us there ceased what we were doing to watch him. We were used to visitors out there, none of them black, but the way he come in kind of caught your eye, regardless of his shade. He had that measure of arrogance that comes from knowing you can do what no other man can.

He pulled up his horse and sat there looking at us for a minute, with a hint of contempt in his eyes, and we looked up at him for some kind of explanation of himself. "I got an act for the show," he finally said.

Well, we sort of figured he must of come for work, but we thought he'd have the cook's job in mind.

"What kind of act?" one of us asked. It was probably Chet, our foreman. With us there was Terry O'Hara, who had been with Zack Mulhall, Bad Nose Bradman, Howard Jones, Charlie-Owns-the-Dog, who was a Injun, and a couple of others whose names and faces have gone back into the mist.

"I invented a rodeo event," he said.

Well, to listen to him you'd think he'd invented the Model A, and to tell you the truth, to us who was listening the invention of a new rodeo event was just as good, for we were always anxious to please the ever-hungry crowd.

"What goes on in this event?" asked Chet.

"It's easier to show you," he said, as though there was something you could show us that we hadn't already seen.

He got himself and his mount in position in the ring. A steer was needed, so I went and got him one that was up to whatever he might have in mind for it. I got the steer in position near the black cowboy. Then he told us to release him and give him

a jolt, which we did and he took off across the ring like a deacon
late to church, the cowboy after him. So far it looked like a
roping event, only Pickett didn't have no rope. He got alongside the steer and jumped off his horse and wrestled him by the
horns to the ground. And then, God is my witness, he sunk his
teeth into the steer's upper lip and let go with his hands and
held him to the ground with nothing more than his bite. The
steer would not *move!* I saw in the animal's face something I
never saw before. He was saying, "Dear Saviour, I know I'm
destined for a short unhappy life that ends up as meat on the
table, but deliver me from *this,* for I am frightened to the
tripe!"

Those of us watching, when we recovered our senses, spit a
few times, punched each other, and kicked dirt at one another,
trying to overcome the effect of what we had just witnessed.

Bill Pickett finally let the steer go, and that poor critter tried
to put a world of real estate between him and that black men-
ace.

We called over George Miller and got a few of the dudes out
and asked Pickett to show us that routine one more time, if he
didn't mind. He obliged, and damned if George and the dudes
didn't spit and hit each other and kick up dirt at one another,
and damned if that new steer didn't register the same unholy
terror of what he had endured.

George signed him up on the spot and billed him as "The
Dusky Texas Demon Who Will Leap From a Running Horse
and Throw a Steer with His Bare Teeth!" But the boys dubbed
him Bulldog Bill Pickett and the word "bulldogging" entered
the Western language.

Naturally, we dared each other to do what Bill had done.
Cowboys find it terrible hard to resist a dare, especially if
sufficiently liquored up, and all of us got as far as throwing the
steer but none of us, no matter how tangled up in the legs, ever
held it down with his teeth, with one exception. Which brings
me to the other person that showed up at the 101 that season.

One evening round about chuck time, Joe Miller returned

from a visit to Oklahoma City and he come in and said to Chet the foreman, "I hired on a drugstore cowboy in Oklahoma City. Put him to greeting and entertaining the dudes. He'll be here in a day or two."

"None of my business, but I thought you said we was over-manned."

"He was tending bar at my hotel. Seemed a natural for the job. We'll see how he works out."

Had I been a mathematician I would have put two and two together and come up with the name Tom Mix. Sure enough, he come riding in on a wagon, Old Blue trailing behind. Sitting next to him was a young unsmiling girl. The innkeeper's daughter, I figured.

"Howdy, Mayor," I said. I promoted him from major to mayor.

He was sure happy to see me and know he had a friend amongst the new outfit. It's a comforting feeling. He jumped off the wagon and pumped my hand. Tom was often a tiring man to watch, for he never simply got on or off a wagon—he jumped. He never walked; he did a sort of trot. He never just came into a room; he *flew* in. More energy than he knew what to do with, it was his nature.

"Meet Mrs. Mix, Kitty to you," he said. "This is Kid Bandera, that I told you about."

"Pleased to meet you, Mr. Bandera," she said, extending her hand to me.

"And me you, ma'am."

She looked bored. She was with Tom but not *of* him. I reckoned at the time it was the long ride or maybe it was her growing up in a city hotel and now finding herself out of the way of things. She was twenty-two, my age. I liked the way she looked, but I could tell that she and me would never be great friends. There was no juice in her, just a touch of acid. It wasn't long before I could tell she and Tom wasn't such good friends neither.

[35]

"So there I was, Kid," said Tom, "tellin' this customer a little bit about myself—"

"My land, that must have called for restraint," said Kitty.

Tom went on as though he hadn't heard her. "Told him a few of my adventures, even told him about bein' Sheriff in Kansas." He turned to his bride. "The Kid here was my deputy."

Same old Tom. "I figured you'd be Mayor by now," I said.

"Well, we did have an election, but they elected Leigh Hunt. I have to tell you, Kid, it soured me on politics. Those people didn't care who was their mayor, all they wanted to do was make cement and make money. I turned in my star over that one. Anyhow, I went on back to Oklahoma City—"

"Only a year overdue," said Kitty.

Tom shot her a look to tell her she was getting on his nerves. "I went back to tendin' bar—"

"And living in my daddy's hotel."

"—and to make a long story short, partner, here I are, at fifteen dollars a month." He rubbed his hands together. "This is what I'm after. Ranch life. I told him. 'Mr. Miller,' I said, 'I got to find me some outdoor work.' Well, hell, to make a long story short, we're here."

"Welcome to the 101," I said, "it's a good outfit. C'mon, I'll introduce you to the honcho."

"Later, okay? I got to get Kitty settled in a roominghouse in town and then I'll hightail it back here. We just wanted to come out here first 'n' have a look at the place."

"Not much to look at," said Kitty.

"Feast your eyes," said I.

And Tom did. He turned full circle slowly, drinking the place in. Home at last. He took Kitty in to town and that night he was with us and slept in the bunkhouse. I reckon I seen her once or twice after that, but I couldn't swear to it. Tom went into town every Saturday night like the rest of us and he must of spent time with her then and looked in on her at other

[36]

times, but I think that once he signed on the 101, she was more or less in the way. Most of the outfit never even knew he had a wife.

Tom was sure disappointed when his duties were explained to him, for he wanted the rough and tumble of the cowboy, but Miller was right; he was indeed a natural. He charmed those eastern dudes right out of their first pair of boots. I come upon him one evening regaling a group of kids with his war stories.

* "The Spaniards had surrendered," he was saying, "and I was picked with the scouts who were sent out to bring in a lot of Spanish sharpshooters that didn't seem to have got word that the war was over. They were always poppin' folks from behind things along the hill roads and stirrin' up considerable trouble and inconvenience for everybody. So we started out to explain to them that it was all over and they could come in and be good. I remember I was going up a hill lookin' around to see if anythin' was likely to happen and I decided I'd never seen such a peaceful, quiet-looking place in my life. Just then I heard a stirring up in a mango tree. A shot came out of it and blew a fair-sized hole in my sleeve, but I couldn't see a thing. No man likes to have somethin' shootin' at him that he can't see to shoot back at, but all I could do was to open up on that mango tree on general principles. Well, we had a lively little argument for a few minutes, and then he poked his head out like a turtle."

" 'Cha get 'im, Mr. Mix?" asked one of the breathless youngsters.

"Son, I made one of the biggest mistakes of my life."

"Whatcha do! Whatcha do!"

"I opened my big mouth."

"Huh?"

"I had just got my mouth open to holler that the war was

*The essential details of this incident were related by Mix to *Photoplay*, and others.

over when he fired his last bullet at me and tore me up in the tongue. Went right out the back of my neck."

The kids grit their teeth in shock and secondhand hurt.

" 'Course, I had him 'fore I hit the ground."

About that time he noticed me listening. You'd expect an ordinary man to be embarrassed in that situation, but not Tom. He drew me in and said, "And here's the man who drug me to safety that day, Kid Bandera. Remember, Kid?"

So I had to either expose him as a liar and disappoint those wide-eyed kids or go along with him and become a liar myself. I reckon I sort of grunted, which is what I usually did when I was put in a position where I had to say something but couldn't talk, which was often, being Tom's closest friend like I was.

"And you can still see where the bullet came out," said Tom, taking off his bandana and exposing his neck. The kids clustered around to see. "You can touch it," said Tom, and the boldest amongst them ventured to do so. I had a look for myself. There sure was an old wound there but it looked to me like what happens when you try to cut a boil off your hide using two looking glasses to see what you're doing. The reason I had that impression is I cut one off my own hind end once that way and didn't think no more of it 'til a couple years later in a Juarez whorehouse when my girl said, *"Pobrecito,* you was shot, no?"

After the kids went on their way, I said, "Tom, why you storying like that to those kids?"

"No harm done," he said. "Those kids come all the way from New York City. It gives them somethin' to remember."

I just shook my head, there was no sense arguing. Besides, he wasn't the first cowboy to tell stories. Hell, it was almost a tradition.

"And, Kid . . ."

"Yeah, Tom?"

"I really was shot through the mouth once."

Well, maybe he was and maybe he wasn't. I know he's been shot *at* a fair number of times, because I was with him when the lead flew, but I can testify to his actually getting shot only three times. The first time was when he was twelve and a chum shot him in the leg, playing with guns they were. They didn't dig the bullet out 'til 1917, by that time he'd been carrying it for twenty-five years. The second time I shot him myself when we cashed in Chance Brothers. The third . . . well, all in good time.

It wasn't only the kids he entertained. He was a man well liked by the ladies, and Tom considered a willing woman one of nature's finest treats, but to his credit he did not touch the women visitors, for they were all married, though some were not in the company of their husbands. He believed it wrong to woo another man's woman, but the fact that he was married didn't seem to stop him from making eyes at an unattached girl, as he did in a big way when Olive Stokes showed up for an overnight visit to the 101.

Olive was sixteen then and quite a natural beauty. She had been away at school and was home for a short vacation. You could say an attraction developed, which didn't weaken a bit when I told Tom that Olive was in line to inherit a fair-size ranch once her mother died.

"Kid," said Tom, "don't tell her I'm married."

"Why not, Tom?"

"Because I'm fixin' to marry her in a couple years, after she fills out some."

"But what about Kitty?"

"That ain't workin' out."

Tom was going to take Olive riding the morning before she was to leave. He had his saddle on his back and was walking around the big cattle corral to get to where Old Blue was kept. To get there he had to walk past a group of the regular wranglers. Tom was not especially liked by the rest of the hands because he hadn't showed yet that he could actually *do* anything besides charm dudes.

[39]

"Where're you going, cowboy?" asked one of the wranglers, in the way you'd call a real stupid feller "professor."

"To get my horse," said Tom.

"Gonna take Miss Olive for a ride?"

"That's what I had in mind."

Olive was watching from the porch of the ranch house. Tom, who had been ready to fight them if it came to that, was taken by surprise when the other said, friendly like, "If you cut through this here corral you'll save yourself some walking time."

Tom saw no harm in that. "Much obliged," he said. The other guy even held his saddle for him whilst Tom stepped through the fence. He put the saddle back on his shoulder and started across the yard.

There was a few head of cattle off in a corner of the corral. Tom caught the eye of one of them. Now, cattle are dumb, and I never heard anybody argue to the contrary. The argument is always in finding what's *dumber* than cattle. But dumb as they are, they're nonetheless curious about unfamiliar sights, and a man with a saddle on his back is to cattle an unfamiliar sight. This one steer moved away from the others and follied after Tom. Tom took notice of him but kept walking at his same pace. Why not? It wasn't nothing but an old steer. The steer closed ground on him. Tom tried to act indifferent, but you could see he was measuring the distance to the rail. The steer come on closer, building up some speed. Tom started walking a whole lot faster. The steer, he too went faster. Well, the steer was all but on him when Tom decided to throw off his saddle and run like hell. He didn't have to look behind him to know where the steer was neither, for it was snorting down his neck. If Tom hadn't flown the last six feet head first over the fence the steer would have stomped him sure.

Laugh, the wranglers fell in the dirt and held their sides.

Tom hated shame worst than pain and suffering, but there was nothing he could do about it. They had had him fair and square, because of his own ignorance, and in front of young Olive too.

That night he come to me after we ate and said, "Kid, I can ride as well as any man here."

"Better'n most, Tom."

"But I got to learn the rest of it."

"The rest of what?"

"Ropin', rodeo—and cows."

I kind of chuckled, remembering what had happened, but Tom was downright serious. "Will you teach me?" he asked.

In the early hours, just before dawn until the dudes awoke and he'd be needed elsewheres, Tom practiced with me the skills of a cowboy. He had a good leg up on the ordinary tenderfoot because of his horsemanship.

As I told you earlier, I knew from the beginning he wasn't no Texan and I suspicioned that he wasn't no westerner neither, or he'd already know the things he wanted me to teach him. Still, he was hell on a horse, so I asked him, casual like, how he come to ride so well.

"My daddy was the stableman for the DuBois family."

"Never heard of them," I said.

"DuBois, Pennsylvania."

"Born there, was you?"

"Nearby. A little town called Mix Run, near Driftwood."

I reckon I caught him in an unguarded minute, but there was work to be done before first light so we let the palaver drop and studied the cattle.

Learning cattle is like learning people: if you know nothing to begin with you can learn a whole lot in a short time, but after that it's a matter of learning as things come up, for just when you think you know them in general some cow will up and show you something you never seen before.

Roping is another matter. There are men who can pick up a rope for the first time and anyone can see that man and that rope belong together. Rope is his talent. In time it will come to life in his hands and he will have a true partner with him wherever he travels. Tom Mix was not that type of man. Will Rogers was, and I never sat down for a chew or a smoke with him when he wasn't also toying with a length of rope. Tom, though, had to work at it, and work he did, with a determination I've yet to see equaled. Inside of two seasons he was spinning a sixty-foot rope, which gave him a forty-foot reach. Most cowboys are happy as whores if they can control a forty-foot rope with a twenty-five-foot reach.

Tom paid the price for every achievement. Once I was heading and he was heeling, and I roped the calf and kept him ahead of Tom so he could rope the hind legs, which he did in admirable fashion, only he made the mistake so many tenderfeet before him have made. He was too slow in dallying his rope around the saddlehorn and when the calf pulled in his legs Tom's thumb was caught between the rope and the horn. Though I haven't had the misfortune myself, I reckon it can cause pain of a real noticeable nature.

The thumb was busted all to hell and burned to boot, and for the next half hour Tom carried it in his armpit. When we finally had a look at it, it was worth the wait, for it was a curious thing to examine.

Years later I was to read in the magazines that Tom always wore gloves because he had overly sensitive hands, or because he was tattooed, or, the one I like, because he had a finger shot off in a gun fight with a desperado. But *I* know why he always wore gloves. He had a thumb that would scare a small child.

We had a squaw at the 101 we called Minnie, who was keen on chewing tobacco. Hell, we had a number of squaws there, but this particular one went to over three hundred pounds. Apart from kitchen words, she didn't have enough English to catch the stage out of town, but Tom got kind of attached to her and often I'd see him confiding in her, and her nodding her head sympathetically, not knowing if he was telling her the Gettysburg Address or the proper way to skin a bobcat. I overheard him telling her how important it was for him to prove himself to the men of the 101 and to himself, how important it was for him to *succeed*. It was a word he repeated over and over again, 'til damned if Minnie the squaw didn't say it clear as a summer's morning: "Succeed."

She could have had sucking seeds in mind, for all I know, but what struck me most about the scene was the ambition coming out of Tom. It was strange territory for me, for I had never had any ambition myself and knew of no others in the outfit familiar with the feeling. Sure, I'd seen how hard he was working but I figured that was just so he could hold his own with the rest of the men and not be made sport of. He had more than that in mind, though I'm not sure that even he knew what it was. All I could tell that day was that Tom was being pursued by demons unbeknownst, and as I watched him over the years I saw the chase grow hotter.

His efforts did not pass unnoticed by the other men, and they could see that he would soon be out of their range, so they planned one last surprise. They got Tom amongst them and soon the blathering turned to Bill Pickett and how it looked like he would wind up the coming season as "Champion All-Around Cowboy," which was a designation the show gave one of us every year. It was our Academy Award. Well, they made on that they were all practicing the Pickett bulldogging technique but couldn't beat his time. Naturally, Tom, who hadn't seen Bulldog in action, was curious to know what his technique was. Someone went and got Bill, who put on a demonstration. Once again he held down a disbelieving steer for ten seconds.

I reckon there was no way to watch Bulldog without spitting afterwards, for that's what everyone did, Tom not the least. The boys went on about how none of them could do any better than five seconds, until Tom said, "I think I can beat five seconds."

Well, they didn't have to have it in writing before they set up. Usually a feller holds his peace during pranks like this, for ranch life often gets tedious and you have to make your own entertainment, but Tom was my partner and I feared he was being tricked into biting off considerable more than he could chew, if you'll forgive me those words.

"Tom," I said, "there ain't a man here with the nerve to even *try* that stunt. They're funning with you."

"I expected as much," he said, though I doubt he did, "but I think I really *can* beat five seconds."

I took one more shot at changing his mind and then figured I done enough.

He come down on the steer like he knew what he was doing, and wrestled him to the ground without any trouble, but then he had a second or two of hesitation before sinking his teeth into its lip. I expect it was that second or two that made the difference. Bill Pickett always made it clear to the steer from the very beginning that there was no contest involved, only punishment for the steer. This steer had another idea. He jerked his head back and Tom, to his credit, held on, but when he brought his head forward hard and stood upright he knocked Tom colder than Saturday's frijoles. He gave him another for good measure before hightailing it back to the pen.

There were three pearly whites on the ground next to Tom and when we brought him to, he spit out a fourth. Daylight was where the bright smile used to be. "Time?" he asked, some blood running down his chin. "Six seconds," I said, but it couldn't have been more than two.

When it comes to conscience and cowboys, you can't generalize. I've seen some outfits that'd laugh at snakebite. In this case, however, everybody was feeling pretty low, for Tom was a handsome man and by their humor they had diminished his good looks, which were necessary for his job. It come fairly close to stealing a man's horse, what they did.

Each in his own way tried to make up for it. One gave him a high-quality rope he had extra. Another offered him a pair of boots but they were too big. Everyone, of course, acted friendly toward him and helped teach him the tricks of the trade, for which Tom was grateful. Somehow, though, it never seemed enough, especially when Tom had to put his hand over his mouth whenever he had the urge to smile. So far none of the Miller brothers noticed that Tom was missing some of the attributes he come with, but it was only a matter of time before they would.

Finally, the boys decided that the only way they could ease their consciences was to pass the hat and send Tom off to Oklahoma City for to be fitted with a set of hand-tooled teeth. I saw him off with Kitty on the train. Two weeks later he was back with a smile even brighter than the original, alone. I reckon Old Blue was his share of the settlement, for he continued to ride him.

The boys sure took pride in Tom's new teeth. They felt they had an investment in him, and later when he became a movie star, damned if they didn't want some of the credit. If they only knew the extent of the damage they had done that man, for the teeth made him self-conscious about talking, afraid they would clack or maybe even fall out. So when he talked he hardly ever moved his lips and he never opened his mouth wider than a cigarette butt, which was all right as long as he was making silents. People say that Tom didn't make the grade in talkies because he had a poor voice, like John Gilbert. Tom himself claimed that the legendary bullet through his mouth had affected his speaking. The plain truth is that there wasn't a damn thing wrong with his voice. He just never learned to trust his false teeth.

With the encouragement of the boys, Zack Miller took Tom off the dudes and put him into the show. Now, Tom had always dreamed of owning his own ranch. I knew it from overhearing him tell Minnie of his dreams and hopes for the future and I knew it because he didn't keep it a secret from me neither. Hell, I reckon most of us had that same dream tucked away somewhere, waiting for it to die a peaceable death, but the difference with Tom was his, what? Vision, you could call it. You knew just listening to him that one day he would have that ranch and the substance he hankered after. He handed me a scrap of paper once and on it he had made a mark: **M**

"My brand," he told me.

See, he was the kind of bird needed a brand even though there weren't a piece of beef he could burn it on.

I told him it was nice enough and had a simplicity I admired.

"I don't know, Kid, it's lackin' somethin'."

I opined as how a bar always gave a brand a pleasurable touch.

Well, that was what he was looking for, and on the spot he created the TM bar brand: **M**

A day later he come back to me and said he come up with a new angle, the diamond TM bar, because if a bar gave it pleasure, a diamond would give it class:

"What do you think, Kid?"

"I think you better settle on it 'fore it gets all out of hand."

That became his brand, and the next time I seen it, it was in neon lights atop his place in Beverly Hills.

He was meant to be the center of attention. I should have recognized it when first I saw him leading the band in St. Louis, or when he rode with me in the inaugural parade, or when I heard him telling his stories. I finally discovered it when Zack Miller put him in the show. Like some men was meant for the rope and others for the plow, he was meant to please the crowd. I think it's the worst of all callings, and I say that 'cause I'm ninety and have had a world of experience with the crowd. The flavor weakens but the crowd don't lose its appetite.

He started out as the fall guy. Ever they wanted to shoot someone off a horse or rope someone right out of his saddle, Tom was it. It's a dues paying sort of job, but Tom loved it, and the crowd grew to love him. He always went that extra distance to make it authentic, and of course nobody knew it at the time, but he was getting his basic training for the stunts he would later perform before the camera.

He had a way of lying still after a stunt 'til just the time the crowd was starting to believe he was kilt or hurt bad, then he'd spring up and do a running mount and ride away. It played hell with little Olive's emotions whenever she was able to catch a show. There was times, however, when he didn't get up and we'd know he broke, sprained, or twisted something, or was simply out cold. Then we'd have to get the bone cracker to set him, tape him, plaster or pill him, whatever, but he was always back in the saddle before the leather cooled.

Every summer we'd go out with the show. Whenever we went east of the Mississippi, he'd use the name Tom Howard, which had been Jesse James' alias. He said he did it as his own way of honoring the legend of Jesse James, but it only went to further my suspicion that he was wanted somewhere. He wasn't the only cowboy to use a summer name, however, so I didn't mull over it. I reckoned he'd come around to telling me all he wanted me to know.

Tom and me was together for three seasons with the 101. They was good days, those. What did we eat? Steak and frijoles mostly, when we was sitting. Sardines if we was saddlebound or leaning against a bar somewheres. To this day my favorite lunch is sardines out of the can.

By this time Will Rogers was a headliner in the east, but he occasionally dropped in to see us poor ordinary folk. He and Tom was once rivals over Zack Miller's daughter Lucille, one of the best cowgirls ever to sit a horse. Zack chased them off the porch with a shotgun, making clear he had more in mind for his daughter than a choice between a half-breed rodeo clown and a no-account drugstore cowboy.

An eastern oil man came to the 101 for to lease some of the land for oil exploration, and he took a shine to Tom, as most easterners did, and offered him and me a chance to invest in his scheme. He was always digging up rocks and carrying them in a sack, pulling one out from time to time to study and explain to us how it told him there was oil somewheres under us. Well, "somewheres under us" seemed like an uncommon big place to Tom and me, so Tom stated our fiscal policy thus: "The Kid and me figure to draw our thirty-five dollars a month and spend it." It's a cowboy's attitude and a hard one to sophisticate. Tom carried it to Hollywood with him, but, hell, how do you spend thousands every week?

Well, that dude went ahead without our capital and soon his wells became Conoco Oil Company and he became a couple hundred million dollars richer. All these years later and I still get the chuckles when I think about it.

* * *

Tom became a favorite of the crowd his first season, but the title of "Champion All-Around Cowboy" went to the Dusky Texas Demon, etc., etc.

Even the spittin' thrill of what Bulldog did eventually wore thin on the crowd so that by the second season he dropped it and began competing with the rest of us in seeing who could wrestle a steer to the ground fastest in an ordinary way. We still called it bulldogging, and rodeo crowds to this day seem to like it well enough, but we were always after gilding the lily.

For instance, we once tried bulldogging a buffalo. Now, there's no comparison between the intelligence of a buffalo and that of a steer. You're probably wondering why if he's so intelligent he's practically extinct, and all I can say to that is that animal intelligence ain't no protection from the bloodlust of man. Anyhow, believe me when I say a buffalo is an intelligent critter, which makes him twice as dangerous as a steer in hand-to-horn wrestling. Only problem is he has a sensitivity and pride to match his intelligence, and once you bulldog a buffalo to the ground he don't want to get up. His feelings are real hurt and he just wants to lie there 'til he dies. I heard 'em cry, and a cowboy, sentimental like he is, can't hardly bear to see a buffalo cry, so we eliminated the buffalo from our bulldogging experiments and went at it in a different way.

A feller came through with a string of camels, his idea being to use them instead of horses in the arid ranges where water ain't plentiful. Seemed like a good idea to us, the only problem from our point of view being that the look of the critters made it unlikely a cowboy would ever develop a feeling of affection for his mount. 'Course their sorrowful faces may have been the expressions of strangers in a strange land, and in time they might learn to love their new surroundings and cheer up.

Tom talked the Millers into buying one of those camels for the bulldogging event, and the focus was turned away from the actual wrestling of the steer and towards the means used in getting *at* the steer in the first place.

[50]

There was no problem finding a rider, for Tom was quick to volunteer, specifying that since it had four legs and a tail and was broke for riding, we should ignore the hump on its back and its woebegone demeanor.

There was some trouble when it come to saddling the creature, since no saddle was sold with him and a horse's saddle was of the wrong fit. We called a saddlemaker out, and I recall he was sorely insulted. His father was a saddlemaker, he said, and he was one too, of more than thirty years' practice; it was a good solid trade, and in two generations of making saddles they had no more disturbance than that which comes out of the ordinary difference in taste. Now we ask him all the way out here to saddle up a critter that could have come from the moon.

"Maybe it's not such a hot idea at that, Tom," said Colonel Zack Miller.

"Colonel, imagine yourself sittin' in the crowd waitin' for the bulldoggin' and the announcement is made that Tom Mix will be ridin' . . . we'll call him a new breed of Arabian, that ain't far wrong. Then out I come on old big hump here and make a dive for that steer . . ."

It sure were a picture. Zack doubled up thinking about it.

We never could get a saddle for him, but the camel was no stranger to bridle reins so Tom rode him bareback, or barehump, as the case was.

Our final problem was fairly conclusive. The steer purely terrified the camel, and Mr. Hump did nothing to still the uneasiness of the steer, the result of which was they spent their whole time wildly racing away from each other. Tom was stranded way up there on the camel's back and could do nothing to spur him closer to the steer, so he waited 'til they passed reasonably close and made his play. He landed three feet back in the dust from the steer's hooves. Dislocated his collar bone on that one.

The other cowboys either felt disinclined or figured they

wouldn't fare no better than Tom did, so the camel camped out with our horses, who took to him better than the steers did, until we sold him at a loss to the first traveling circus that crossed our trail.

Tom admitted to being wrong in the particular about the camel but insisted he was right in a general way: the real crowd-pleaser was in the method of getting to the steer. To that end a long series of misadventures commenced, which would be going on today if the 101 hadn't fallen to the force of the times.

We tried a bicycle first, which the steer hooked and trampled, and the gas-driven motorcycle didn't last much longer. Each of the Miller brothers owned his own automobile, but none of them would let us use one of them, in spite of Tom's pleading. We finally built a catapult and Tom was already perched on the end of it, ready to spring after the steer, but Zack Miller forbid us its use and ordered it to be dismantled. He later took credit for saving Tom Mix's life, and I'm inclined to support his claim.

Years later, Tom and me went back to the 101 to see the first big show of the new season. Movie stars now, we were. I was a bit uncomfortable that the boys there would make fun of us, but Tom put on one of his gaudiest outfits. What he wore on his back would cost those cowboys a couple years' wages. And there was a touch of undisguised mocking too when they saw us moving picture cowboys. "Good God," said Zack Miller, "whatcha doing with all those brass buttons on your jacket, Tom?"

"They ain't brass," said Tom, "they's *gold.*"

Would you believe that those cowboys, and most of them was new to us, was still doing what Tom had started years before: trying to make the bulldogging event more exciting. Believe it or not, partner, they had got themselves an airplane brought in from Tulsa and was fixing to bulldog a steer from it.

[52]

Not being one to miss new thrills, Tom had already been up in the air, a few times even taking off and landing himself. But he gave it up. He told me, "There's no sport to it, no more than riding a horse where you have no place or reason to ride him to."

What we were about to witness here, though, gave the airplane new potential that Tom had never considered, and I could tell he wanted a shot at it. He did his best to talk himself into that event, but the young feller who devised the scheme wouldn't hear of it.

They cranked the prop and started her up. The pilot pulled his goggles over his eyes and the cowboy behind him held onto his hat. They sped across the field and up into the air. They made one practice pass over the ring. Fired by the cheers of the crowd, they was ready to bulldog. A length of rope was lowered from the airplane and the cowboy slid down to the end of it. Tom listened to the frenzy coming out of that crowd and jabbed me and said, "See, I *told* you so!" The plane circled round and they released the steer. Now, I blame the pilot for what happened next. He made his pass into the ring over the "101 WILD WEST SHOW" arch that stands maybe twenty feet high, and the cowboy hanging from the rope wasn't more than that off the ground himself. He went smack through the sign, sending splinters halfway across the ring, and landed in a reduced state of physical well-being. Some bulldogger.

Tom supported the young cowboy's idea, and having some aeronautical experience behind him, offered his advice and counsel on the next try.

"One try's plenty," said Zack Miller, preparing to pay off the pilot for the use of his machine.

"If you was to put a plank between the wheels, the bulldogger would be in closer control by your pilot, which I think was the only flaw in the plan. And if you're jumpin' from a solid place 'stead of a danglin' length of ladder, you stand a better chance of hittin' the target."

Like most times, Zack was swayed by Tom's words.

"Who's going to do the jumping?"

"Me," said Tom.

Forget the fact that Tom was already in his late forties and hadn't had to bulldog for on to ten years, and remember that I had promised Sol Wurtzel, who was heading up the Fox outfit in Hollywood, that I would protect Tom from himself and bring him back to the cameras in one piece. And remember also that Tom was the idol of children everywhere and Zack would have known the consequence of having him kilt on his show.

Over Tom's loud objections, he let another man volunteer for the job. It's always a puzzle to see a man volunteer for a stunt that just may have been the Big Casino for the last man to try it. The cowboy was named Shady, and after they had set up the plank betwixt the wheels, Shady squeezed on top of it and yelled, "Let 'er rip!"

The plane took off, like before, and made a practice run over the ring, like before, and they released the steer, like before. There was some problem maneuvering over the steer, who was terror-stricken by the sound of the motor over his ass and ran everwhichway. They made a number of passes, but none came close enough for Shady to risk a jump. The crowd was growing impatient and finally it was "die dog or eat the hatchet" with Shady. Some twenty feet up and forty feet back of the steer he took his plunge. He come down on the steer's neck with his knee and broke it—both the neck and the knee. The steer was kilt straightaway, but the last time I saw Shady he was walking like one foot was in a trench and the other had an orange crate nailed to it. And as if that wasn't bad enough, when Shady removed his weight from the traveling airplane, it must of called for some quick calculations on the part of the pilot, who failed to make them, owing I'd reckon to an omission in the correspondence course he must of took to learn the flying trade. Nose up and tail under, the plane went, and in that position it was evidently unfit for flying, for it coughed once and died, falling back to earth on its tail and changing in the process its whole configuration. God looks over fools, so the pilot lived, but fear of flying, so I heard, kept him close to the ground thereafter, too afraid to even climb up on a barstool, choosing instead to drink his tangleleg off in the alley.

But I sure got ahead of my story. I was telling about how Tom had learned the skills of a cowboy and had become top crowd-pleaser of the 101 Wild West Show. In 1908 he made "Champion All-Around Cowboy," and none of us ever disputed the Pennsylvanian's right to the title.

Winter came and most of the hands was either laid off or they drifted away of their own accord, to return again in the spring. Tom and me stayed on at reduced wages, reduced to nothing. So when the offer come to go up to Medora, North Dakota, for to fetch two carloads of horses back to the Cherokee Strip, why, we jumped at the chance. We didn't know who'd be paying us, but covering ground has always been a pleasure, and doing it at another's expense does nothing to diminish the joy.

North Dakota was a cold and bony sort of place and we arrived with a blizzard just after Christmas. Who do you suppose was at the station to meet us? Olive Stokes, a pretty little round-faced item all wrapped up in skins against the cold. She was just eighteen.

Tom looked at her for a long time, then whispered to me, "Well, I reckon she's ready."

Tom took the reins, she sat between us, and we rode off to a ranch belonging to Nels and Katrine Nichols, friends of the Stokes family. Seems Olive was there to find some horses for her own spread back in Oklahoma.

"I should have known I'd need help selecting and transporting them," she said.

Tom allowed how he and Kid Bandera were about two of the best horse selectors and transporters in the west.

The Nichols house was well appointed and warm, what with a fire going in each of its rooms and hot punch ready and a turkey done up and a pig roasting and potatoes in the coals. It was a cold and craggy land outside, so folks made the most of the inside. We stayed there for over three weeks and every day people kept dropping by for a drink and a smoke and a leg of something or other. Whenever enough had gathered we'd take down the fiddle and the guitar, somebody'd shake out his mouth organ, and we'd commence to dance the bejeezus out of the polka. What a good life was led there.

Tom was out every day with Olive, looking at horses to buy. I figured it was my job to go along with them, but Tom reckoned they could manage without me, and Olive was not quick to argue the contrary. I didn't mind a bit. I huddled round the house and took on ten pounds of winter fat that visit.

Finally, the horses was bought and sheltered in town and we was ready to go back to Oklahoma. The Nicholses threw a farewell party for Olive, though seemed like to me every day there was a party anyway. They pulled out all the stops on this one. People come from all over the territory and fought a raging snowstorm to get there too. Olive was gussied up and danced every dance with Tom, who was as good at dancing as he was at most things, save singing, for he sang like rolls of barbed wire drug across a cement floor.

You didn't have to be a musician, though, to see that Tom and Olive had struck responsive chords in each other, and all assembled commented they'd be man and wife before winter came another time. It was because of this that I mentioned to him casual like, in the interests of friendship, that a man twice burned should be doubly warned of the fire.

"I hope that don't mean you wouldn't stand up for me if I took another run through the flame," said he.

"Well, sure. I was only making an observation on the game of matrimony," said I.

[57]

"Any game worth the losin' is worth the tryin' of it again. Here."

He handed me a gold wedding band.

"What's this?" I asked him.

"Well, you practically agreed to be the best man, and the best man always takes custody of the weddin' ring."

It was a mite unusual, but I reckoned any man that'd have a brand long before any hopes of having a cow would be apt to have a ring long before the bride to wear it.

The fiddlers had folded, the fingers of the pickers and kettle whackers had grown heavy, and the jug blowers had all gone dry. No one wanted to face the driving snow outside, so most all of them lay about where they had dropped. The rooms sounded like so many sawmills. The Nicholses, Tom and Olive, myself, and a collie pup was still awake, so we waddled into the kitchen for something to eat. Folks in bedrolls laid all over the floor and we had to step over and between them with considerable care.

Mrs. Nichols put a plate of ribs on the table, along with a goose and what was left of a turkey. She poured us beer and coffee and hot rum. We sort of sat silent around the table and nibbled and sipped the way you do at the end of a real good time. Nobody had much to say until Tom asked Nels how long he had been in the married state.

"Thirty-two years this June," he said.

"The Kid here don't believe in marriage," said Tom, and then I had to explain myself, and everyone else had to offer up his opinion on the subject. Olive was the last to speak and she said that she certainly approved of the institute of marriage and looked forward to it someday for herself, but what bothered her was the way some men were quick to marry but slow to assume the responsibilities of married men. It was a right little fancy speech and I wonder if Tom heard a word of it, for he started in talking about the wedding ceremony as it's done in the Cherokee nation, which his grandfather married into when he took a squaw as his wife. (Truth is his grandfather was an Irish lumberjack who never got farther west than Pittsburgh.)

"But I kind of like the simple way white folks do it when they get married in their houses," said Tom. "Like for instance here, if we wanted to have a weddin', why, all we'd have to do is . . ." Suddenly he was on his feet. "Here, Nels, you can be the preacher. You would stand here."

"Never had much time for preachers," said Nels Nichols.

"Justice of the Peace, then. Don't need a preacher."

"Oh, okay," said Nels and he took his place in front of the big cast-iron stove.

"And you, Mrs. Nichols, you could be the matron of honor and stand right over here, next to the bride."

"Who *is* the bride in this ceremony of yours, Mr. Mix?" asked Olive.

"Well, I don't see anyone who'd make a prettier bride than yourself, Miss Olive."

She flushed up pretty red, but finally went along with the game. "Is it asking too much to inquire the name of the groom?"

"Well," said Tom, "Kid Bandera here is against the whole idea of marryin', so I reckon it'll have to be me. You can be the best man, Kid."

We all got in our places like you would for a real wedding, but there was no bouquet of flowers for Olive to hold, so Tom fetched her a handful of carrot greens.

"Now, the Justice of the Peace says . . ." started Tom.

"Reckon I know what he says," said Nels, who began to say the words of the ceremony, sometimes interrupted by the giggles from Olive or a wisecrack from me. Tom, though, was the mask of a serious nature and Mrs. Nichols was such a good actor she had already wet one hanky through, as women do at the real thing.

We got around to the "I do's," which is like the climax of the ceremony, and Olive by this time was in character and offered a nervous little "I do."

"The ring," said Nels.

Tom gave me an elbow and I said, "Whaddaya want?"

"Give 'im the ring, Kid."

So I rooted through my pockets 'til I found the ring and I handed it over to Nels, who gives.it to Tom, who slips it on Olive's finger. The deal over with, Nels folded his hands and said to Tom, "You may kiss the bride."

Tom attempted to do just that, but Olive was embarrassed and got out of his way. "It was a lovely little play, Tom, but let's not carry it too far," she said. She tried to take off the wedding ring but it was stuck on her finger.

Mrs. Nichols had dried her tears and was smiling now, along with Nels and Tom, all of them looking at a puzzled Olive. Me? Oh, yeah, I was beginning to catch the drift of it.

"Leave it on," said Tom, "it's yours."

You can appreciate her confusion, can't you?

"Looks like we're married now," said Tom.

"If that's the case," she said, "then I'm married to the neighbor boy, for it seems to me we played this game when we were six."

"It wasn't no game," said Tom.

Mrs. Nichols began blubbering again and took Olive to her breast, and it was this that convinced Olive it was no game.

"I *am* a Justice of the Peace, Olive," said Nels Nichols.

"What about a license?" I piped up.

"Right here in my pocket," said Tom, drawing it out for us to see.

His third, her first, as they say in *Newsweek*.

Nels uncorked another jug and it took Olive most all of one drink to assess the situation. "Tom Mix, I don't even know you so well," she said.

"Being married'll help that," said Tom.

Well, we had another snort, and Olive looked like she was

trying but could find no real good reason for not letting the marriage stand. After all, she *did* love him. We finally saw the couple off to their bridal chamber, and I crawled between two cowboys on the floor and was soon asleep. Some Tom Mix.

Tom and Olive decided to take a long trail back to Oklahoma, as sort of a honeymoon, so I had to hire another wrangler to help me get the horses back. On the long ride back I got to thinking. Olive was bright and pretty, with the resourcefulness of a girl of the plains, and Tom and her looked good together. But, damn, ain't it hard to see your partner married off, for you know you're more or less in the way now, a reminder to him of the footloose state he put himself out of, and a threat to his wife that he'll want to be free again. I gave some thought to moving on, Texas maybe.

We got the horses to the Stokes place all right. The other wrangler turned around and went back up north. I stayed on with Ma Stokes for a time. I had to tell her Olive wouldn't be along 'til later. "She got married up there," I said.

"Who to?" asked Ma Stokes.

"A feller name of Tom Mix."

"Tom Mix? Why, ain't he the cowboy over to the 101, always trying to get himself kilt somehow?"

"That's the feller."

She sighed long and weary, like, hellfire, there's nothing she can do anyhow.

Tom and Olive come back by way of Miles City, Montana, where Tom knew of a saddlemaker said to be one of the best in the country. He picked up two silver-mounted saddles and a pair of hand-tooled chaps, as wedding presents to each other, though he handed the bill for $600 to Olive, for he had spent the last of his own money on the wedding license and the ring.

Ma Stokes took him in, but she wasn't hiring no band for the occasion. Like it or not, he was her son-in-law now and she figured he'd last a little longer on her spread than on the 101, but Tom developed a proprietary attitude toward the ranch, and Ma Stokes didn't take to that one bit. She'd done all right on her own for years and expected to die before taking a partner.

Tom didn't see it that way. As far as he was concerned, he had become a rancher, the goal he had set for himself.

"I guess this is it for you, Tom," I said. "Looks like you got what you been wanting."

"Looks like it."

"Wear it well."

He wasn't smiling. I could see in him already the seeds of dissatisfaction, for no man can be handed his dream. Lord knows he was not the feller to miss an opportunity, but I knew he could never enjoy what he didn't work to get. Worse than that, he would come to hate the dream of his youth. I didn't want to see it happen, I had grown to like the cuss. I reckon I'd made up my mind to move on. What he said next clinched it.

"Kid, I got a foreman here who don't know his sombrero from a cow chip. I'd like to fire him and give you the job."

I was afraid of something like that and I couldn't figure out why, for my whole life it seems has been spent in a single pursuit: looking for work. But I didn't want to work for Tom. Not then anyhow. You know what I mean?

I wished him his first loop would always hit, and he wished me my dally would never slip, and I was on Toby and riding out again.

I got to Texas all right, but felt no welcome in the place of my birth. I passed on through and continued to Mexico, where the beer is best. I spent the rest of the winter there, living off exhibitions of roping and shooting, and off the chili of them that took a shine to me.

With spring I started to slowly wind my way north again, hoping to get up to Seattle where the Lewis and Clark Exposition was to be held and I knew there'd be something for me. On the road outside of Denver I saw a little campsite off in the field and figured to stop for a cup of coffee. Within earshot I picked up some bickering in progress betwixt a man and his woman about who did such and so when he should of done this and that. The voices were not strange to me and when out of the bickering came a raucous laugh full of sharp edges, I knew it was Tom. I couldn't understand how their station had reversed itself so fast, from a good working spread on the Cherokee Strip to a bitty fire somewheres outside of Denver.

Well, they were happy to see me, if for nothing else but something new to talk about, but I couldn't get halfway through my story 'fore Tom said, "Goddamn that Wilderman!"

"He's entitled to run his business how he sees fit," said Olive.

"Ever I have my own show," said Tom, "I hope I'll be man enough to be open to good suggestions."

"Tom, you weren't just suggesting, you were ordering his people around."

"Well, it was about time *some*body did."

"If you weren't so quick with the ordering, we'd still be home."

Which was about the tone of things when I come in.

"I'll never work for a woman. Never have, never will."

Seems Tom and Olive's mother found it well nigh impossible to live on the same ranch, so Tom and Olive mounted up and joined the Wilderman Wild West Show.

"He half-killed a man in the lobby of the hotel," said Olive, "just for looking at me."

This was what must of caused Tom to laugh as I come upon them, for he did the same exact laugh again.

"When you got Indian blood in you, you learn to hear the language of looks," said Tom.

"Well, I *got* Indian blood," answered Olive, "and all I could hear was nothing, 'cause the man only looked at me."

"You got Indian blood?" asked Tom.

They had signed on with Wilderman and had an acrobatic riding and lariat-twirling routine.

"Ran into Will Rogers in Kansas City," said Tom. "He was playin' at the Orpheum. Ain't he somethin'? Now, who ever thought he'd amount to anythin'?"

From Kansas City the show was to go to Napa, Idaho, but in Colorado Wilderman put them off the train.

"Someday, Tom Mix," said Olive, "I hope you'll learn to use your mind as well as you use your fists."

Poor Olive. I reckon she was having second thoughts about what she got herself into that snowy night in North Dakota.

I told them I had a loosely held notion of catching the

fair in Seattle. Well, nothing would do but that they go with me, and by the time we had rode halfway to Denver, Tom come up with the brainstorm that we take advantage of the big crowds that would be there and put together our own show.

"We'll round up the talent soon as we get there and put together the acts and have us one hell of a show," he promised.

You don't just slap together a wild west show with talent and enthusiasm. It involves stock and props and advertising and advance work and a world of finagling that I never cared to learn.

"It'll take money," I said, figuring that would put an end to it.

"Well, Olive here has a purseful of the stuff."

"Tom, that's money to *live* on!" she protested.

Her protesting did her no good, for at the Denver station Tom told her to get the horses aboard the train to Seattle and get tickets for us humans, whilst he and I repair to the bar to celebrate the formation of this new partnership.

"Goddamn, Kid, it's good to see you," he said. "I was dyin' on that ranch. Now we'll get doin' what we *ought* to be doin'."

He was right on that count. He was never so much alive as when risking his neck in front of a crowd. That was his nature, I reckon, and anyone who fights nature is going to come out second best.

At the bar we met a touring Englishman who had just spent a month in the Rockies shooting game and was busting out with stories of the west to tell his countrymen. He called us "old chap" and talked about how he might want to write a book about his adventures in the west. As I mentioned before, Tom was never very slow off the mark, and he started right in working this Englishman over, telling him about his exploits as a Texas Ranger and as the Sheriff of LeHunt, Kansas. Why, it wasn't long before this English

[65]

gent was crying, "Splendid, old chap," and taking down notes. Then Tom got to how the last hope of preserving the great history and romance of the Old West was through the traveling wild west show, which he and his partner were now in the act of forming one.

"I say, old chap, forgive me my temerity, but I wonder do you need any financial backing?"

Well, we ordered up another round and took in another partner. By the time we was ready to go to Seattle, the train, with Olive and our horses, had already left. We went back to the bar and waited for the next one.

On the wall of the bar was a poster showing the rear view of a cowboy bulldogging a steer. Tom took it down and wrote on the bottom of it: TOM MIX, WORLD'S CHAMPION BULLDOG-GER. He was going to have copies made and it would be our advertisement for the new show.

They poured Tom and me and the English lord off the train in Seattle, and we couldn't hit the floor with our hats if they gave us three tries. Olive was sitting in the depot waiting for us; the look she gave us I never seen before, and pray God I never see it again, but when Tom saw her and realized how long she must of been burning just so, he fell on the floor laughing.

Our show, the Tom Mix Wild West Show, included a totally new act, never before seen in any wild west show. Our Eng-lishman partner had described to us some stunts performed centuries ago in his homeland by cowboys called knights. The routine that caught our fancy was called jousting. All it was really was two fellers each with a long stick trying to knock the other off his horse. Turned out to be a real crowd-pleaser, but it was as hard on the participants as any bull or outlaw bronc. We put a ball of rags at the end of the stick to prevent putting out the other feller's eye, but it didn't seem to soften the blow much. I took one of those in the gut, sent me off the horse like

I was hit by a cannonball. I couldn't take solid food for three days and I wondered that it might have flattened both sides of my stomach together.

In spite of that jousting number, the show was a bust. The rainy Seattle weather was against us and the crowds just didn't show up. It was a good example of the jinx that attached itself to Tom all his days. He did damn well for others, making them rich and himself rich, but whenever he set out to do something on his own he went bust. I've seen it happen to farmers, I've seen it happen to shoe clerks, and I've seen it happen to movie stars.

Another thing became very clear in Seattle, if it wasn't already. Young girls were crazy for Tom. They took to hanging around the show, sixteen, fifteen, as young as fourteen they were, and they had notions, those girls. You should remember that Olive herself was still only nineteen, and here were all these other girls even younger than her making eyes at her husband, and he not doing much to discourage it neither. Lord, did she ride herd on them.

We managed to repay our Englishman, which was a point of honor with Tom. He did not want him to go back to his country thinking ill of the American cowboy. But Olive's money was gone, and amongst the three of us, we had just about enough to get to the Frontier Days at Cheyenne, where we hoped to pick up some prizes.

I entered the calf-tying and bull-bucking events. I wasn't on the bull long enough to feel any body heat, but I did pick up fifty dollars first place for my calf tying.

Tom entered the bronco-bucking and bulldogging events. Me and Olive stood together waiting to watch him take his ride. A Wyoming cowboy standing next to us made a remark complimentary to Wyoming broncs and belittling to Oklahoma cowboys.

"You a betting man?" I asked him.

"Do a bear have claws?"

I bet him my fifty dollars that Tom would ride the bronc 'til it got boring.

I'm forced by all I know to be real to admit that it must of been my imagination that made me see smoke coming out of the nostrils of Tom's bronc. The outlaw turned and bucked as if Satan himself was in the stirrups, and I could tell that Tom was seeing nothing but daylight between his legs. Tom had his teeth clamped hard and his eyes wasn't more than black slits. But he stayed on him 'til the gunshot and then hopped off onto one of the wrangler's horses.

Afterwards I told Tom of the fifty I made on his ride and he was touched by my faith in him. He made me promise to bet it all on his bulldogging event. I was feeling mighty high with my fortune and his confidence was not to be denied. I sought out my Wyoming cowboy and offered him the chance to get even by betting a hundred on the bulldogging. He took it too quick to please me, and I wonder if he could of knowed something I didn't, for when Tom dived off Old Blue he rose up out of the dust looking at his empty arms in wonder that a thing so big could of slipped through them. Good-bye, hundred. Some World's Champion Bulldogger.

Besides the aches and bruises, which don't count, all we had was the fifty Tom won in the bucking event, and we contemplated it back at the hotel wondering where our future lay. That's when a telegram come for Tom from Will Dickey, who ran the Will A. Dickey Circle D Ranch Wild West Show and Indian Congress. But he didn't want Tom for the show, as you might guess. He said in the telegram that he had a line on something new, something with real money in it. Tom was to go to Chicago and check into a swell hotel there, all expenses paid.

"What do you reckon he's got in mind?" asked Tom.

"Beats me," I said.

"Well, he's a damn good showman. You think we should go, Kid?"

"Telegram don't ask for me, Tom."

"I ain't goin' to Chicago alone. I'm gonna need some moral support."

And there was Olive sitting like a dipper in a bucket, but I reckon she knew what he meant for she made no objection when he sent her packing with the horses back to her ma's.

We got to Chicago, checked into the swell hotel, and started right in charging our grub and drinks to Will Dickey whilst we waited for that gentleman to contact us. Too soon to please me, for the Chicago chuckline was fine indeed. When he finally come he wasted no time in telling us of his interest.

"Moving pictures," he said, "the ultimate in pleasing the crowd, my boys."

Tom and I looked at each other full of the perplex. Of course, we had had a look at this thing called motion pictures, and granted it was causing a bit of talk amongst folks, but we didn't see as it offered much thrill to the spectator. It's kind of hard now to describe my feeling on first seeing a movie. I reckon it was like most any other cowboy's. I looked at the thing like I might a five-legged calf, said, "Ain't that amazing!" and went on without giving it much thought.

Will Dickey, though, was sold on the idea and had affiliated himself with a company that made the pictures, known as Selig Polyscope Company. Tom wanted to know where he come in, and I was interested myself, knowing that's where I'd come in too.

"Well, Tom, they'd like to make pictures that involve action, and that involves danger, which your ordinary actor ain't up to, so what they want to do—it's the damnedest thing, but it works—they want to get another feller about the same size and configuration as the actor in the movie, and then when there's something dangerous to do, they'll call in this other gent and take the pictures so's you never see his face. The audience'll figure it's still the actor. Get it? This other feller, they call him the double."

*And that's what they wanted Tom for, 'cause he resembled the feller in this movie they were making and he was known to have some affection for danger. We was led over to the studio and the director, a feller named Francis Boggs, checked out Tom against the hero of the movie. Only one thing was noticeably different. The actor had curly black hair and Tom's was straight. Well, right there I figured Tom had lost the job and we was stranded in Chicago without our horses or other means of transportation out of all its civilization, but the director ordered a little gal there to put a curl in Tom's hair. Tom objected, saying he was willing to do the dangerous part in the movie, but this other stuff was plain unnatural and unmanly. It called for quite the conference, during which I whispered to Tom that we sure needed the money, which they promised would be plentiful. He made me swear on the graves of my dearly beloved that I'd never tell a soul about it, and I never did, 'til now.

So while they were fixing up his hair, Tom inquired what it was they wanted him to do for them.

"Our story," said the director, "is about a banker ravaged by the wolves of Wall Street. In desperation he leaves it all behind him to escape to the mountains and live like a hermit in a mean little hut. One day while out hunting his meat, a pack of wolves

*The following incident, in its essential details, was described in an article, "How I Was Roped for the Pictures," which appeared in *Ladies Home Journal*, March, 1927.

attack him and chase him back to the hut." Here the director's voice took on the excitement of the chase. "He gets back in time, only he forgets to shut the window and the wolves jump in after him!"

"Sounds like a right educational movie," said Tom. "Looks like he's beat by one pack of wolves only to go off and find himself face to face with another variety."

"Exactly!" said the director, pleased as a dog in fresh cow-shit. He looked around him nodding his head, as though to say he knew the audience would understand the complexities of the scenario. "Exactly. He fights the real wolves with his bare hands and comes out the victor. He decides then and there to return to Wall Street and take on that other bunch of wolves!"

"There's only one thing wrong with your story," said Tom.

The poor director's face just kind of all shifted down like a mound of loose mud. I since learned that that's what always happens when a director hears there's only one thing wrong with his movie.

"You can't fight wolves with your bare hands," said Tom.

"I beg your pardon," said the director, who was now shrinking at the rate of one inch per sentence out of Tom's mouth.

"You maybe can finish off coyotes that way, if they're near tuckered out to begin with, but not wolves. Right, Kid?"

"I never heard of it being done," said I.

"Who the hell are you?" said the director, in a twit. It was bad enough he had to contend with Tom, but he sure wasn't going to put up with some trail tramp about to put a chew in his cheek.

"I'm his manager," I said. I don't know what come over me to say such a silly thing, but it hit me that since a boxer who gets in the ring with another feller always has to have a manager, then an hombre about to fight wolves ought to have one too. Oh, I was reasonably sure that Tom would fight the wolves, and it wasn't the money he'd get that convinced me of that. It was when he said you can't do it that I knew he'd want to try.

He fell to laughing when he heard I was his manager.

"Well, good fucking night!" cried the director.

I reckoned it was movie-making lingo. Not a one of the ladies present seemed outraged by it.

"Look, cowboy," said the director to Tom, "we need this scene. Without this scene we don't have a picture."

"I'd sure like to oblige," said Tom, "but you really can't ask a man with his full senses to try to kill a pack of wolves with his bare hands."

"Two wolves," said the director. "Forget about the pack of wolves. The pack chases him, but let's say only two get through the window. Two little wolves. What do you say, cowboy?"

"Excuse me, mister, but so far nobody's mentioned the pay."

"Colonel Selig!"

Colonel Selig come out of the shadows and it seems he's the honcho of the outfit, only I reckoned he was the money honcho 'cause he had nothing to say on any other subject.

"One hundred dollars," said the colonel.

"Hell," said the director, "that comes to a whopping fifty per wolf."

I all but swallied my chew. For that kind of money I'd razzle those critters myself. The heat of easy money brightened Tom's face too and he was set to jump up a-lookin' for wolves, but I stepped forward and said, "You'll have to make it two hundred."

"Who are you birds?" said the director. *"Pistoleros* from the Wild West? Did you come here to rob us?"

"Can you replace Tom's hand, if the wolves bite it off?" I asked. "Can you mend his hide if they tear it to shreds? Can you bring him back to life if your wolves cash him in?"

I come close to overplaying my hand, for Tom was about to contemplate the visions I had conjured.

"Two hundred dollars," said Colonel Selig.

"All right, *bandido,"* said the director, "you win."

They fixed Tom up in a suit of clothes to match them worn by the actor in the piece. They had the banker's hut right in the studio, with one wall removed so you could see what was going on inside. They rigged up a chute that opened at the window of the hut and went back to where they kept the wolves in a cage. The whole business had a wire fence around it so the wolves couldn't get at the movie-making people.

Whilst they were getting Tom ready I ambled behind the hut to have a look at the critters. Little, he called them. They was two big hungry timbers, snarling and occasionally taking a snap at each other out of frustration at being caged up. Good fucking night, I thought. The influence of movie people was already upon me.

Tom took his place in the hut, all smiles and curls. "Let 'er rip!" he yelled. The director informed him that *he* would be the one to say when it all began. Finally he said, "Action!" and the feller tending the wolves opened their way to the chute.

One thing you should remember about wolves, which Tom and me forgot and the director never knowed. They're cowardly devils and won't risk trucking with another creature unless they're right sure the odds are with them. When it comes to human beings, they ride wide of them unless they're laying injured.

So when those two come flying in the window the first thing they did was try to get away from Tom. He had to chase one of them in a corner to get aholt of him. The other jumped back out the window and crawled back the chute to his cage.

Though cowardly, once he has to, a wolf can put up one hellacious fight. Tom had him by a hind leg and the scruff of his neck. The wolf turned and bit Tom a good one on the wrist, at which juncture Tom started looking for something to kill it with. A cabinet of dishes come down on them and broke in a thousand pieces, since movie furniture is not built to last. Me and the movie folks yelled our encouragement to Tom, whilst the director kept telling him where to take the animal and where to turn his face, as though he had a selection.

The cabinet falling on him at least served to stun the wolf long enough for Tom to rip off a leg of the eating table and whack him on the head with it. The table wasn't built no better than the cabinet and the leg broke to pieces in his hand. The wolf got in another snap and come within a two-days' beard of Tom's throat. Tom managed to get aholt of both his hind legs and he commenced to swing him around in a circle.

"Fantastic!" yelled the director. The rest of us cheered. "Don't hit the wall!" offered the director. "It will knock it down and we'll have to do the scene over!"

Well, you could tell that's exactly what Tom had in mind, but he was not about to run through this again. He looked like he was getting a mite dizzy twirling around that wolf, who kept trying to get his teeth back to Tom's hands. Finally, Tom circled him up over his head and cracked him down upon the floor. That finished off old Lobo.

A man come in to bandage Tom's hand, the director said, "Terrific, cowboy," and got his actor to come in and put his foot on the wolf's head for the next scene. Will Dickey congratulated Tom on his performance and introduced us to the paymaster, who made good on the two hundred dollars.

Not a minute too soon neither, for when the actor began emoting, telling about how he would go back to Wall Street and do to them what he done to this dead wolf under his foot, the wolf come to life and sunk his fangs right into the feller's leg, causing a commotion better than "Rattlesnake in the bunkhouse!"

Tom grabbed his clothes and together we scrammed out of there and to the nearest bar, for to celebrate what we reckoned was Tom's entire career in the moving picture trade. Tom weighed his two hundred dollars, not to men-

tion our short stay in a classy hotel, against the few minutes' work he had done and his partially chewed hand. He
concluded that all in all the movie business had done well
by him. I drank to that.

When we had it, we spent it. We took the long way back to Oklahoma and arrived with hardly enough to put a down payment on breakfast. I signed on with the 101 again, and after checking in with Olive, Tom did likewise. It was back to bull-dogging and tall-tale telling, the first of which was the story about how Tom fought the wolves in Chicago for the movie cameras. He added back to the two the pack which the director had subtracted, so that now it was a pack of seven he kilt. By the time he kilt the fourth wolf all the cowboys feigned sleeping, snoring like fat old dogs.

The days took on a likeness, all to each other and Tom seemed a satisfied man. He was content with Olive, if not with her mama. If he was returning to the lady dudes any of the energy they was sending his way, I didn't notice it.

Then one day Zack Miller come to Tom with a telegram in his hand. "Since you're the local authority on the movie business, Tom," he said, "I thought I'd check this out with you."

I believe he thought that some of us boys had sent the telegram as a joke. The Selig Polyscope Company of Chicago was asking permission for to use the 101 in a movie they wanted to make. What made him think it was a joke was that they offered him $100 a week plus $1.50 a day for every horse and $1 a day for every cow they used.

"Ask them for two hundred a week," said I. I was sure finding the range on this managing trade.

Tom agreed with me and we convinced Zack it was no joke. "The Kid's right," said Tom. "The way the movie business works is they offer you one hundred dollars to do somethin' that nobody else can do, and you tell them you won't do it unless they give you two hundred, and then they give you the two hundred and you do it."

Partner, you might think that's an oversimplification of it, but in every oversimplification you got that hard brassy knot of truth. Anyway, Zack did what we said and by return telegram the Selig people sent him an advance of $200 for their first week. The drinks were on Zack and by the time the cock crowed we was on our knees on the road, looking for our eyes which we imagined we had lost.

In due time the company arrived and all the cowboys gathered down to see them unload, figuring the first thing they would do would be to slap a hand across their breasts and start in emoting. It was a disappointment to see that movie folk was just like anyone else, people who had looked for work and found a job. When we saw the director alight, Tom and me tried to cover our faces with our hats and melt back into the crowd, for it was Francis Boggs, the same director who did the wolf picture in Chicago. He caught us, though, and yelled to his outfit, "Pack it up! We're getting out of here!" He was only funning. Turned out his wolf picture was very well received and he credited Tom's fight with its success.

The story they was to do at the 101 was also of an educational bent. Since books was able both to entertain and educate, they figured movies ought to cover as much ground. This one was to be called *Life in the Great Southwest,* and it was to give an account to folks who didn't know any better how a calf born in Oklahoma winds up a steak on your table in New York City.

In the beginning, when we cowboys got in front of the camera we froze stiff-necked and stern of face, as we had been used to doing whenever our picture was took, but Mr. Boggs explained to us that our posture defeated the purpose of motion pictures, which was supposed to give the illusion of *motion*, after all, the more natural the better, so after a while we loosened up and soon we ignored the paraphernalia all together and went about what we had to do.

Tom was given the part of the ranch foreman, which the real foreman took as a criticism of his work. Poor Mr. Boggs spent a lot of time explaining movies to cowboys, more time than the cowboys spent explaining their work to him.

Mr. Boggs had heard a good bit about cattle stampedes, and he said he'd be obliged if we could provide him with one so that he could get it in his film. It's kind of hard to explain a stampede to a feller who never been in one. It's exciting, I'll admit that, but it's the kind of excitement most cowboys could do without.

It's not the sort of thing you can just start for the camera and turn off when the picture's took. It's riding back and forth, back and forth, most all the night, hoping your pony don't trip and leave you under the hooves of the cattle. It's to prevent a stampede that cowboys take to singing, though whistling or reciting poetry would do as well, anything to let the slumbering cows know where you are.

When the director asked for a stampede, we made polite excuses. Mr. Boggs started carrying on again, the way he did when Tom told him in Chicago that you can't fight wolves with your bare hands.

He tried to shame us by saying that it was his opinion that, without a stampede or two, working cows was a pretty dull line of work. He got no argument from us. Truth was, it was as dull and as lonely a job as man could be condemned to. Still, when we wasn't out with the show, it was what appealed to us.

To give the story some excitement, Tom talked Mr. Boggs

into featuring him in a bronc-busting scene and me in a bull-dogging scene. He was much obliged. It gave his film some needed excitement. But it wasn't enough. He wanted a stampede.

But for Tom's compromise, he would of gone home mad and Tom Mix and Kid Bandera might of wound up living their lives as two cowpokes, sitting on the top rail, chewing sticks of straw and swapping lies. We had a great compost heap on the spread and it was the closest thing to a hill within one hundred miles. Tom told Mr. Boggs to aim his camera at this compost heap so that it well nigh filled his looking hole. Then we got twelve head and raced them round and round the compost heap 'til they was ready to drop from the exhaustion. On the screen it looked like a herd of thousands gone wild, with scores of sweaty cowboys intermingled in the clouds of dust, risking their lives to bring them under control.

Mr. Boggs, he sure was pleased, and so, evidently, was the audiences, for some weeks after the movie outfit left the 101, we got wires from Chicago, both Tom and me, offering us parts in a movie being done in Flemington, Missouri, called *The Range Rider.* Straight as a shot, we quit the 101 and rode off to Flemington. Half the boys at the 101 thought us crazy to get involved in such foolishness. The other half was jealous they wasn't asked. This time Olive came along, thinking it wise to keep Tom in her sights.

The director in Flemington was a feller named Otis Turner, and I reckon he had to do pretty near as much explaining to me and Tom as Mr. Boggs did the 101 cowboys, for we was now getting to the finer points of play acting. For instance, the lady in the movie was named Myrtle Steadman and the story called for Tom to kiss her. Now, Tom was never one bashful about kissing pretty girls. I think he'd ruther do that than shoot out the lights. But the lady's husband was standing nearby, along with Olive and about fifteen other members of the outfit, and it seemed to Tom not the most romantic of situations in which to taste a little kiss. Mr. Turner had to get Myrtle's husband to say it was all right with him, and he had to get Olive, which was a good bit harder, to give dispensation for Tom's bit of infidelity. Finally, Tom did what they told him and kissed the lady, but movie kissing made no sense to him. It was a prelude to nothing.

That night, sitting around our chuck, Tom said, "This has got to be the damnedest way for a fit man to make a livin'. They're makin' me chase people I ain't after, fight people I got nothin' against, and kiss ladies I don't have a cravin' for."

The next day they had him ride a horse off a thirty-foot cliff into a lake. It was his first western stunt in a movie, if you don't count the bronc busting he did for Mr. Boggs, which was only all in a day's work for a cowboy. This here, though, this was something special. He had never done nothing like it before, and it fairly set him on fire. Why, he couldn't hardly see a river or lake without wanting to jump Old Blue into it.

I guess I did passable in my role for nobody fired me, but near the end of our time in Flemington, me and Tom over-heard one of the outfit comment to Mr. Turner, "This cowboy Tom Mix photographs like a Greek god."

Tom was all but ready to take his head off, believing there was something fruity in what he said. There was definitely something fruity in the feller that said it. Mr. Turner calmed him down and told him that if everyone agreed with that comment Tom would find himself a rich and famous man.

When the picture was finished Tom was offered a job to go to Florida and make a jungle picture with an actress named Kathlyn Williams. No one offered me anything. Tom spoke up for me, and they said they were sure they could find me some-thing to do, but I decided to go back to Oklahoma. It wasn't that I felt slighted, hell, my head don't work that way. It's just that I believed I'd had enough. The pay was good, the work easy, and the company congenial, but I never got over feeling like a stranger.

[81]

So I went back to the 101 and Tom and Olive went on to Florida, for to make the jungle picture, a thing called *Back to the Primitive*. I reckon he did all right. From there, he was asked to do another and another. He and Olive must of done nine or ten of them that year of 1910. I was out on tour with the 101 Show, but we managed to keep in some kind of touch through postal cards that crisscrossed all over the country trying to catch up with us.

We was doing a show in Washington, D.C., when I received a handbill from him advertising one of his movies. I have to make it clear that he still wasn't what you'd call a star, and had never played a leading role, so I reckon he was proud of the handbill, which said at the bottom, "Also featuring Tom Mix, former Texas Ranger and Rough Rider." Same old Tom.

I knew he wasn't neither of those things, and I didn't need any proof. For what? Who cares? A man's fantasies are his own business. So why did I go over to the Army Department in Washington claiming I was Otis Mix, trying to find out what happened to my long lost brother Tom? I was never very proud of that little errand.

Well, a feller there found his record and sort of breezed through it before he handed it over the counter to me. "When you find your brother, Mr. Mix, tell him we'd like to see him too." Uh-oh.

October 25, 1902, two years before I met him, Tom deserted the army, out of Fort Hancock, New Jersey.

I don't know what I expected, but I sure as hell didn't expect anything like that. All I wanted to do was see for myself if he ever rode with Teddy like he said. But the danger in snooping is how you often find more than you care to know.

I had always thought of desertion as the cowardly thing to do, but I knew Tom was no coward. In fact, he's the only man I know who was fearless, in the true sense of that word. He didn't know what fear was. He had the normal misgivings any man has over the twisting trails of his life, but he never knew fear of life or limb. How many other men could claim that? So why did he desert?

A service record is a cold and orderly thing, a listing of dates and places that don't tell you nothing beyond that. But if you know the feller, and you read it careful, it can tell you more than it means to.

For instance, I read that he enlisted on April 26, 1898, a five-foot-eight boy of 147 pounds. That just happened to be the day after the Spanish-American War was declared, so my guess would be he enlisted at that time to get himself in the fighting. They sent him to Delaware, right through the end of the war. He didn't get to see a bit of the action.

He made sergeant the last day of 1898, eight months after joining up, and was transferred to Fort Monroe, Virginia, where he sat out the Philippine Insurrection. He was honorably discharged on April 25, 1901, at Fort Hancock, and by that time he had reached his full growth of five feet ten, 174 pounds.

Now, why he up and reenlisted, only to go over the hill a year later, is anybody's guess. Mine is he reenlisted to get in the Boer War and when the army let him wilt away in New Jersey through the end of that one, he decided the hell with them, and frankly I can't say I blame him.

I can picture young Tom Mix sitting in his barracks in Delaware or Virginia or New Jersey, dreaming about battles he'd never fight in. I can understand his gathering up his first bride and heading west to the Oklahoma Territory, where the army would not be apt to find him. It's his making himself out to be a war hero that kind of confuses me.

12

Between shows at the Garden a bunch of us went out and found a movie house where they was playing a picture of Tom's. We walked in like a forty-car train, spurs jangling, the room shaking under the weight of our boots hitting the floor. The movie houses in those days weren't more than neighborhood stores that went broke and was converted into dark rooms with benches and called themselves theaters. We sat down, rolled a smoke or set in a chew, and waited to see Tom.

The movie started and the first thing you see is this lady on a runaway horse, just shy of slipping off. Tom goes riding after her and pulls her onto his horse. It's a wonderful thing to see someone you know on the movie screen. Makes it more fun somehow. We cheered, lord, what a good time. When Tom helped the lady to the ground and flashed his smile, the boys stood up and waved their hats and yelled, "Lookit our teeth! Lookit our teeth! Gee, don't they look grand!" I can tell you the rest of the audience didn't know what to make of us. Truth is, we could not contain ourselves, and by the time we seen that little Olive was made up to play the part of Tom's mother in this movie, why, we started pounding each other and rolling on the floor amidst the feet of others. The owner of the place called the police and they come and removed us, so to speak.

Not before most of us made the new acquaintance of a billy club on the head, and the police of New York sampled cowboys' knuckles. Zack Miller had to bail us out, and for the rest of the season we was dragging a dead horse, as far as any salary was concerned.

I stayed with the 101 through the next season, 1911. Tom and Olive spent most all that year in Canon City, Colorado, where the Selig outfit had set up a studio.

That studio didn't last long, and was phased out in favor of locating in a clearing in some orange groves outside Los Angeles called Hollywood. Selig's would be the first movie studio in town. No sooner was they set up than a crazed Japanese gardener who worked at the place shot and wounded Colonel Selig and kilt Francis Boggs, who had directed the picture on the 101. I always like to think that crazy Jap gardener kind of established the pace the town was to live by.

Anyhow, for whatever reason, Selig did not invite Tom out to Hollywood and did not renew his contract when it run out, so he and Olive come back to her ranch on the Cherokee Strip, their movie career finished, at least for the time being.

Movies at that time was, like the wild west shows, seasonal work, and I don't believe more than a handful of people across the country was fixing to make it their lives' career. Oh, there was folks saying that movies were here to stay, but I've seen lots of things come and go and in all the things that went there was folks claiming the thing was here to stay. You see, even though Tom had made a string of movies long enough to make him a seasoned hand, by today's standards anyway, he never thought of himself as a movie actor. He was only picking up easy dollars until something else came along.

Back in Oklahoma, there was nothing for him at the 101, so he did odd jobs, breaking horses and such, for various ranchers in the territory. By this time Olive was pregnant and Tom was thirty-two years old, and I thought I noticed growing in him some notions about the future and his responsibilities.

My mistake, I reckon, because in March of 1912 he come up to me and said, "Kid, you ever been in Canada?"

"No, got as close as Buffalo, New York."

"Let's go."

I thought about it most all of a minute and said, "Okay." I packed my gear and said good-bye to the Millers. "Be seeing you," they said. "Most likely," said I.

Since I was fifteen, the 101 was the closest thing to home I had. I reckon I kind of counted on its letting me go when I wanted to and its receiving me back again when I needed it. Turned out that this time I was saying good-bye to it for keeps.

You could say Olive was not in favor of Tom's taking off to Canada; you could say she disapproved of it; you could say she grabbed a knife, stood at the door, and threatened to find his heart with it if he tried to get past her. You could say all these things and you'd be speaking the truth. Now was not the time for him to be doing this, she said, not in the condition he was leaving her in. He'd take her along, he said, but for the condition she mentioned.

"You've dragged me back and forth across this country," she cried, "—shows, rodeos, moving pictures, and plain old wild goose chases—well, now I'm ready to settle down."

"I ain't," said Tom.

That was near where they left it, for there was no place to take it from there. She put up her knife, and I believe Tom told her not to fret, that he'd be back home before the baby came. She acted like his leaving in the first place made talk about his returning an uninteresting topic of conversation.

Guy Weadick, who had his own show, had sent Tom a telegram telling him he had something big brewing in Calgary. So that's where we headed, with enough money to take us and our horses to within sixty miles of the place, where we had to offload and ride in the rest of the way on Old Blue and Toby.

Next time you open a magazine and see one of those six-page

spreads advertising Canada for your summer vacation, look at the page that tells about Calgary. It'll say that back in 1912 four ranchers passed the hat and raised a few grand to start the Calgary Stampede, which is today the greatest outdoor show on earth. I can testify to the truth of that. What they don't mention is the actual organizers of the First Annual Calgary Stampede: Kid Bandera, Tom Mix, and Guy Weadick.

They wanted something to commemorate the passing of the rough and ready days of the Old West, and maybe in the process hit on something that could put Calgary on the map. We promised them we could round up five hundred cowboys who would come to Calgary in July and get the place all western-flavored in a hurry. Then if they could provide us with stock and equipment we'd put on a show they'd want to repeat every year.

Well, everybody lived up to their promise and when the big day come we had a parade of cowboys on every breed and color of horse imaginable and with every kind of rig that leather and silver made possible. Where there wasn't cowboys there was Indians and where there wasn't any Indians we filled in with Mounties. For good measure we even elected a pretty little thing as Miss Calgary, who somehow later turned up in Tom's bedroll. We elected Tom as World's Champion Roper and myself as World's Champion Bulldogger, or maybe it was the other way around. Didn't matter. We lost our titles in the events that followed anyway.

Tom got gored in the jaw and was cooled out for a few minutes, and after the bucking events I started pissing blood, but neither of us was willing to sit out the grand finale that we had come up with: the chuckwagon race.

We had outfitted three chuckwagons, from flour to jerky, from Dutch ovens to tin coffee cups, and our plan was to race them three times around the ring, the winner to receive a bronzed plate of beans or something.

A chuckwagon is a powerful built thing, requiring a team of

six horses to pull it, for it is heavy indeed, carrying as it does the provisions and bedding for all the roundup cowboys. On the trail it's the cowboy's kitchen, social center, post office, news bureau, first-aid station—if it had tits it'd be his sweetheart. It's meant to move about as fast as a horse thief on his way to the noose.

Tom, his face most all in bandages, was to race one of them; me, my kidneys cinched up tight, was on another; and the third was rode by some local talent, who was the crowd's favorite to win and I reckon technically he did, as he was out in front when the competition sort of fell by the wayside.

We all made the first turn proper enough, more or less necks to necks, dropping behind us assorted campware large and small, and enough grub to feed the Cherokee Nation. The noise up on the hot seat, of all the pots and kettles slamming the sides of the wagon where they hung, was enough to make a dynamite man cover his ears.

At the start of the second lap Tom had a nose on the local talent and I was bringing up the rear. Coming around the turn, the local feller started to pull ahead on the inside. Now I was not in a position to see what went wrong, but Guy Weadick later told me that Tom's face wrappings from his gored jaw started to unravel and was blowing over his eyes, and him with his hands full of reins could do no more than try to shake them free of his vision. The chuckwagon fishtailed and rolled over, pulling over with it all but the lead horses and burying Tom underneath wagon, gear, and horseflesh.

I was right behind him and had to turn my team into the infield, which sent my rig in on top of Tom and his. I knew it was going so I sprung off it, with considerable push from the force of the wagon, and I found myself brother to the birds. I let myself go limp as I always did when throwed and waited for the ground to stop me.

They had dug him out by the time I got to my feet, feeling tolerably busted up inside. I went over and looked down at him and joined in the consensus of the rest of the witnesses. "He's a goner." A newspaper reporter was already writing up the death notice. But the fall had opened up the wound on his jaw and it was bleeding, which I took as a sign of life.

A doctor looked him over pretty good and determined he might still be worth a hurry-up to the closest hospital. A horse-drawn ambulance was brought into the ring and they loaded Tom in it. The doc eyeballed me and said a hospital wouldn't be a bad idea for me neither, so I crawled in after Tom.

I reckon it was that loud clanging bell on the ambulance that woke him up. "What the hell hit me?" he wondered, reasonably so.

" 'Bout two chuckwagons and four horses," said I.

Tom sighed and laid back, as if to say, well, I made it through this, it'll take the Union Pacific at full speed to finish me off.

"What's this contraption we're in?" he asked.

"Ambulance. They're taking us to the hospital."

I wasn't too keen about going neither. When you've never been in a hospital, after healing from a dozen things that could of put you there, you sort of feel you got a record to maintain.

When the ambulance stopped for some sheep on the road, me and Tom crawled out of it and made our way to the nearest bar. The first drink went into Tom's wound, which we covered with a clean bar rag. The bartender was sure taken with us, and a small crowd gathered when we started to describe the accident that had put us in our present unenviable condition. The truth of it was so good that we was hard pressed to find any embellishments. The best we could do was slow the story down enough to give them opportunities to buy us drinks.

We got a couple cans of sardines for nourishment and took them with a bottle of Sinner's Cider to a table.

Now that the excitement of the Stampede and the chuck-wagon race was behind us, I could see Tom go down into himself. I waited him out, either for the mood to pass or for him to talk. The mood wouldn't pass.

[89]

"I ever tell you 'bout my father?" he said finally.

"Not that I recollect."

"A good man, hard-workin', knew his oats. I—wanted to be like him, like kids do. He was a stableman for the DuBois family. DuBois, Pennsylvania."

"Ah, now I remember."

"Well, once Mrs. DuBois asked me into her house for some cookies. You got to remember that in that town the DuBois house—hell, it was a mansion, we were proud just to live in a town that had a mansion like that in it. And then one day for no reason she asked me in to get cookies. I held those cookies in my hands and I couldn't eat them, lookin' at the house with everything in it so thick and soft and shiny and gold. I couldn't tell you what all was in it because I didn't know such stuff existed. All I remember was being overcome by this feeling that I wanted such stuff for myself. I wanted someday to ask some little boy into *my* house for cookies and have him feel like *I* did that day. So at that time, I stopped wantin' to be like my father and started in wanting to be like Mr. DuBois, who owned such a grand house."

"What kind of gent was DuBois?"

"I thought I had pretty much outgrown that ambition," he said, paying no heed to my question, "but then last year making those movies, the feelings started coming back on me. Those actors were talkin' about salaries of one hundred, two hundred, three hundred dollars a week, like it was sawdust. I started thinkin', maybe *this* is how I can do it. I started seein' it as the *only* way I could do it. The things you and me do best, Kid, are hard learned and admired by them that can't, but in the marketplace they just ain't worth that much. So just when I'm startin' to think I got a chance at the big pot, they fold their hands and that's that. I can't help myself, Kid, it bothers me. I ain't used to losin' once I set my mind to succeedin'."

It was about the longest, and for sure the most personal, conversation we ever had. I was hard put for something to say, since I couldn't appreciate his sense of being thwarted and how it must of et at him. I reckon I just urged him to take another drink and the misery would go away.

Good advice, because finally he concluded he was probably well out of the movies, if they held the power to stir him up inside that way. Only trouble was, he said, that forgetting about wanting something is hard as getting the thing in the first place.

All in all, it was a bad night and could have ended up much worse but for some good Samaritans who loaded us in a buckboard and took us to the hospital themselves.

1916. His last year with Selig Polyscope Company.
(*Courtesy of Tom Mix Museum*)

left:
1916. Descending a sheer wall in *Texas Ryan*.
(*Courtesy of Tom Mix Museum*)

1917. The car is a Locomobile belonging to Tom. The photograph is probably from *Six Cylinder Love*, one of his first two-reelers at Fox.

A cello for mood music. Usually a cello, viola and violin accompanied the film group.

Tom Mix and Old Blue, 1918. (*Courtesy of Tom Mix Museum*)

Lunch from the chuck wagon. On the set of *Wilderness Trail*, 1919.

Erecting a monument to himself, while on location in Arizona, 1919.
(*Courtesy of Tom Mix Museum*)

13

We laid up in that hospital for most all of a week, Tom with four broke ribs, a concussion, assorted sprains and abrasions, and some stitchery in his jaw. I come in for three broke ribs myself, and my plumbing was all out of kilter. We was twenty-nine and thirty-three, young, but how many years can you go on the way we was? When would it finally get the better of us?

What got us out of our doldrums and the hospital itself was a telegram from Olive saying she had delivered a healthy baby girl. When darkness fell, we checked ourselves out, claimed our horses, and hit the trail for Oklahoma.

Naturally I went right to the 101, but the show was on tour with all the men they needed and the ranch had no place for another hand, so I was reduced to living in town, performing odd jobs. Tom stayed close to wife and child for a week or two. Then one day he come riding into Dewey on a new surrey Olive had bought so's she could take the baby riding. He looked like a proper gentleman.

We sat around the Dewey Hotel for a time, just chewing the fat, and then took us a stroll about town. Earlier, I had taught Tom how to twirl a six-gun, sending it spinning from hand to hand and back in the holster. We hadn't had much chance to practice lately, so as we walked we each twirled a gun.

We discussed the finer points of this occupation, about to conclude that it was one more thing with no value beyond itself, when two desperadoes backed out of the First National of Dewey, moneybags in one hand, guns in the other. When they turned to make their escape, wasn't they surprised to come face to face with two cowpokes who had the drop on them!

It's a singular feeling to be funning with your gun and the next minute find yourself pointing it at a feller who throws down his own, mistakenly convinced you know what the hell you're doing.

"Hands up!" yelled Tom, crouching behind his iron, and the two of them reached right smart. Mr. Peabody the banker and his teller come running out, thrilled to have their money back. We marched our prisoners over to the Sheriff. Soon Mayor Woodard was there congratulating us. Within minutes half that sleepy town had gathered and the atmosphere grew fairly heroic.

"I wouldn't be surprised if there wasn't a reward out for these two birds," said Mayor Woodard.

"Mayor," said Tom, playing it slow for the crowd, "we couldn't take no money for doin' our duty as citizens."

Well, it was news to me that we couldn't. The Mayor's mention of reward was the first good words I heard since getting back to Oklahoma, and here was Tom acting like we was the idle rich.

"Ain't that right, Kid?" he asked.

I'd have to be a turd to say what I was thinking.

"That's right, Tom," I mumbled begrudgingly.

It played well. The crowd loved it. Of course, we didn't know it then, but what we was doing was playing a scene from almost any one of Tom's pictures. He trusted the formula and years later would explain it to anybody that'd listen: "I have always showed the value of stayin' in your own sphere," he'd say. "I am always just a wanderin' cowboy. I ride into a place ownin' only my horse and saddle. It isn't my quarrel, but I get

[93]

into trouble doin' the right thing for somebody else. When it's all ironed out I never get any money reward. I may be made foreman of the ranch and I may get the girl, but there is never a fervid love scene."

Now, I ask you: ain't that one shit way to run an airline?

It seemed to work, though. Works still, on the rare occasions when they try it. It gives the crowd what they can't give themselves: the selfless desire to do what's right.

And as it come out, we was given a job too. We was made night marshals under Sheriff Jordon. The occasion of getting a new job was one always to be celebrated and this time we figured on two extra excuses for a celebration: we were returning to our earlier trade of lawmen, and since it was a night job we had only this last night free to howl.

We got a couple bottles from a local bootlegger, who would become our first official arrest, and went about in Tom's new surrey getting peaceably realigned. He seemed a far sight happier now, at ease in his own element, than he was in Canada when he was still brooding over his failure at the movies.

It must of been three, four in the morning, and Tom was driving us out to Olive's spread where he expected her to fix us up with breakfast. He ran hell out of the horse. A low-hanging branch took off the canopy of the rig, and by the time we finally arrived the rest of it didn't look like much neither. For that matter, the passengers wouldn't of got into the Cowboy Hall of Fame neither.

Tom stepped down to unlatch the gate, singing something about the correlation betwixt women, brandy, and trouble, when damned if someone didn't take a shot at him from a window of the house. He flattened out behind the fence post, which still provided plenty of target even for a shooter of less than average talent. For some reason I started to laugh, in the crazy invulnerability that booze provides. The next shot come my way and tore up the seat next to me. Once again I was reminded of the sobering properties of gunfire. I dived off the surrey and took refuge behind the horse, trusting that the bushwhacker would have the good sense and common decency not to shoot a fine animal just to get a clear shot at a drunk cowboy.

The shot at me gave Tom a chance to make it to a nearby tree stump. We held fast for a minute or two and when nothing happened, Tom raised his head. A shot rang out and whittled down his cover by a few splinters. A Winchester 30–30, I reckoned.

"That you, dear?" yelled Tom.

"You woke up the baby!" came Olive's voice from the house.

"Well, do you figure shootin' like that is gonna put her back to sleep?"

I reckon she didn't care for his logic, for she sent another one his way. Every time he moved a horsehair's worth, she pinned him back again.

"Look here, Olive," I yelled. "There's an innocent party here."

She put one on the ground close enough to start me and the horse to dancing. Some innocent party.

God, I don't know how long she kept us besieged like that, but it was long enough for Tom to trot out every apology and promise in his inventory. All shopworn goods, evidently, for she flew the lead as freely as ever.

We'd be out there yet but for Tom finally saying, "I'll have you know you're shootin' at the law."

She ceased out of curiosity if nothing else.

"Me and the Kid was today appointed Marshals of Dewey," he said, rising on one knee. When no shots came he stood up real slow.

"Why would they do a fool thing like that?" she inquired. I bear her no grudge. Considering the characters we were, it was a reasonable question.

"Why?" asked Tom bewildered. "Because we just captured two notorious and desperate bank robbers, that's why."

[95]

Well, that brought her rifle back to life again and sent Tom belly-down behind his tree stump.

"It's the truth!" he pleaded.

"I'm so sick of your lies!" she answered.

"Ask the Kid," said Tom.

"It's true!" I said.

"He'd lie and you'd swear to it," said she.

We batted it back and forth like that for a while until Tom, painful as it was, told her *how* we captured the bandits, and that she could believe. Started her laughing out loud.

The really incredible thing is that she wound up making breakfast for us.

14

So now we was night marshals, Tom and me. Oh, the pay was next to nothing plus a percentage of nothing, but the work was about as hard as the cracking of eggs. On any given day you'd catch somebody walking on his ankles, but officially the town of Dewey was dry, so our chief duty was to curb bootlegging. After that the only illegal activity that had to be birddogged was gambling. There was a cowboy whorehouse on the way out of town, but that had been there forever and folks more or less was used to living with it.

The first thing Tom accomplished was to make our load lighter by legalizing gambling. (He wouldn't dream of trying to make legal the other, for all his life he tried to give the impression to decent folks that he was a teetotaler.) It involved many meetings with the Sheriff, the Mayor, the Council, and finally the townsfolk themselves, but Tom convinced them that if a few games were allowed under the strict supervision of himself, on behalf of the town, the evils generally associated with gambling would disappear. He was right too.

After setting up the games so nice, you'd think Tom would cut himself in for a percentage, as I suggested. He wouldn't hear of it. Said it would be dishonest.

I could see him wistfully eyeing the Mayor's office. Funny thing about the law, those that get involved in it, from defending it to practicing it to controlling it, all figure that the next step is politics. Tom could have been a crackerjack politician. He had the gift of making the most outrageous claims sound like gospel. Though finally the political life was denied him, he put those gifts to good use in an allied art.

After legalizing the games, we was left with precious little crime fighting to engage ourselves in. Sheriff Jordon's son Sid, a taciturn cowboy of about my years, drifted back into town with nothing to do so we took him in as a third marshal, and we mostly just sat around with our feet up, an occupation better than most, I reckon. I've always enjoyed police work.

Our biggest arrest was of an Italian bootlegger we collared with ten barrels of beer. Tom, Sid, and me took him to jail, but he refused to go in, and I can't say I blamed him. Our jail there was nothing more than a concrete box, about eight feet by ten feet and no more than six-foot high, sitting out in a field. The door was a heavy iron grid of about four feet by two feet. The jail was seldom used and the weeds grew high around it.

"You gotta go in," said Tom.

"I ain't gonna do it," said the bootlegger.

"Well, I reckon I'll have to shoot you then," said Tom.

"Shoot," said the bootlegger.

There was wasp nests in the corners of the jail and kids too lazy to make it to an outhouse was using the place to shit in. I wouldn't of gone in neither.

It put us in need of some sort of executive decision, and Tom finally decided to lock the bird up in the Mayor's office up on the second story of the bank. We did just that and went downstairs to pour out his ten barrels of beer. We opened them in the gutter next to the bank and went back upstairs to check on our prisoner. There he was smoking the Mayor's cigars and drinking of his private stock. Well, that wouldn't do neither, so we figured we'd have to make the jail fit for human habitation, and be quick about it.

Down on the street every loafing Indian and out-of-work cowboy had an old tin can and was having a party on muddy beer, along with the town's chickens, dogs, and other staggering feathered and tailed friends. It was near the most disgusting sight I ever seen.

Tom, Sid, and me mucked out the jail, not escaping wasp stings in the process, and all in all it had not been a pleasant evening. We got Jake the barber to give us a bottle of tonic that was slow to sell and we splashed that about to give our jail some sweet-smell. Then we throwed the Italian in there, and I think he knew that this time someone *would* shoot him if he balked.

That done, we repaired to our little office across the street, all of us in a sour mood, to bicker over what we'd have for supper. We had cooking gear and had been taking turns cooking a nightly meal. None of us felt like the ordinary beans or sardines or fried bread. We thought we deserved something a bit fancier that night, due to the discomfort we'd been put through. We all come up with various suggestions, none of which hit the mark with our stomachs. Then Sid said how he could go for a supper of spaghetti.

Darned if that didn't sound good! Only trouble was cooking wasn't what we was noted for, if we was noted for anything in those days, which we wasn't. None of us could handle anything as fancy as spaghetti. Then Sid remembered that our prisoner was Italian, maybe he would know how to fix it. Well, we marched over to the jail and our prisoner tells us he's been bending spaghetti since before Maggie lost her drawers.

First to Greenbriar's General Store for the makings, then back again to the office where we set around the table and waited for our grub. Soon it was ready. He had put an onion in some tomato sauce and gooped it all over the spaghetti and over that he spread out some kind of cheese.

I opined that it was the best dish of its type I ever tasted. Tom said it was good enough, but he'd had better. Sid said, "Well, that's amazin' because I suspect you never et it before this day. Otherwise, you'd know you ain't to slice it up like that but should wrap it around your fork."

Tom claimed he was eating it Mexican-style, where the dish was invented. To this the Italian cook said, "Up a piggy's ass." I laughed, Sid made some remark about "hoof in the mouth" disease in connection with Tom, and the next thing I know Tom's plate of spaghetti was all over Sid's face. The table got overturned, I got one in the eye and one in the gut, and gave out likewise, one to each. We threw our punches without discrimination at whoever was within receiving them, until we noticed that in the confusion our prisoner had escaped.

We fanned out and it took most all an hour to find him; finally we located him playing the piano at the whorehouse I told you about. We had to wake up Greenbriar to give us more makings, and this time we locked the Italian up just as soon as he finished ladling out the provisions, and then we took our plates to neutral corners and et in silence.

It was not a bad life, the peacekeeping trade, but the winter that come was so bitter and blizzardy it put the moonshiners and bootleggers out of business and the peace sort of kept itself. Out of work again.

For a time I lived on icy air and the cuff, and then was took in by Tom and Olive. Sid stayed with his dad. We missed the job we lost, but there was nothing to do but bundle in for the winter.

Maybe a man gets an inkling when something's about to land on him, for one day Tom said, through his chattering teeth, "Someday, Kid, what do you say we go where the winter's warm."

"Sure, Tom."

The next morning he got a telegram from Colonel Selig the movie man. Seems folks all over the country was wantin' to see more of the feller who did all that riding, roping, and shooting in the movies Selig put out. So Selig offered him a one-year contract and promised him his own unit if he'd come out to

Hollywood, California, and star in movies for him, at $100 a week, fifty-two weeks a year.

Tom wasn't quite positive what a unit was, but he knew that $100 a week was close to a presidential salary.

"Pack it up, Kid, we're goin' where the snow don't blow."

Again, the telegram made no mention of me, but Tom always took for granted that any good luck that fell his way fell mine, and I was free to take it for granted too. Only, damn it, I didn't want to go. There wasn't a doubt in my head that Tom would succeed out there, and that there was something in it for me. Only I didn't want it. Wasn't my pride, neither, but I suspect an abiding fear of ambition. You can only ride one horse at a time. If you got to have two, then you got to have two hundred, two thousand, and no cowboy with that many horses ever made for very good company. It's a sorry fact of life that ambition is a bushwhacker, and I just wanted to make a small and moving target, though in the end, hell, it got me too. But that day I told Tom I had other plans.

He tried his best to convince me to go with him, and I made excuses.

"I hear this place has oranges growin' from trees," he said. "You want one, you just pick one."

"Hate oranges," I said.

"But just think of seein' 'em grow."

"Sounds unnatural to me."

"Why, an orange is a wonder of nature."

"I couldn't stand seeing oranges growing," I said.

Well, it was plain I wasn't going to California with him, and we kind of awkwardly looked away from each other, like friends do when they figure they're saying a final good-bye.

"See you in the movies, Tom," I said at last.

"I wouldn't be too surprised, Kid."

15

It was this farewell I remembered twenty-five years later in a small Arizona town, standing in an open hangar by the airstrip, Tom's coffin under my elbow. I smoked a cigarette and waited for the private plane to come from Hollywood for to fetch his body. The years, I reckon, fall down quicker the fewer are left to run. Time decides everything for itself. "Kid, I moved as fast as I could," he had told me, "and it still caught up with me." And now overtook him.

Way off in the distance I could see the dot of the plane get bigger 'til it landed and pulled right up to the hangar. The pilot was a pal of Tom's, a stuntman named Paul Mantz. He looked at me and the coffin and his eyes filled up. He turned away for a minute, then shook my hand, and I helped him load up. We got aboard and left the town of Florence below us.

I stayed with Teddy Eason at her house in Hollywood. She had Tom's old rolltop in her living room. The room had no other purpose but for a place to keep the desk, which Teddy had already established as some sort of shrine.

We rode to the cemetery in the back of the same black Cadillac. Efficiency often gives the look of strength and I took for granted her control over her feelings. 'Course there was a

mob at the first service at Pierce Brothers over on Washington
Boulevard, and Teddy was always one concerned about how
things would look to the public. I didn't know she was crum-
bling. I'm glad they put me with her. I reckon I was the only
friend she had there.

She cried softly in her handkerchief at the Masonic service
at Forest Lawn, but by the time we got back to the house she
was pretty much herself again.

"I half expected him to jump up and say it was just a joke,"
she said. I forgot how warm October could be in California
when the Santanas blow. We sat on her front porch drinking
cold beer.

They had buried him in his white ranger coat and white
riding britches, stuck in a fine pair of hand-worked boots.
White came to be his favorite color. He wore his belt buckle
that spelled out TOM MIX in diamonds. Well, he was sure
dressed for the part, but the life had gone out of him, and it
was the excess of life in him that made him Tom Mix. I wanted
to slam shut the coffin. What I was looking at was not what I
cared to remember. I could go to the wax museum to see that.

"I tried to give Tony an apple last night," she said. "He
wouldn't eat it."

Teddy was taking it well. She was on my mind. The wives,
the kids, the friends and fans who had remained devoted, they
all had somebody else, but Teddy was her own.

I got her to talking. All the long afternoon and into the night,
when we had to go in out of the cold. We spent that night with
hot coffee on the table between us and I got her to talk on
about the Tom *she* knew, when I was still punching cows in
Oklahoma and thereabouts.

She'd started out to be an actress and worked for a year on
The Diamond from the Sky, a serial starring Lottie Pickford.
That's where she met Eugenie Forde, at the Flying A Studio
in Santa Barbara, as beautiful an actress as ever flashed a smile.

She kind of looked after Teddy, and I reckoned she needed looking after.

The serial was directed by William Dean Tanner, who come to be known as William Desmond Taylor. In 1922, he got himself murdered and became one of the first of many unsolved Hollywood mysteries. The whole place is an unsolved mystery, if you ask me.

"Unfortunately," she said, "I made six movies before I had the opportunity to see myself in the first. By that time it was too late. I could not return from the exile of immature dreams."

When the serial finally ended, she joined the others in taking it in a philosophical way, like a good trouper, but secretly she was relieved. She went back to Hollywood and stayed with Fordie, as Eugenie was called, and her husband Arthur and daughter Vic in the big house they had bought on Bronson and Carlton Way when they were in the chips.

"Early every morning I would go out with the others to look for a part. In those days there was no central casting, the studios posted their needs on a blackboard at the gate, not unlike any other factory, and one scurried from blackboard to blackboard, looking for his 'type,' in my case: female, mid-twenties, plain.

"At the first gate I would lose myself in the crowd, emerging finally alone, in an orange grove or the park, away from all the Napoleons and Cleopatras and Neros and Union and Confederate soldiers that jammed the trolleys and streets hurrying to and from assignments. Not to mention the hordes of Indians in warpaint, all of them bruised from taking falls, trying to win the three-dollar bonus for the best fall."

With the help of that bonus, a half-blind cowboy could take a single shot and hope to knock fifty Indians off of their horses.

"And cowboys!" she said, remembering them underfoot.

It was the opening of a lush new trail, and every other cowboy in the west had drifted to Hollywood, like crows following a plow. There was more cowboys shuffling along Sunset Boulevard than there was on the length of the Chisholm Trail. Most of them found work too. Some of them made easy livings. A few made and spent millions.

"But there was only one Tom Mix," said Teddy. "No one ever came close. No one ever will. Why? Art Acord might have been better-looking. Hoot Gibson might have been a more skillful cowboy. Bill Hart might have been a better actor. Why Tom? I'm sure Mr. Autry is a fine man and his voice, I'm told, is quite pleasant, but he should bow his head at the very mention of Tom's name and should desist from referring to himself as a cowboy, out of respect for the truth. Oh, there will be other cowboy stars, Kid, but none as bright as Tom. Why? *I* know why."

He come upon her once as she was sorting out a mountain of his fan mail, and he stopped to read over her shoulder. He laughed, in that way he had, like he was the holder of the patent, and said, "Teddy, people just seem to love me, all kinds of people. And I guess I should confess to bein' pretty fond of myself. You know why?"

"Oh, yes, Mr. Mix—"

"Because I ain't afraid to take a chance. People love the fella who risks something, because they're ashamed they can't themselves. There's too much to lose, they figure. Well, what's to lose really? Your life is all, and that's not yours to keep; that's lost from the minute it's given to you." Tom was never afraid to bounce an idea around.

"And yet there were those who accused him of simplemindedness," said Teddy. "Jealous, all."

Fordie became a gypsy type at Selig's, and her daughter Vic became a comedienne with Al Christy, at Sunset and Gower. Teddy? Well, she kept to herself. "I was twenty-four and living off their charity, helping to clean and cook in return for room and board while I attended secretarial school in Los Angeles. Though I adored the company of actors and actresses, I could

not be one myself. Rather than languish about Hollywood with
so many other screenstruck girls, younger than I, I determined
to cultivate a negotiable skill with which I might at least pay
my own way through life, should my gentleman fail to find me,
and by the look of things he had lost his compass in a distant
forest."

One day Fordie came home and found a note from Arthur
stuck in her pin cushion: "Have gone to China." They asked
around and learned, sure enough, that's where the old bird
went. No hearts and flowers here, I'm only pegging the time.
Because shortly after Arthur left, Fordie began bringing Tom
around, that's where Teddy first saw him.

Fordie was only thirty-three, and like I said, a beauty and a
half. Her daughter Victoria was only fifteen years younger and
they were girl friends. "A common enough friendship, when
you think of it," said Teddy, "when one girl is peppy, self-
reliant, and pretty, and the other is fragile, dependent upon
others, and not as pretty."

Fordie favored cowboys, as did her daughter. She was a
robust woman, free-thinking, with the appetite of a man.
Men wanted her. I would become one of them.

"I came back from classes one night and noticed the new
twelve-cylinder Packard parked out front. Upon stepping inside, my eye was drawn to the piano bench on which sat a large
white sombrero. Curious, I stepped inside the parlor. A cowboy was seated next to Fordie, a tall drink of whiskey on his
knee. My God, he took my breath away. I must have cut quite
a ridiculous figure. I was overwhelmed by him. I could hardly
speak."

At this early date I reckon he was dressed like any other
cowboy along the boulevard, in coarse serviceable clothes of
drab color, though Teddy remembered that the sombrero on
the piano bench was bigger than any she'd ever seen on the
other cowboys.

He rose to his feet and Fordie introduced them.

"Pleased to meet up with you, Miss Teddy," he said, in the self-conscious manner of most cowboys.

"Of course, I fell in love with him," she told me, as though I didn't know it these many years. "Just another ga-ga kid, another twitchy virgin? Wrong on both counts. It happens, Kid. It happens just that way, but only to the fortunate—or doomed, depending upon your point of view. Gone now, lost before I found him, really."

For the first of many times, I had to reach across the table, grab her hand, and give it a squeeze and a pat.

"At that time his name and face were not particularly well known," she said. "Most of his pictures had been directed by William Duncan, who also starred in them. He had only recently moved into starring roles, and they were just one- and two-reelers. But later that year the exhibitors, in one of the first of such polls, voted him among their ten favorites.

"I learned that Selig had found him out in Oklahoma and coaxed him away from his ranch, giving him free run of the studio in Edendale. He was in complete charge of writing, directing, producing, and starring in his own movies. I'm afraid those early films suffered because he was left so much on his own, but he was learning, he was learning, and no matter how poor the film, audiences could not help responding to him personally.

"They use the phrase 'captured on film,' and it's an apt one, but Tom transcended the very film he was on. Nothing could capture him. He could alternately send an audience shivering against their seats for fear he would ride his wild horse right through the screen and thunder over their bodies, or rollicking in laughter at his boyish simple ways and his good-natured infectious smile.

"I can't even remember what I said to him. I was too nervous for small talk. I imagine I said I was happy to make his acquaintance and excused myself to go to my room. Some time

[107]

later Vic knocked on my door and excitedly said, *Teddy, did you see mother's new boy friend?*

"Well, I met a Mr. Mix, I said. Oh, God, I was afraid she had fallen in love with him herself. Somehow I could bear Fordie having him and my wanting him, but the thought of his possibly preferring Vicky made me weak in the knees.

"Isn't he about the handsomest cowboy you've ever seen?

"What about the cowboy you already have?

"Already forgotten, evidently.

"I just know he's going to be a big star, she said.

"Well, she didn't have to tell me *that.* I saw him first.

"I've decided I'm going to marry him, she said.

"So had I but, alas, without her conviction."

Neither of them knew at the time that Tom was already married. Fordie might of known, but to her it wouldn't have made no difference. When Teddy discovered it, the news of Tom's wedded status gave her a sense of hope. She hoped it would derail Vic's campaign for him. "Does anyone anywhere really care about the person who lives in a world of false hopes?" she asked me. I had no answer for her.

"He took a room in our house. There were three women living there, and I can only speak for one of them when I say there was no hanky-panky going on, but I feel reasonably sure the other two were not passing him back and forth either. Tom Mix was a man of high principles." She waited and watched me. "Kid, I'm so glad to see you didn't smirk, as others have. I will go to my death believing in the basic integrity of Tom. He was a pioneer, you know. No one had laid out a trail for him, no one knew the long-term effects of movie stardom. Today's stars have his example and the examples of many others. They will be able to avoid the pitfalls their predecessors could not know existed. But in the Twenties . . . well, things were different then, and Tom had been a simple cowboy adept at riding and with a natural knack for comedy. He fell into certain excesses, but basically he was a good man. He was."

"Sure he was, Teddy."

Nightly she would look for his sombrero on the piano bench in Fordie's parlor. He showed interest in her studies and always asked her about the skills she was learning, admiring of their complexness and usefulness. "Why, Teddy," he told her, "you keep this up and you'll know how to do stuff that darn few people can handle. That's my definition of genius. I believe that the man who can do what no other man can do is a genius."

"I believe it too, Kid," she said, "and someday even the pirates of this sad world will have to proclaim Tom Mix a genius."

Ah, well, what's another pirate, more or less?

One night she came home and there on a table in the parlor was a brand new Underwood. "I never seen anyone up close a-workin' one of these contraptions, Teddy," said Tom. "I'd love a demonstration." He was always crazy about gadgets and motorized or mechanical things. Think of the fun he'd have today. Teddy sat down and made that typewriter sing. He couldn't hardly keep up with the words as they was typed.

"Okay, Teddy, okay," he said, stopping her, "it's yours."

She told him she couldn't accept it, but he insisted, pointing out it would give her the chance to practice at home. She wanted it real bad, for a couple of reasons, but still was slow to take it. "Tell you what," said Tom, "I'm startin' to get a lot of mail and I'd like to answer it all, but I ain't got the time to sit down and write back. How'd you like to answer some of my mail for me on your machine there, and we'll call it even?"

It was one of the brightest moments of her life.

"But it was Vicky he wanted," she told me. "All his life he had been hopelessly attracted to childlike women. Fordie would have been better for him. So many women would have been better for him, and he could have had any one of them. All he ever had with Vic was an enormous physical attraction, and even that I could not comprehend. True, she had a youthful, sensuous figure, but, my God, she was all teeth and nose."

Well, I won't lie about her teeth or her nose, because the camera's work will find me out, but there was more to Vic. There was about her, I don't know, a delicacy that was hard to overlook. A fragile lost little girl about her that you wanted to wrap your arms around and then find—I reckon—that doing so did more for you than for her.

She carried with her, always, a look of desperation and it kind of called out to men. Her father was an Englishman. I never met the man, but I understand he was a charmer, calm in a crisis, fit for his role: "producer" or "manager," depending on his wife's job at the time. He enjoyed a pipe and a pint and figured man's only occupation was nothing, if he was wise enough to master it. He thought his best shot the discovery of his child bride, and of the fireworks at the core of her. When other men were drawn to her it only convinced him of his own good judgment.

Together they dragged their daughter through a string of stiffed-and-strandeds from Buffalo to Manitoba, often with the lack of not only train tickets to a larger town (the only real social security for vaudevillians) but also food for the stomach, a situation Arthur faced with customary good cheer, and Fordie considered just another occupational hazard. Hunger, after all, always ended with eating.

Victoria, though, was to keep from those years of repertory companies, music halls, and one-night saloon stands a solid abiding fear of poverty, and at the time of Tom's funeral, with over a million in cash, diamonds, and real estate, she dreaded with knee-buckling terror the sure morning when the money would be gone.

When Fordie saw the attraction between Vic and Tom, she did a funny thing for a woman whose boy friend was being stolen by her daughter: she encouraged it. She always had a sense of humor. And a pretty sophisticated notion of revenge.

At that time Vic was seeing a cowboy in his late twenties

named Bosco and Fordie asked Tom to "counsel" her and warn her of the dangers of older men, and cowboys at that. What she was doing, and she knew it, was throwing them closer together. The suspicion was growing in Teddy that they'd already got as close as you can get.

"Tom found Vic's cowboy at Nat Goodwin's Café on the Venice pier," said Teddy, "and told him to stay away from the young and innocent Victoria. Bosco's reply, though it lacked a certain refinement, was to the point: *If they're old enough to bleed, they're old enough to butcher.* Tom nearly killed him, to judge from the blow-by-blow descriptions of the encounter. The cowboy left Hollywood and Tom became known about town as a man as fast and effective with his fists in real life as he was on the screen. Vic was thrilled to have been the cause of the fight." The rumors of romance, though, were still all about Tom and Fordie. Things was finally brought to a head by a young columnist in New York named Louella Parsons, who was in the business of writing quick jabs about the private lives of movie stars. She used to be the story editor at Essenay, Broncho Billy Anderson's company.

"Louella began what will, I'm sure, become a tradition in this town. A girl who wants to act or write or do something that will express the talent she imagines she's full of fails to break into the business. Find one who will not return to Indiana but has to stay here adding to her considerable supply of bile, gall, and the other bitterly brewed acids, and give her access to a newspaper's audience. She'll do a fine little job on those who have moved into the creative circle denied her. Power of a sort will accrue to her, thanks to the desire in us to see the mighty belittled, and soon she will be extending her hand at parties and premieres for all assembled to kiss. And I imagine she will consider herself a success. She will write books about herself and the stars she has abused. Watch, you will see a continuous string of them, distorted souls, pilot fish feeding off the scum on the backs of nobler creatures."

Louella wrote an item linking Fordie and Tom, though both were married, she said, to other mates. Well, you'd think that Tom would find himself in a position where some explaining was necessary, not that Tom didn't have a knack for that sort of thing, but Fordie, Vic, and Teddy were all suckers for him.

Little Olive was another matter.

He had invited the three girls to lunch at the studio, during the shooting of his current two-reeler. Selig had built for him a western town of some fifteen acres, complete with saloon, general store, jail, and what all. There was stables for the horses and bunkhouses for his cowboys, about thirty of them. Sid Jordon was there, and Pat Chrisman and Terry O'Hara and Minnie, the Indian squaw, all sent for so's he'd be amongst people he trusted. They were calling the place Mixville.

The scene they watched called for Tom, the Sheriff, to be shot by the outlaw, but saved because the bullet hits his silver star. Tom didn't want to have to explain to the audience with a dialogue card that the Sheriff was saved by his badge. He wanted them to *see* it, to see the bullet hit the badge. He told Sid Jordon, who was a sharpshooter, to stand behind the camera and take a shot at him. Sid wanted to use a .22, but Tom, though he felt sure about Sid, didn't much trust the .22. He finally decided on a 25-20. Hell, this could of gone right through the badge and probably the thickness of Tom's chest, so he got a stove lid and slid it under his shirt and took his place in front of the camera for the close-up. Sid stood some twenty feet away, the rifle at his shoulder.

In silent pictures there was always as much action behind the camera as in front of it, and the crew felt free to cheer the actors during a scene. This time there wasn't a sound. Tom said, "Let 'er rip." The cameraman started turning. Sid aimed and fired. The shot sent Tom three steps backward and to the ground. Once again the crowd thought he was a goner.

They clustered around him like three old-maid sisters over the corpse of their reckless brother, the darling of the family.

[112]

He came to finally and yelled, "Somebody get me a five-pound sandbag." He was going to put the sandbag between the badge and the stove lid and try again.

Looking back at where they had been standing, Teddy saw an intense young woman about her own age. She was holding the hand of a little girl about three years old, neither much moved by the scene they had all just witnessed. There was a defiant yet troubled look about her. "Which one of you ladies is Mrs. Forde?" she asked as they came near her. Her voice had the same twang as Tom's.

"I am," said Fordie, "and this is my daughter Vicky and our friend Teddy Eason. I don't believe we've met."

"Not likely," she said. "I'm Mrs. Mix."

Fordie looked her over. Please, God, prayed Teddy, don't let her say *You must be very proud of your son.* Teddy knew she was planning something like that. Olive might have sensed it too, because she said "Tom's woman" before Fordie had a chance to answer.

"How do you do?" said Fordie.

"Hi," said Vicky.

Teddy couldn't speak. She was ashamed to be facing the wife of the man she loved.

"Mrs. Forde, where I come from a woman respects the marriage vows."

"Ah, you're a long way from home."

It's played thousands of times since, the confrontation between Oklahoma values and Hollywood morality.

"I know he's a weak man—"

"Hardly."

"—and I don't hold him fully responsible."

"As you choose."

"But you—"

"Yes?"

"Out in the open like this. You'd think you'd sneak."

"That appeals to you?"

[113]

"I just want you to stop it, that's all, I want a stop to it."

"To what, dear?" said Fordie, unruffled.

"You, you *hussy!*"

"Quaint."

Teddy wanted to shrink out of sight. She knew Olive wanted nothing more than to strangle Fordie. Vic had been digging about in her purse. "Gum?" she offered, handing a stick to Olive like she hadn't heard a word.

Olive looked from one to another of them. She looked at Teddy for a second, an enemy by association, though Teddy hadn't said a word.

"Missy," she said to Vic, "stick your gum up your ass."

A shot rang out, followed by cheers. They turned and saw Tom waving to them, pointing to the hole in his Sheriff's star. The others crowded around him, congratulating him and Sid on the stunt, before setting up for the new scene. By the time Teddy turned back to Olive, she was gone.

"Two days later Tom came into the parlor with Fordie," Teddy said, "a box under his arm. He threw his hat across the room as usual and it landed, as usual, on the piano bench.

"Vic around? he asked me.

"She's upstairs in her room.

"Be a pal and give her this, will you, Teddy?

"He gave me the box, and I had to deliver it for him. I did what I could for Tom. Let them put those words on my headstone.

"I gave Vic the box and she jumped on the bed, giggling. She put the box between her spread legs and put her nose in the air and said, *And where is Mr. Mix, may I ask?*

"Downstairs with your mother.

"Well, I suppose I have to open it, she said haughtily.

"Then she tore into it. A beautiful pair of hand-tooled western boots. Her mouth was agape at the sight of them, and she said they proved Tom must love her. Then what about the typewriter he had given me? She ran to her bureau for socks, so she could try them on. The lid to the box had been thrown to the floor. I bent down to pick it up and noticed the writing in wax pencil on the underside of it: *I do and you know I do.*

"Can you hear my heart shatter, all over again?

"Do you need the box, Vic? I asked.

"No, no, she said, waving me away like a servant. Everyone was a servant to her. *You may have it.*

"Yes, I took it and I have it still, and when the nights seem without end I read the words. They would have been wasted on her."

But the message itself must have finally found its mark, for soon Vicky did her last comedy for Christy and became Tom Mix's new leading lady, replacing Goldie Colwell. He moved the unit out of Mixville and went on location in Newhall, twenty miles away, near Harry Carey's ranch and where later Bill Hart and Jack Ford would play at being ranchers. It was a good location for westerns, but the big attraction was that there Tom and Vic could begin their love affair away from Olive.

Which isn't to say Olive never hired a carriage to take her out to Newhall. She became the butt of the cowboys' jokes, which in matters of the heart display a humor with few redeeming qualities.

Well, there's Tom Mix with a new woman and a new way of life in California, and old Kid Bandera is still without chick nor child living like he'd always lived in Oklahoma and surrounding territories, and without many complaints. Whilst Tom was making his mark on moving pictures, I was at best making another six miles before sundown.

After Tom and Olive moved out, I moved in with Olive's ma. We got along fine, she saying nothing to me and I saying less in return. I split winter wood right through spring, when I signed on with the Will Dickey show, that gent having decided movies wasn't all he had thought they might be. I must admit

I shared the same attitude, but lately I could sense that the show we dragged across the country wasn't having a satisfying effect on the crowd. They was all gathering in those dark little rooms to watch illusions on a screen. Was I the one out of step? I mean, I could be watching a real lovely up there on the screen, but if the ordinary filly across the aisle happened to flash a little ankle, she had my complete attention.

I never intended to do more with my life than punch cows, until I got a taste of the wild west shows. Now I couldn't escape the feeling that ranch work would be second best. And the wild west shows was already petering out. Hollywood was starting to look more inviting to me; as long as you didn't take it too seriously you could probably have some fun out of it, I was ready to wager. Tom, as I saw it in his movies, wasn't taking it too seriously neither. Most of his movies was in a lighter vein, with fewer adventure stories and most of those was centered around riding stunts on Old Blue. This one I saw, *Bill Hayward, Producer,* has him coming upon a stranded movie company out on the plains. He's just a wandering cowboy, but he decides to make the movie for them. He sits down and whips out a script, then he puts all the actors where he wants them to be, and he shoots off his six-gun to start the action. Well, naturally that starts a stampede and all his good efforts are reduced to pandemonium. I had to hold my gut. That picture spelled out pretty close the kind of partnership I thought a cowboy would have with the movies. What the hell, I had near forty-five dollars in my jeans. If I had to I reckoned I could eat an orange with the hungriest. I saddled up old Toby and headed towards the ocean.

That would have been 1917.

"I became his personal secretary that year," said Teddy. "I had already been answering his fan mail on the machine he had given me. *Dear Bobby, Well, here's the autographed picture you hankered after. I'm right proud to be there on your bedroom wall. Your pal, Tom Mix.* I had mastered his signature, if not his syntax.

"I became his liaison to his growing public, and because he and Vic were so busy I began to perform certain personal services. I found them a private little love nest, for example, and went about buying furniture and food and supplies. Whenever Tom would send me out on these errands, he would dig into his pocket and pull out a big fistful of cash and hand it to me, bills spilling out onto the floor. His salary had gone to a hundred seventy-five a week, while William S. Hart, who was the nation's number-one cowboy star, was earning only a hundred twenty-five, though of course he was being screwed by Thomas Ince, his producer. Tom had more money than he had ever seen as a cowboy, and he just stuffed it into his pockets or his suitcase or his tin coffee cup.

"*Mr. Mix,* I said, *don't you think it would be safer to put all this money in a bank?*

"I called him Mr. Mix in those early days, and in public I always have.

"*Reckon so,* he said, *only what if I needed it right away?*

"I explained to him the principle of bank checks, but he stopped me and said, *I'm pretty good at minutes and seconds, but get throwed early on dollars and cents. How 'bout you cart my cash on down to the bank and make the arrangements?*

"And so I began to handle his checkbook. In addition, I kept track of appointments and professional obligations for him.

"*Well, Teddy, looks like you've become my secretary,* he said. *If old Zack Miller could see me now, my own private secretary. You decide what you want to be paid every week and just write yourself one of them checks.*

"Since even he couldn't tell his own signature from my forgery of it, he encouraged me to sign his checks for him. I didn't bother drawing a salary, just enough for my simple needs. A wise decision, if I do say so myself, for soon he would need the money."

Wouldn't you guess that's where I'd show up. Good timing has never been one of my talents.

Selig had been falling into financial trouble, and had formed a film trust with Edison and Vitagraph and Essenay, combining his output with theirs. Selig's main dish was newsreels, and they were still active in that department, but the only entertainment pictures coming out of the place were Tom's, and they were made too fast, with no attention to detail. A scene left over from some earlier picture would be stuck in a current one, without any mind paid to the difference in costumes or background. You might see Tom lose his hat as he galloped along the road and yet, by God, he'd be wearing it when he pulled up at the ranch house.

"In spite of their quality," Teddy reminded me, "the pictures were bringing money in to the Selig sagging fortunes. Tom's personal magnetism was worth the price of admission."

Selig deserves fair credit for giving Tom a start and setting him up in Hollywood, but the truth was he was on a treadmill and would have stayed so, kept to a studio like Selig's. Selig took the money Tom made without ever sinking any back into the source. The cowboys even had to trade hats and clothes and horses just to give the pictures a bit of variety. Finally, Selig asked Tom to trim his overhead. Tom was always willing to take a cut in salary himself, he would do it later in a pinch, but when "trimming the overhead" meant firing friends and cutting loose good horses, there was no decision to make.

So there I was. I had found my way out to Mixville, but a Marshal stopped me out front. I reckoned he was there to keep out any more crazed Japanese gardeners who might have a notion of finishing the job on Colonel Selig. For a while it looked like that might be as close as they'd let me get to my old friend, but the Marshal sent word over to the unit and shortly Teddy come to the gate and fetched me inside.

"I'm Mr. Mix's secretary," she said, with considerable pride. "He's spoken of you often. I'm sure he'll be thrilled to see you."

"Well, I'm kind of looking forward to seeing him too, ma'am."

"Unfortunately, you've come at a bad time."

I followed her past painted castles, phony forests, and buildings of only one thin side, right from the sidewalks of old New York. Finally we come out on a dusty street not unlike one I recollect from my boyhood in Bandera. In front of the saloon it was crowded with cowboys. A goodly number of them I recognized. I even picked out old Minnie the squaw, though she was easy to locate in any crowd. Tom stood on the boardwalk, his arm around his leading lady, Victoria Forde.

Me and Teddy sort of hung back behind the crowd and listened.

"Boys," said Tom, "we've had us a pretty good drive. You all worked hard, but I think we had us some fun at it and I think you got a few more dollars in your jeans than you come with."

They was no more a stranger to layoffs than I was. They started shuffling about and whispering short comments to each other.

"Colonel Selig has told me to let you all go."

Well, there was a fair total of sorrowful sighing.

"But I told him I'll go first, and I'm a-goin'."

The fellers all laughed then. Friendship's the only stock that keeps going up.

"Now, you boys can get back on the trail if you want to, but I'm stayin' where the movies are. I hate to tell you this, but I believe the wild west show is goin' the way of the buffalo. We're sittin' on the greatest form of entertainment devised by man. We can stay here and do what we do best, and still do our share in keepin' the Old West alive. I believe there's some money in it too. Anyway, my plan is to find another big sugar to take us on.

"You all know the feelin' that just around the bend is cool, sweet water. Well, that's the feelin' I got with me and the movies. If you care to hitch your wagon to my star, I'll make sure you got shelter and grub 'til I get a producer. If not, well, much obliged for all you done."

He gave them a minute or two to saddle up, if they'd a mind to, but not a one of them made a move.

"Thanks, folks," said Tom. "I won't let you down. In the meantime, you need anything, just yell."

"Well, I ain't et in a day 'n' a half," I yelled, like he said to.

He squinted his eyes against the sun and when he saw who I was knocked over two wranglers in his jump from the board-walk to get his arms around me.

He put me in his big car with Vic and Teddy and drove on out of Selig's outfit. Now, the way he laughed when he saw old Toby tied outside the gate you'd think he never saw a horse before.

"You came out here on horseback?" he asked.

Always seemed like a reasonable method of transportation to me. Gives you some company to talk to along the way.

Well, there wasn't a thing I could say that wouldn't have Tom laughing himself out of the car, and the two ladies with him. Keep up like this, I told myself, and you'll be giving Will Rogers a run for the money.

I could say it took me some time to sort out Tom's situation as far as the ladies was concerned, but the truth is I never did get it straight, not from the beginning. For instance, he put me up with Olive and then disappeared, back to Vic, I reckoned.

Olive seemed genuine glad to see me, like maybe this old Texas trail bum might remind Tom of who he really was and put the whoa to his headlong fall out of her life.

"Anyone who ever saw Tom and Vic together," Teddy told me, "would have known that Olive was odd man out in the game of love. I should have felt some sympathy for her. We were members of the same lodge, as Tom would have said."

It got uncomfortable, my living with Olive when Tom wasn't around, so I went on downtown to Spring Street, turned over my hat, and put on an exhibition of roping. With the proceeds I rented a room on Yucca Boulevard.

Two days later Tom showed up there and fitted me out in a black tuxedo. I'll admit to having had aspirations of wearing one of those rigs, but only for the special occasion of my burial.

Now I wasn't even sure about that. But we was headed for the premiere of a Doug Fairbanks picture and word was you couldn't get in without one.

I pulled on my boots and friendly old hat. I'd no more go outside with my top showing than I would with my bottom showing. From Tom's reaction you'd of thought I was the wit of the nation. But after he got hold of himself again, he said, "Leave it on. It's perfect."

Well, I don't know about that, but I had no intention of doing otherwise.

We drove by and picked up Olive. I reckon he had to take her, for appearance's sake. It was the last time he ever went home.

At the premiere he was mobbed going in and mobbed going out. Me and Olive was a step behind him, fighting our way through the crowd of fans. A fearful feeling went creeping up my back, the old familiar one that came whenever I was riding a spooky herd just on the shy side of stampeding.

Tom smiled and waved as the fans shoved their autograph books towards him. They may have been asking him for something, but they was giving him life, and the expression on his face was a richer rendition of what I seen on him that first time in St. Louis, when he broke his arm and the crowd cheered him for his ride. It worried me some, that early. Life's got to have other roots; public praise is a shifting soil.

Somehow we got to the sidewalk. Tom stepped into the waiting limousine and was driven away, never noticing he had left Olive and me standing on the curb.

"I'll get a cab and take you home, Olive," I said.

"I wouldn't want you going out of your way, Kid," said she, almost in a daze.

"It ain't out of my way."

"Oklahoma?"

[121]

16

"Olive went back to Oklahoma," said Teddy, "and no more was heard from her."

Not even when Tom kept pressing her for a divorce, I pointed out.

"Whether from resentment or Catholicism I cannot say. Maybe it was the subsequent discovery of oil on her property that softened her and led her to agree."

Agree she did, and free of her Tom popped the question to Vic. Wait until we're established with a new producer, was her answer.

"For the next two months Tom supported his cowboys while he thought about his next move," said Teddy. "Once again he would stuff his pockets with cash and drive along Sunset Boulevard, stopping whenever he saw one of them to press some money into his hand, though the cowboys always tried to refuse it, claiming they were getting along fine."

Come to think of it, I reckon I was.

"I kept him apprised of his dwindling savings, and when the money was nearly gone he sat down with Vic and me and had a conference.

"I think I'm about to find what I been waitin' for, he said.

"Many thought him ignorant and slow-witted, but they were wrong. He had his own brand of shrewdness.

"William Fox is comin' out here from New York to look over the new West Coast studio. Everythin' I hear in town tells me he's the fella to watch.

"Would you like me to arrange an appointment for you? I asked.

"Won't work. He's got to come to me.

"How do you expect that to happen? asked Vic.

"I ain't worked it out yet. Maybe I can meet him halfway.

"We discussed options and procedures and inherent difficulties in each and then sat in the timely silence that always occurs in such conferences, when the real solutions are invariably found. His head came up from the table and he looked at me. *That blouse you're wearin', Teddy?*

"Yes? I was embarrassed under his scrutiny. I had worn it for him.

"Where'd you get it?

"I made it.

"What do you call the color of it?

"Magenta.

"You got any more of the material?

"Vic looked on, as perplexed as I.

"No, but the store had plenty.

"Could you make me a shirt out of it?

"I laughed. In the midst of our worries, he suddenly decides he wants a shirt of magenta silk. Vicky, more instinctively attuned to show business than I, reached over and laid a hand on his shoulder. *Tom, that's a wonderful idea.*

"And it's gonna work too.

"We went out and bought yards of material in the brightest of colors. Back at the house Tom stood in his union suit as Vicky and I measured and cut and sewed. Tom had drawn on a piece of paper a design for the shirt he wanted. It had two slash pockets and rows of decorative buttons and six buttons running up each wrist. *Tight, girls, I want this pullin' against my skin.* We finally made up a magenta shirt like none other ever seen before. Little did we know we were ending an entire tradition and starting another. He wanted the shirt embroidered and knew just what he wanted, swirls to follow the line of the yolk and over his shoulders, roses under and over the breast pockets. When we told him such fine work would take weeks, he settled for an embroidered monogram over *each* pocket: ◁M▷ It had been his brand as a rancher."

Same old Tom.

"We made him riding britches that tapered at the legs, to be worn inside the boots. They were made of white cotton and then dyed to match the shirts."

When William Fox was driven to his studio at Sunset and Western, Tom was waiting for him, leaning against a lamppost and smoking a cigarette. Fox was slowed some by the sight of him, like every passerby within two blocks. There just never was a cowboy like that before. But he didn't stop the car. Maybe somebody back in New York had warned him about Hollywood. Always the optimist, Tom suited up in a new outfit and took up his place next day at the same light post. Poor old Fox, what did he think, seeing the same cowboy in a different outrageous outfit, day after day?

Finally, after a week, the car passed as usual, but this time the chauffeur stopped and backed up to Tom. Bill Fox leaned out of the window and said, "Excuse me."

"Whatcha do, partner?" asked Tom, like he hadn't seen him before.

"May I ask your name?"

"Sure may. My answer'd be Tom Mix."

Fox thought for a moment, then began nodding his head. William Fox was two years older than Tom, born in a village in Hungary. When he was a boy he broke his left arm and the doctor took out the elbow joint. It weren't never the same and in time the arm withered. Now, the only thing he ever wanted

[124]

to be in life was an American cowboy. He knew that in spite of the costumes Tom was the genuine article. He'd seen his pictures and liked them. This meeting was to pay off handsome for both of them.

"You ride very well, Mr. Mix."

"Had some practice."

"I've seen you here daily. What are you doing?"

"I'm lookin' you over."

"Me? Why?"

"Well, I figure to come work for you. I got thirty cowboys and forty head of stock. I got a girl friend and I got her mother. I got an Indian squaw and I got me a personal secretary."

"You've got a nerve."

"Yeah, I got that too."

Fox laughed and thought it over some.

"You've provided the country with a good deal of entertainment lately, Tom."

"Well, there's lots more where that come from."

"What do you require for salary?"

"I'll need two hundred a week. 'Course I write and direct my own stuff."

"Put out your cigarette," he ordered.

"Wha?"

"What if some young boy sees you smoking? He'll think that he should smoke too."

Tom hadn't ever thought about it, but he stepped out the cigarette he was smoking.

"I'll pay you *three* hundred a week, provided you do *not* direct or write. Be a cowboy."

"I will," said Tom, confused as a feller who lost his gum in the chicken coop.

"Remember what you mean to youngsters."

"Yes, sir, Mr. Fox."

"You start tomorrow, you and your thirty cowboys and your —whatever."

[125]

He tapped the seat in front of him and the driver pulled away, leaving Tom happily bewildered.

"William Fox loved Tom Mix," said Teddy. "Tom represented all he ever wanted to be, not an immigrant glove maker, not a maker of movies, but a *cowboy*. How sad he must have been, ten short years later, to tell Tom it was all over. To tell the man who had made a giant out of a small struggling studio that would surely have collapsed without him that he would have to go. I think it broke his heart. It should have anyway. It broke Tom's."

It didn't start me to singing neither.

17

Now, William Fox did not stay long in California after hiring Tom. He went back to New York, which he considered the major branch of his outfit, and didn't set foot in Hollywood for another ten years. Much of that time Tom was about the sole support of the studio. Fox left his personal secretary in charge, a twenty-five-year-old man named Sol Wurtzel. Winfield Shee-han, who used to be the secretary to the Police Commissioner of New York, was made Chief Superintendent. Fox managed his spread by means of long letters and wires, cleverly worded to keep Wurtzel and Sheehan working with one eye on each other.

"Sol was a decent man," said Teddy, "eager to please his boss, but he lived in a world of budgets and profits. Tom re-sented a hundred-dollar-a-week bespectacled youngster from New York making any suggestions relevant to the filming of a western story. Basically, that was the only contention between them. Oh, I know there are those who say Tom was anti-Semitic. He may have committed the sin of calling Sol a Jew-boy. Well, he was a Jew and in Tom's view a boy, so where is the sin, where is the prejudice in calling him a Jew-boy? In 1939, when Tom was in Denmark, being entertained aboard the *Graf Spee*, Hitler phoned and asked him to tour Germany. Hitler actually stuttered, he was so nervous to be talking to Tom. *Tell him I'll tour Germany over his dead body*, said Tom to the translator. Would an anti-Semite have said that?

"He made Sol's life miserable, but Sol's life would have been miserable anyway, answerable as he was to William Fox. I believe Sol was the first person I ever met in this business suffering from stomach problems. Certainly not the last. He didn't like Tom either, you know. Why do you believe, Kid, he pulled you out of the unit and tried to make you a star? When that didn't work, he tried Buck Jones. He wanted to find someone who could put Tom out of business, as Tom had done to Bill Hart. But I'm getting ahead of my story and telling you things you already know. Oh, my, you didn't know. Does it really matter now?"

Now it doesn't. When you're ninety, not much does. But *then*, goddammit, it mattered, which only goes to show you that when someone drops the promise of fame and fortune on your lap, why the weight of it near keeps you from ever standing up.

"I can't help believing that Mr. Fox knew from the start what he had in Tom," said Teddy, "even though the two-reelers he was making now were just like the one hundred sixty-odd western comedies he had made at Selig. At least now he was able to devote a full month to each film; at Selig he had to make one a week. Still, I think he would have come to a dead end there just as surely as if he'd stayed at Selig. He made only five for Fox, who let him direct them as well, contrary to his earlier wishes, which makes me believe this period was just a warming up for greater things to follow."

The Fox outfit, unlike Selig, had the means to get their product to hell and gone and Omaha on Sundays, so in quick time the public was clamoring for more of Tom Mix.

Sol Wurtzel called him into his office. "Mr. Fox is very pleased with your pictures here, Tom."

"Great, ain't they?"

Tom never thought modesty was such a hot virtue.

"But he wanted to know where are the fancy outfits you used to wear?"

"Them? Oh, they was just to get his attention."

"Don't you think they might also get the attention of the audience and the public?"

While Tom thought about it, Sol said, "The audience has things on their mind. They are worried about their lack of funds or their Aunt Tillie's ulcer or their wicked boss or their wayward brother. . . . Your job is to take their attention away from those troubles and pin it to yourself. You ever watch Doug Fairbanks?"

"Not bad."

"He doesn't give you a chance to think of anything else. Bill Hart, now, is going to run into trouble. He makes them think of too many things, unpleasant things."

"I like to keep 'em happy," said Tom.

"Dustin Farnum's about to start a five-reel feature."

"Nice fella, Dusty."

"Durand of the Badlands, it's called."

"Catchy title."

"Mr. Fox wants you in it, in a supporting role."

"Dustin Farnum had fallen out of favor," said Teddy, "and Mr. Fox wanted to see him and his new discovery in the same arena, like Roman gladiators. Oh, there will always be a Fox Studio."

I played second or third heavy in the shorts we did before the Farnum picture, but none of the unit was in that one, only Tom. After, things were pretty slow, waiting for the public's reaction.

The closest Tom had ever come to a car in our days in Oklahoma was when he tried to talk the Miller brothers into letting him use one of theirs for the bulldogging event. Now he had already gone through three or four of the things and

[129]

had just bought himself a new Stutz. He took me out for a ride in it and we passed the bottle back and forth as we rode. All of a sudden he hit the brakes and I all but went out of the Stutz.

We had just drove past an Italian vegetable vendor on Vine Street. Tom jumped out of the car and ran back to the vendor. I expected him to buy the whole supply. He did that once with a flower cart, showering them all on Vic. He was mighty fond of that gal. But he wasn't interested in the vegetables at all. What caught his eye was the horse pulling the cart, a sorrel gelding with hind white sox. Tom said something about the animal being much too smart to be wasted on the drudgery of pulling a cart. He had a way with horses, of looking past their beauty and finding their intelligence, a talent that sometimes failed him when it come to humans.

Tom took a carrot from the wagon, tossed a silver dollar to the owner and fed it to the horse, who nuzzled him like they could get along if they had to.

"Tell me there, partner, would you like to sell this here horse?" Tom asked the vendor.

The Italian said, "I don't know," in the hesitating way of a man who'll sell anything if the price is right.

Tom reached into his pocket and peeled off a ten-dollar bill.

"Worth more," said the vendor.

Tom peeled off another ten. He'd peel off bills 'til that horse was his.

"Sold," said the vendor, and he began to unhitch him.

Tom was right pleased with his bargain. "What's the fella's name, partner?"

"Don't got a name."

"Hell, how can you have a horse without a name?"

"Don't need one."

"Well, what the hell is your name? I 'spect you need one."

"Tony."

"Good enough."

There was a rope in the Stutz. Tom tied Tony to the door handle and led him to his new home.

"Tony the Wonder Horse," said Teddy. "Eventually he would receive more fan mail than any other animal in films and more than all but a few of the human stars. Like his human colleagues he did not escape unscathed the pitfalls of stardom. He became an insufferable ham and accomplished upstagings that would have put a Barrymore to shame."

Tom walked away with the Farnum picture, and I reckon the trail Fox had to follow was marked clear.

"You'll recall what they did with Theda Bara and Annette Kellerman," said Teddy. "Theda, née Theo Goodman, was all the rage and through the success of her pictures made the financing of other, more serious ventures possible. Annette had been brought to the verge of major stardom, though unfortunately failed to get over the top. These two were among the first of the manufactured personalities created by anonymous publicity people more skillful in deception than even they realized. They took a dark-eyed shy little beauty from Cincinnati, who had in her face the hint of mystery, scrambled the letters in *Arab Death,* and came up with Theda Bara, the Egyptian vamp. And Annette? Besides her good looks, she was almost totally without distinction. She did show some slight affinity for swimming, however, and the publicity hawks pounced on this, turning her into an Olympic champion, a veritable mermaid.

"So it's not difficult to imagine the scene between Tom and some young man or woman assigned the duty of writing the official studio biographical sketch of the newest Fox contract player.

"Born?

"El Paso, Texas.

"It seems now so small a fib, the consummate cowboy trying to escape the onus of an eastern birthplace, but Tom had no way of knowing how a thing like that could get out of hand. They soon wanted to make him the adopted son of Buffalo Bill Cody. Tom was sorely tempted too, because he loved Buffalo Bill, and when as a child he saw him in his traveling Wild West

Show he said to himself, *That's what I want to do.* Isn't that the way most little boys take their first step? They read a book or watch a painter or travel with a tinkerer and say, *I want to be like this.* But Tom resisted, thank God, the suggestion that he call himself Cody's adopted son. Instead he compromised and settled for a captain in the Seventh U.S. Cavalry. I suppose that in his naiveté he thought his real father, a simple stablemaster, would either not hear about it or pay no attention if he did. Tom, unlike Will Rogers, believed none of what he read in the newspapers."

Speaking of Will, he might have been as big a dreamer as Tom, or maybe he was telling the truth about himself, but there sure are some peculiar similarities in their stories. My hunch is that Tom borried what he liked from Will's background and used it in his own. Other cowboys, those who came later, borried from Tom's. They probably thought it a sign of friendship or admiration, like sharing a woman.

Tom's Indian blood, for instance, must of come from Will, because it sure didn't come from his forefathers, who was English, Irish, and Pennsylvania Dutch. And I know the site of his birth, a log cabin, was Will's. Writing in *Photoplay*, Tom said, "I've heard a lot of times . . . that being born in a log cabin is one of the best ways to cinch success later on in life. It's now regarded as a heap more lucky than being born with a gold spoon in your mouth. A lot of men would have laid the scene of their entrance into this sphere in a log cabin if they'd been writing their own scenario."

Well, of course, he was, with a hand from the Fox publicity department. He always felt free to use personal experiences as material for his films, and it wasn't much harder for him to take movie scenes as part of his personal experience.

Back to scene, as the writers say.

"What occupations did you pursue prior to your contract here?" asks this young man or woman that Teddy has gathering up information for the official biographical sketch.

"Wal', you might say I pursued quite a few."

"Anything we might use for promotion?"

"Colonel Selig used to bill me as an ex-Texas Ranger and U.S. Marshal."

Which ain't necessarily the same as having been those things.

"He *could* have filled those jobs," claimed Teddy. "I mean, he certainly proved he had the ability. And you know he was a lawman, and acquitted himself with honor in the role. Who knows better than you? What difference does it make if they sweetened the thing with those impressive titles, as long as it brought people to the box office?"

Back to scene again, 'nuff said.

"Military duty?"

"I was a scout with Teddy in Cuba."

I reckon I smiled the wrong way 'cause Teddy piped up, "Now that was true. How often have I kissed the wound on his neck that he sustained there?"

"Any awards or honors or medals, etc., in the military or elsewhere?"

"Does National All-Around Champion Cowboy count?"

I can see this young man or woman running with his notes to Sol Wurtzel, all excited. "Holy shit, chief, we've got the real item here."

"They did, you know," she said, "but it was only a base for them to build upon, to create a glittering attraction that people would *pay* to see. That is the fundamental bedrock of this business, Kid, and the key to success in it, so simple really. Just find that which people will *pay* to watch. The possibilities are frightening."

Theda finally laughed off the monster created for her. So did Annette. But Tom came to believe it. In a few years Vic would give him a baby girl. On her birth certificate Tom would write his own birthplace as El Paso, Texas. The danger, or blessing, of lies is the way you come to believe them.

One war, one major battle was not enough. They put him in the Philippines, they put him in the Boxer Rebellion in China, they put him in the Boer War in South Africa, breaking horses for the British. This last one was also Will's contribution to Tom's history. A few years before Tom died, broken derelicts, veterans of every war and insurrection since Grant took Richmond, would show up and rehash with Tom campaigns neither of them fought in, each claiming to know the other well, all of them crediting Tom with saving their miserable lives in one or another scrape.

Tom welcomed them all. "Will you have a bit of the white or a bit of the red?" he'd ask, a fifth of gin in one hand, a fifth of bourbon in the other. A bit of the white, a bit of the red.

The anonymous Fox publicity folk elected him Sheriff of half a dozen counties throughout the Southwest, appointed him Marshal in others.

"Why didn't they leave him alone?" sighed Teddy. "You would have thought that his killing the nefarious Shonts brothers in the line of duty would have been enough. How many people realize how sensitively he was affected by that deed? Because of it he would never kill a villain on screen. He had taken human life, and in the process tasted lead himself. He knew the truth of such an act and knew that it had no place on a theater screen."

I nodded in complete agreement. It's the kind of bird I was.

They put him with Madero's forces in Mexico and sentenced him to a firing squad, then saved him a second before the command to fire.

They gave him a military academy education (Virginia Military Academy, the same school they graduated Ken Maynard from) and they told him he could speak Spanish and a bunch of Indian dialects. Tom could speak enough Spanish to catch the Aztec two-step in Tijuana, and as for Indian he couldn't even make sense of Minnie, nor she him, which is the arrangement he preferred.

They settled on what he used to be, so they turned their heads to what he would become. Tom loved the Old West and he wanted people to remember those times with reverence. Even he had to admit that Bill Hart's hard-drinking, hard-fighting cowboy with a shady past and a shaky future was pretty close to the mark. The problem was how to improve on Hart's character.

"Do you mean to tell us that all cowboys smoked and drank?" they asked him.

"Yup, kind of helped clear out your pipes."

"You never met one or heard about one who didn't?"

"There might've been one or two, but I can't recollect their names."

"Well, supposing we make you a cowboy who doesn't drink or smoke?"

Tom had some real misgivings about that.

"One who doesn't curse or take advantage of girls."

Tom worried about stretching the limits of believability.

"One with a bit of flair."

"And a sense of humor," added Tom. "Like in my other pictures."

"Absolutely. Hart is morose and moody. He has a sense of humor like the rug on this floor."

"I'll wear fancy costumes."

"That's the idea. Give him some dash and color. A mysterious stranger who shows up in town and has to save everybody's bacon."

And so they took it to William Fox and he found it good.

"Tom liked the idea too," said Teddy. "Of course, the ever-virtuous, courageous, good-humored, sartorial cowboy they created had nothing to do with authenticity, but once he was created Tom received him with the observation that *The Old West is not a certain place in a certain time, it's a state of mind. It's whatever you want it to be.*

"With that convenient explanation he set the pattern for

[135]

cowboy heroes that has remained substantially unchanged to this day. Mark my words, Kid, the future cowboy heroes will either be more like Hart or more like Mix, that's all there is.

"I called it a 'convenient remark,' and that smacks of sarcasm. He was right. Once there was a place called the West, in a time when people moved toward it in order to prove something. Finally, so many had done it that it no longer became a proving ground. The era had already passed by the time Tom was born. Still, those with something to prove continue to move westward, some until the ocean stops them. Here.

"What the West was really like, what it meant to those who settled it, now exists only in our imaginations. Who, after all, is locked into his own history? Why shouldn't each of us write our own scenarios? Shall I tell you why most men cheat on their wives? Their wives know them too well. With another woman they have a chance to be someone else. That's the last I'll have to say about it."

Now, Teddy never had much going for her, but one thing she didn't have going against her was stupidity.

18

Tom's first starring role in a Fox feature was in *Cupid's Roundup*. Ed LeSaint directed it, and Ed became one of Tom's favorite directors. After that, in roughly one hundred features, Tom always had the starring role. They bumped his pay to $400 a week. The leading lady in *Cupid's Roundup* was Wanda Petit. Vicky could have had a supporting role, but turned it down. Fordie took it instead. Vicky might of been miffed 'cause she wasn't offered the lead, but I don't think that was it. I think she saw her future didn't lie in an acting career, leastways not hers. She played only one more role before quitting for good, the lead opposite Tom in *Western Blood*. That one introduced a cowboy named Buck Gebhardt Wurtzel seen with the Barnum and Bailey Circus. When I couldn't be a star, in my style, they made this feller into Buck Jones, and gave him Tom's style. Nice feller, though. Died like a hero, pulling people out of a burning nightclub in Boston.

Vic and Tom finally got married on location in Las Vegas, New Mexico. We was there for to shoot a number of films under the direction of Lynn Reynolds.

Lynn directed more Mix pictures than any other director. Later, Sol Wurtzel would try to force down Tom's throat directors who had their own ideas, but Lynn was agreeable to whatever Tom said.

It was a workable arrangement. Like most of the cowboys he directed, Lynn had no ambitions in movies. He wrote if he had to, directed when he could. His wife, Kathleen, did some acting, a few times as Tom's leading lady. It was a good living. If Lynn wanted something done one way and Tom wanted the opposite, it was always, "Sure, Tom, why not?" He never believed the work he did would be preserved in granite.

"Familiar with the volatile nature of film," said Teddy, on the subject of Lynn, "and the fickle attitude of its audience, he correctly assumed that he would never belong to the ages. If anyone today remembers poor Lynn at all it is for the mysterious circumstances surrounding his death, and even that is an in-house speculation since reports of it were kept from the press at the time. Of course, I know. I happened to have been there."

All in good time, partner, all in good time.

"I suppose at one time Lynn was enthusiastic and full of promise and ideals," she went on. "You never start out a cynic, do you? But by the time I met him he had already drunk with a few too many producers, held hands with a few too many starlets, and lunched with a few too many actors. Tell him what to do and who to do it with, and he'd take care of pointing the camera at the action and bringing the film in on schedule. At the end of the picture he'd take his pay and go out on whatever new one you assigned him. They were all the same to him.

"Naturally he drank. No more than Tom, I'd judge, but few men drank more than Tom. Unlike Tom, however, who drank only to amuse himself and others, Lynn became morose, insulting, and finally obnoxious when he drank. It must be a progressive disease, for over the years I watched Tom become more like Lynn, and Lynn . . . well, Lynn became dead."

Lynn was the first director I knew of who tried to organize the story into numbered scenes. It might be fair to say he gave

[138]

rise to the format screenwriters and directors have been using these many years.

From New Mexico we moved on to the Grand Canyon. Tom loved the canyon and wanted to use as many natural wonders and national parks as he could. He wanted for people who might never be able to visit them to see them and appreciate their country.

It was about the happiest time in Tom's movie career. He was back in his own element. We loaded all our supplies and cameras and the portable piano and stringed trio we needed for mood music on mules and horses and wound our way to the bottom of the canyon where we made camp. Tom's laughter echoed off the walls of the canyon whenever he looked at the expression on Vic's face. She was a New York City girl seeing the Grand Canyon for the first time, and from the back of a mule.

"It was a hard life," said Teddy, "with few comforts or diversions, but I loved it. In the mornings I would take care of Tom's correspondence or any notes he had dictated, but by the afternoon would be free to watch them shoot the movie, and sometimes themselves."

She made sure that remark went home. Well, yeah, I did happen to fire too close to Tom's face. Blacked his ear with powder burns and all but bust the eardrum. They had to shoot from Tom's other profile for the rest of the picture. Me and Sid Jordon was the two sharpshooters in the outfit and I reckon we had a little friendly competition going seeing who could come the closest without drawing blood.

Hardly a day went by there wasn't some injury, usually to Tom, since he wouldn't hear of being doubled for the stunts. As pliable as Lynn was, he worked on Tom to use a double.

"We can always get another double," said Lynn, "but if you kill or maim yourself, good friend Fox is out a valuable piece of property."

"When I'm old and gray I'll give some thought to it. 'Til then,

I reckon I'll do the stunts, because to tell you the truth I don't think nobody here could."

So there you'd find Tom, dangling down the sheer canyon wall, his arm caught in a loop in the rope. By the time he'd get down a brown path was burned round his wrist.

I lost track of how many blows, sprains, and cracked bones Tom collected down on our Grand Canyon location. After the day's shooting was over, he'd be up to boxing with Dan Clark, our still photographer. Dan became a favorite with Tom, and was later made the assistant cameraman. By 1922 he was head cameraman for the unit and solely responsible for the fine photography of all Tom's later pictures at Fox.

Evenings was our best time. We'd watch Tom and Dan spar, read the papers and mail delivered by the cowboy who was dispatched daily to the top, for to deliver our film. Then we'd shower before dinner. It's a habit I fell into in Hollywood, one of a few.

We had two showers set up on the perimeter of the camp, one for men and one for the ladies. Tom stood in line with his cowboys, he never tried to place himself above us. At the time, he was very keen on a soap called Packer's Tar Soap, a mean-smelling item. I remember one evening in line when he turned back to me and said, "You see this soap?"

I looked at it in his hand. It looked as awful as it smelled. "Yeah."

"Well, I been usin' this soap for close on five years."

"Ain't worn much, is it?" I said. I always found something to amuse me.

Showered, we'd sit around the chuckwagon for our grub. It was close to being on the trail. We had an irascible old cook named Dried Apple Pete, who's since opened a restaurant in Burbank. Everyone enjoyed chucktime so much that when we finally got back to Hollywood Tom ordered a chuckwagon built on the chassis of a Studebaker, and the actors and crew always et their lunch from it.

After our grub we'd sit around the campfire. Usually we'd sing, you feel an obligation to sing when faced with a campfire, and a group sing does wonders for sagging spirits. Years later we lost a girl in a river stunt and the company sat around the fire crying about it 'til Tom led us in a sing.

We was there seemed like forever, and like on the range it got boring. We'd have to invent our own diversions, practical jokes usually, most making use of the snakes and other wildlife of the canyon. Tom hates snakes more than telling the truth, but he had to suffer the pranks along with the rest of us.

Betting was popular too. One night Tom bet he could stand on one foot for an hour. All the bets was covered and we made a circle around him, sitting on the ground and doing nothing but watch him stand on one foot. We tried to make him lose his balance by warning him of the rattler creeping up on him, but it didn't do no good. At the end of an hour, he calmly put his foot down, lifted the other and stood there for another hour.

Another night, whilst jawing around the chuckwagon, one of the boys observed, "I reckon Fifi's tail to be about ten inches long."

"Ain't no longer'n eight," I said.

Fifi was the camp cat.

"Well, you're both close, but I'd bet money it's nine," said Tom.

Soon everyone made his guess, to the quarter-inch, and tossed a dollar in a hat. Then it was after Fifi with a ruler to find our winner. I recollect it was Benny Kline.

Benny was the unit cameraman, and a helluva betting man. He'd won a fair total betting on the dimensions, speed, colors, and habits of canyon flora and fauna. Late one afternoon he looked at the high sweeping bluff on the other side of the river and said, "Say, look up there, ain't that a man?"

We all gathered at the river and squinted our eyes where Benny was pointing.

[141]

"It sure looks like a man," said some.

"That's not a man," said others.

"Well, if it is a man," said Benny, "he must be dead."

It sure looked like a man, but most of us thought it was an unlikely spot to find a man, dead or alive. "Wonder what it is, then," said Benny.

"Probably an old tree that fell there," somebody suggested.

"Sure looks like a man, though," claimed Benny.

Tom snuck over to his tent for his binoculars and focused them on the thing across the river. It was a prop dummy. We used them whenever we had to throw a man off of a cliff or into a raging river or anywhere else a man wasn't apt to survive.

We had a ranger staying with us. Tom got him and asked him off by himself if he happened to know how one of our dummies found its way to the cliff yonder. The ranger quickly 'fessed up that Benny Kline had paid him to put it there.

Tom put away his binoculars and went back to join Benny and the rest of us still perplexed and looking across the river. "How big do you suppose that thing is?" asked Benny. "I'd say it was about five feet."

"Oh, no, that's six feet at least, likely more," said some cowboy.

And soon we was off again, each of us guessing at the size of the unknown thing, which is what Benny wanted to get to in the first place.

"That's six feet long," said Tom, "or Texas ain't my home."

He said it with some authority and most of the bunch agreed it must be six feet. Benny was sure that it didn't go more than five-four. 'Course he had the advantage, since he knew it was a dummy and he knew the dummies was never taller than five feet.

"Who's willing to bet?" asked Benny.

All of us went along with Tom that it was six foot tall, and Benny covered all bets. The ranger volunteered to fetch the object. We watched him cross the river on a small boat and

[142]

slowly climb. Nobody wanted to eat 'til he came back. Finally we saw him next to it. He waved to us and hoisted it on his shoulder. Sure did look like a man.

He come back to camp and laid out the dummy before us, stretched to six foot two, just as Tom paid him to. Poor Benny, the money he lost was exceeded only by the damage to his pride.

"It was idyllic, our time there," said Teddy, "and I could have stayed forever, but Vic grew irritable. She did not marry Tom, and abandon her career, she said, in order to live at the bottom of the Grand Canyon in the company of gamblers and pranksters, standing in line to bathe and eating greasy food with ashes in it. She wanted to see people again, go to parties and night clubs, she missed her mother.

"*Well, we ain't gonna stay here forever, darlin'.*

"*We've* already *been here forever. I want to go home.*

"*Stay here, baby, it won't be the same without you. Don't leave your big boy lonely.*

"It was one argument I wanted Tom to lose, and he did, but imagine my horror when she said she wanted me to return with her.

"*Teddy ought to stay here,* he said. *What if I need her—to spell a word or something?*

"*Lynn can spell,* said Vicky.

"*Only one of my numerous talents,* said Lynn.

"Tom insisted he needed my services close at hand and Vic was sent off pouting with a cowboy escort. Tom was heart-fallen, it was his first separation from his new wife, and he never fully regained his sense of humor.

"One night, after a particularly hard day, a group of us sat around the fire. Tom stretched out and in the most natural and unassuming way rested his head on my lap. Just as naturally I stroked his hair. Let me be his sister, then, I asked fate, anything.

"He held in his hands Will Rogers' first book, delivered that

TOM MIX DIED FOR YOUR SINS

day by our own version of the pony express. It was the year before that Will had made his first picture, a debut without distinction, and Tom had recommended that he concentrate on other pursuits, perhaps the stage, since Will seemed to do so well face to face with people. Now he had written a book and Tom was overwhelmed by it. *To think that old Will could put all these words together and have them make sense to folks.* He flipped the pages and shook his head in wonder. *There was times on the range we might of made good use of these.*

"*If ever you grow tired of breaking your neck,* said Lynn, the booze-sodden words slowly degenerating, *perhaps you too could become a cowboy philosopher.*

"*Hell, all cowboys are philosophers,* said Tom. *It comes from all the time spent alone.*

"*Perhaps I could become the director philosopher. There's a paucity of them.*

"Tom reached up and drew my head to his. I was sure he was going to kiss me. *What's paucity mean, Teddy?* he whispered."

It could of been the proof that Will, in his fumbling, unsophisticated way, got himself an audience, not with death-defying feats from the back of a horse, but only with words, that made Tom want to write. Tom was basically a physical person, and he wasn't about to change the rhythm of his life and body now, but he sure had a fondness for literary gents and he'd of liked to join their lodge. What he never understood was that a writer who commits his thoughts to paper takes a risk greater than riding a horse through a window. Like many a writer before him, just sitting down and dashing off a bit of harmless satire, he would destroy himself.

Teddy went to the rolltop and opened a drawer. She took out a letter.

"I have a sample of his first work, written there at the bottom of the Grand Canyon," she said. "It was sent in a letter to Vicky some time after she wired, demanding that I be sent back to her. She claimed that the household simply would fall apart without the secretarial skills of Teddy. Such nonsense. She wanted me away from Tom. Even Tom, as he sent me packing, laughed and said, *I do believe Vic is jealous of you, Teddy.* You all laughed too, as though such a situation were the most ludicrous of possibilities. I had to laugh or die of shame. I laughed.

"It takes the form of a personal credo, although he modestly dismissed it as *Some little things I wrote.* Ignore the part at the bottom."*

> To think only of the best, to work only for the best, and to expect only the best.
>
> To forget the mistakes of the past and press on to greater achievements of the future.
>
> To think well of yourself and proclaim the fact to the world, not in loud words, but in deeds.
>
> To give so much time in the improvement of myself that I have no time to criticize others.
>
> Write me dear and be a good girl as everything is coming our way, and I love you so much, need you so much, miss you so much.
>
> Your husband,
> Tom

I read it and handed it back to her. It was Tom all right.

We went back to Hollywood from the Grand Canyon just in time to find out that the studio was in financial troubles. They asked us to take a voluntary pay cut. This wasn't an order to cut overhead, just a request to take less 'til the crisis passed. In this day of unions and greed you can only wonder what color shit would hit the fan if they made that request today. Tom

*This letter, and others written by Mix over a ten-year period, was made available through the courtesy of his granddaughter Victoria Midgley, with permission of his daughter Thomasina Mix Gunn.

volunteered to take a fifty percent cut, and the rest of us followed suit. It was that kind of industry then.

By this time Tom was a major star in close contention for the champion belt buckle. Colonel Selig started to re-release some of his old pictures. In *Twisted Trails,* Selig spliced a one-reeler of Bessie Eyton's with a one-reeler of Tom's with a two-reeler they done together. After running the first two reels, neither having anything to do with the other, he stuck in a title card, "Thus did their twisted trails meet." Then he ran the two-reeler they both appeared in. You could say Tom was money in the box office.

Selig, though, was all but out of the business. He sold Mixville to Fox, a nice piece of irony, and Tom was able to move the unit home, so to speak, and start up shooting there again.

The financial crisis passed and Sol Wurtzel was given the go-ahead to raise Tom's pay. He dickered the figure with Tom.

"Well, Sol," said Tom, "when I was a cowhand I often used to dream about someday makin' a hundred dollars a day. I reckon it's my idea of what a success is, a fella who can pull down that every day."

Hell, when he was a cowhand he used to dream about making *five* dollars a day.

Since Tom worked six days a week, Sol raised his salary to $600 a week. He bought Vic a house at 5841 Carlton Way, and he bought himself another car, a Duesenberg, custom fitted with calfskin and silver accessories. He fixed steer horns to the hood and a holstered .45 dangled from the steering column. He dressed all in white, tailor-mades.

Tom did some hairy stunts in his career, some I had a hand in, some I only watched, but that year, 1919, he did what for my money is the best stunt ever. The picture was *The Wilderness Trail.* The leading lady was young Colleen Moore, Hollywood's first flapper. Tom sat down with her and explained what they was going to do. She warn't no more than eighteen, with eyes big as saucers, and a faith in Tom that made them blind to danger. She would have rode into hell sitting behind him on Tony.

Come to think of it, this particular stunt was so dicey Tom wouldn't use Tony. They got some other horse and made it up to look like him. Put the real Tony in a sour mood for a week.

The story had Colleen kidnapped by Oriental dope dealers and hidden away in Chinatown. One of those bad Chinamen was yours truly, Kid Bandera. We took Colleen and held her captive on the fourth floor of an opium den.

Everybody at the studio gathered down at the set for to see this stunt. They'd built for us a four-story cutaway building.

Tom rode his horse up four flights of stairs and swept Colleen up in one arm, putting her on the horse behind him. A section of each floor was constructed of plaster and chicken wire, just strong enough to hold up Tom and the horse, but with the added weight of Colleen they fell through. They dropped to the next floor and fell through that, and fell through the next floor too, until covered all over with plaster they landed on the ground floor and galloped away.

Folks was screaming as they fell through, and I could feel the hairs on my neck stand up. By the end of the year Sol started paying him $1,500 a week.

19

In his position, Tom came in for a lot of complimentary tickets. He almost always gave them to Teddy, figuring that free tickets was usually for a show worth nothing. There was a young big player joined the unit, a quiet, lonely kid, eager to see all he could of the world. He kind of reminded me of Tom, except for the quiet part, and I think Tom also saw in him a younger edition of himself. They called him Dusty Fields and Teddy took to mothering him. He was a good bit younger than her. Let's see, in 1920 she was thirty. He must of been about twenty. With Tom's tickets she'd take him to concerts, plays, exhibitions, stuff like that. I always halfway hoped there was a romance betwixt them.

"He respected me," said Teddy.

Women always have put great store in respect.

"We did not meet under circumstances which could be called auspicious," she went on. "The cowboys in Tom's unit were loyal to him, and loyalty is a virtue, one of the finest. I have often, however, questioned their reasons. Let us say they were expedient when it came to holding their jobs, present company excluded. Anyway, if they were truly loyal out of simple strength of character, it was one of very few virtues

[148]

they possessed. Most of them were crude, cruel, and cowardly, and pain was a pleasure to them, especially another's, though their own seemed to assert some principle of which they were proud. They were generally prejudiced, against Jews, coloreds, Catholics, people who couldn't ride, people who could ride better than they, people who weren't cowboys, and cowboys who weren't in their unit. Their idea of a good time was a kangaroo court followed by corporal punishment for the accused."

Well, on with the story, partner. I ain't here to defend cowboys.

First day on the job, Dusty was accused of spitting his gum in the path of progress, by a cowboy who found a glob of it stuck to his boot.

"Wasn't mine," said Dusty. "I'm still chawin' the stick I come with."

"You the only bird I see jawin' on the stuff."

True enough, the rest of us chewed tobacco. Well, it got to be a heated argument.

Dusty was a boy, but not a small boy. "You're a liar or a fool," he told the accusing cowboy, who toed a line and told Dusty, "Cross this line and say that."

Dusty stepped across the line and said, "You're a liar or a fool."

Well, the cowboy was outraged. He looked around at the rest of us, as if to say, can you beat *that!*

He picked up a twig and laid it on his shoulder. "You better not knock this off and say that."

Dusty knocked it off and said that.

I was ready to set down and watch a succession of lines in the dirt followed by a trail of twigs all the way downtown, but the cowboy wisely brought his case to the bar and court was convened. We was on our lunch break so the proceedings were brief. Dusty was found guilty of haphazardly discarding his gum and was sentenced to a chapping, count of ten. Three fellers held him face down across their laps. Jimmy Mann was to do the honors. He selected him a pair of chaps studded with silver medallions along the sides.

"I believe he could have disfigured a man with those chaps," said Teddy. "Dusty seemed resigned to paying his dues to the pain-lust of his new partners, but I couldn't tolerate the idea of them brutalizing that young boy. Jimmy took a practice snap and I cast an anguished look at Tom."

Just as Jimmy was set to snap the chaps against Dusty's bottom, Tom stepped forward.

"Boss?" asked Jimmy.

"What's fair is fair," said the cowboy with the gum on his boot.

"You go ahead, Jimmy," said Tom, putting his hand on his gun.

Well, Jimmy didn't know what to make of it, and neither did the rest of us, but we all sensed it would be a big mistake for Jimmy to start without something more from Tom. When Jimmy finally looked like he was going to let fly the first snap, Tom pulled his gun and aimed it at Jimmy's foot. "Only I don't want to hear him make a sound."

"Hell, Tom, ain't that the gun you shot me with in our last picture?" Jimmy smiled, figuring the gun was loaded with blanks.

Tom fired and nicked the edge of Jimmy's boot. If there's anything respected by all cowboys, across the board, it's live ammunition. You might recollect, too, that Tom weren't all that terrific a shot.

Jimmy, as skillful a chapper as ever plied the craft, laid ten good ones on Dusty without raising nothing brighter than a smile.

That afternoon Tom rode a wagon down a steep hill and through the walls of the heavy's cabin. Broke his arm, two ribs, and gave the doctors a suspicion of internal injuries. Dusty spent the long night by his side at the hospital, and when Tom woke up thirsty, Dusty went out and smuggled back a bottle of tangleleg for him.

"Shortly after," said Teddy, "we became friends and together made use of Tom's complimentary tickets. On the night before Prohibition took effect we had attended together a concert of Wagnerian music. Afterward, he suggested a final drink at an institution which would be no more—the American saloon. I recommended Ship's Café in Venice. Had it been Saturday night I would have been almost positive that Tom would be there, since I was familiar with the timetable of his Saturday-night circuit. As it was Thursday, I was only reasonably sure that he would be there.

"I wanted him to see me with Dusty. There was a time I would have died rather than to confess that pathetic ploy. That time is far past. I know they say I never had another man, but they are wrong. There was another man, just one, before Tom. I've forgotten his name.

"He was there, alone, talking to the owner, who was behind the bar. He was glad to see us, and not at all surprised to see us together. I mean, it meant nothing to him. Why should it? Did it? He told Dusty to save his money, that he would buy the drinks.

"Put your money in some real estate round here, he told him. *Someday Hollywood is gonna grow all the way around L.A. and land here'll be worth more than water on the Mojave.*

"Which is essentially what I had been telling him for some time. Land was cheap. He had surpluses of cash. These pretty hills could have been his without any drain on his comforts and hardly any cutting back of his ostentations, but he insisted on keeping his money in a bank and in his pockets, simple and uncomplicated. Land required lawyers and agents and papers to be signed and a watchful eye to be kept, all things naturally in opposition to one's personal enjoyment of daily life.

"Here's to you, Colonel, said Dusty, *and Teddy, happy Prohibition!*

[151]

"*No, no*, said Tom. *Mulhall was a colonel, Teddy a colonel, Selig a colonel, all friends of mine. I was just a lowly major.*

"*Here's to you, Major.*

"We drank. He may have been a bit tipsy. Tired, probably, and hurt. He had his leg in a brace to correct some faulty treatment of an earlier injury.

"*A drink with friends*, he mumbled.

"*Yes, sir*, said Dusty.

"*And it's a great pain-killer, medicinally taken.*

"*It is, sir, yes.*

"*But I'm not sorry to see it go.* He ordered another round. *If we learned nothing else in the war, we learned that a country drinkin' whiskey is not at the top of its preparedness.*

"He was speaking rather formally, like a demagogue, a pose he often fell into with young people.

"*We gave 'em what for*, offered Dusty.

"*Pantywaists. What would happen against a real enemy? Let me tell you somethin', son. It's good to share a drink with a friend. It makes kind of a warm glow in your gut, and what the hell, we don't have little kiddies at home worryin' about us spendin' our paychecks at the saloon.*

"*No, sir.*

"*But put booze in your body and you're no longer in charge. There's only one thing you got to depend on in this world. You can't depend on a gun, it'll misfire. And you can't depend on a well-trained horse, he'll stumble. And you sure can't depend on another person. . . .*

"He looked into my eyes, wondering if he was revealing too much. And he was, but, really, what could he reveal that I hadn't already seen or guessed?

"*You can't even depend on your own mind, it often plays tricks on you. All you've got is one body per person.* He slapped his chest to indicate the reliability of the one he had been issued. *And the booze, my friend, will slow it down considerable, if you don't watch out.*

"Just as his voice was slowing down in the telling of it.

"*Well, then, here's to Prohibition,* said Dusty.

"*I'll drink to that,* said Tom.

"The owner overheard them and spoke out against the new law, angry at the hypocrisy of it, and ruing the effect it would have on his business.

"*I'm sorry, partner, for your loss of revenue, but for the public good some of us have to make sacrifices.*

"*Hell, Tom, I'm stuck with two truckloads of booze in the cellar. What the hell am I supposed to do with it, drink it?*

"*You have two truckloads?* Tom asked, rising higher on his barstool.

"*Twelve thousand dollars worth of the stuff.*

"Tom stood up and took a roll of bills out of his pocket and counted out twelve thousand dollars. *Here's a couple hundred for the truck. Deliver 'em to my place before midnight.*

"He ordered another round and expounded, sincerely, on the many benefits to be derived from life in a dry country.

"Few of which seemed to accrue to him.

"As a contract player Tom was paid fifty-two weeks a year, but the studio worked their money's worth out of him. He made eight pictures in 1919, as many in 1920, all of which made huge profits. We worked six days a week. Evenings and Sundays there were interviews to endure, personal appearances to make, openings, weddings, and funerals to attend, flowers to be sent. I took care of all the details, leaving him free to his art. Still, one would have thought it a relief to spend a quiet evening at home. He seldom did.

"I try to be, I've always tried to be, as objective as I can, under the circumstances. Tom had a wife and home, an enormous salary in an exciting profession, the adoration of most of the country. What he wanted most then was an occasional quiet time to try to write his thoughts. I don't profess to know why he had to come to me to get it, but come he did, and I let him in. I don't castigate Vic. Tom seldom talked about her and I never asked. Time was too precious.

"*I'm afraid I don't have a drink to offer you,* I said.

"That's all right. I reckon I've had my share for the night.

"I can make some coffee.

"Good. Make it strong.

"He followed me into the kitchen.

"Nice little place you got here, Teddy. You fixed it up real nice.

"Tom had given us a lift from Ship's, dropping off Dusty first. I made the coffee, put some Chopin on the Victrola and cranked it up.

"Ah, now that's what I call music, he said. *Modern music convinces me that we have slipped back a few centuries. Modern music is quite similar to the kind the Indians and cannibals used to enjoy.*

"It was the tone he usually reserved for interviews.

"We educate ourselves, he continued, *up to the point of appreciatin' symphony orchestras, grand operas, and chamber music, and then we slip back to the crude jangle and dumdum-dum of our primitive ancestors.*

"Tom, please relax, I said. *It's just you and me here, in my home. You can relax.*

"I knew that one of the attractions of The Little Mill, the colored place in Watts, was that the drummer there always graciously permitted Tom to take a turn, and Tom was always good for a hundred-dollar tip in return.

"Nice, he said again, looking about my very simple apartment. *What's the rent?*

"Twenty-five.

"Do I pay it?

"Well, through my salary, I guess you do.

"No, I mean I want to pay it, above your salary.

"Why?

"It seems right. Like a business expense.

"As you like.

"Okay, let's do that. As though to pull the added expense into proper perspective, he said, *Vic just bought us some gold table service.*

"Gold?

"Most folks got silver. I found out which fork to use for what, so I reckon we'll get invited back again. But we plan on throwin' a few of them dinner parties ourselves. You know what I had 'em do? I noticed how folks like to cup up the salad with the edge of their fork. Ain't always easy, so I had 'em file down the edge of all the salad forks.

"Yet there were those who called him inconsiderate. Insensitive themselves, if you ask me.

"Yeah, I'm travelin' in some pretty fancy circles these days.

"You're a star.

"Reckon I am. Vic is studyin' French. Got me readin' up on Shakespeare. I don't mind. I kinda like the yarns he tells. You take Hamlet, *now, right fine. It'd make a good western. You got this young wrangler, see, who's reduced to a hand on his own spread by a wicked uncle who kilt his daddy and married his ma. Only this wrangler knows that the uncle bushwhacked his pa. But he's a good lad, knows his right from wrong, and every time he gets the drop on his uncle he finds a way out of dealin' him misery. Like when the uncle's prayin' and Kid Hamlet can't bring himself to ambush a prayin' man. I wish the uncle and Hamlet was in competition for the fair Ophelia. That'd make a better story. I don't reckon I'll ever do it, though, 'cause in my mind Hamlet's got to be a shy, hesitatin' lad of fourteen or so.*

"Not bad for a cowboy with only a fourth-grade education.

"Tom, I've known you for several years, I said.

"Been that long?

"You've never been to my place before.

"Hadn't much call to.

"I wanted to ask him, why now? To discuss Shakespeare?

"I'm a fella of pretty big appetites, he said, patting my back like a pal.

"Oh, it was coming, it was coming, I knew, but God, in the wrong way. He was going to tell me he dearly loved his wife but was incapable of excluding all other women. He was going to tell me he *needed* many other women in order to truly *love* one woman, and Vicky was the woman he loved. God, didn't I have eyes, didn't I have a heart? Hadn't I seen the inevitable petty romances blossom between him and his various leading ladies. It starts early, the first day of shooting or before, with the laying on of hands, that gradual taking possession. A hand on the shoulder, the elbow, the cheek. And then she returns it. Her hand on his knee, against his arm. Have I never seen that mating dance, nor borne it? This business is not buying and selling, sowing and reaping, measuring and making.

"And there I was, tentatively placing my hand on his knee, like just any other leading lady. No, I wanted more. I took both his hands in mine.

"Tom, how could you not know I love you?

"He smiled. Only one long accustomed to being loved would have been able to smile.

"I kind of suspicioned it, he said.

"No one ever called me Tom's mistress, not in my presence. But if they had, it would have filled me with pride. Somewhere I was called that, if only in the foul mouths of his cowboys. It is enough."

20

Well, frankly, there was some of us who figured that's what she was to Tom, but most of us didn't give it a thought 'cause they seemed such an unlikely couple. Teddy was a dear girl and I was real partial to her, in a brotherly sort of way, but the truth is she was meant to be an old maid, nice but as plain and ordinary as the road home.

Even those of us who sized up the situation couldn't guess what she was giving him that he couldn't get at home or other places. And close as we were, Tom never talked to me about it, though he weren't near as bashful about other dallyings.

That night in her parlor Teddy said it and for the first time I knew the answer: a quiet place.

"I tried to be a comfort to him," she said, "a refuge from the demands of a pressurized occupation, a clamoring public, a socially ambitious wife. And, of course, I was convenient."

Tom had just reached forty and was still in top shape. Blow for blow, I couldn't keep up with him, though I was four years younger. He was still doing all his own stunts, and on Sundays he'd get drunk with the rest of us and join in an innocent pastime of beating each other witless. He had his share of back-alley brawls too, and never come out second best. But as early as this his body must of been telling him something. Maybe the injuries was taking longer to heal. Could be his breath was harder to come by. All I know is that more and more he hankered after the writing life. He looked at Will and seen the freedom he enjoyed and measured it against what he was doing, six days a week, fifty-two weeks of the year.

We didn't get to see much of Will. Betty Rogers disapproved of Tom and in her book he was a bad influence, and Will himself seemed to grow a mite wary, since his own public image was halfway round the bend from Tom's. As popular as Tom was with the plain folks, he couldn't get a rise out of the sophisticates, who was flocking to listen to Will. And, 'course, it was important for Will to stay spotless. Tom was already a bit —excessive.

Will didn't fare too well in films and went back to the stage. Then he come to be a lecturer in great demand. When he was in town me and Tom would meet him Sunday mornings on a goat pasture. There we'd hold goat-roping contests, racing after the critters on foot, just the three of us.

Neither Tom nor me could ever understand how Will always managed to rope his goat, while half the time ours slipped away from us.

Tom finally had to ask him his secret, since he was using the same technique as Will, but with no success.

"Well, Tom, would you fish for trout with a whaling line?" asked Will.

"Not hardly."

"Which proves you're a better fisherman than you are a roper."

Tom examined Will's rope and found it to be soft and pliable, not like the stiff cowropes we used, which gave the goats a chance to shuck them off.

After that Tom ordered silks and took up polo, and I spent my Sundays playing faro down to Gardena. Some years later, he convinced William Fox to relocate his studio on that goat pasture. Fox wasn't too keen on the idea because it was so far

TOM MIX DIED FOR YOUR SINS

out of the way of things. Give credit to Tom's foresight. He told him that someday it'd be in the center of things.

Apart from all those Selig films which even Tom never thought had much to do with writing, his first try at something for public consumption took the form of a Christmas card. It was hanging in a frame on Teddy's wall.*

The Bells of Christmas

When the final curtain boomed down upon the Great War there were those blind enough to say that never again would the Bells of Christmas have the same meaning to the world.

The war-makers had proven their power, Brotherly love was a joke, when dollars, francs, marks and pounds were at stake. What was the lesson of Gallipoli, of Verdun, of Ypres, of Chateau-Thierry? Christianity was a failure, a farce, a laugh. Thereafter Christmas Bells and Christmas Carols would fall upon deaf ears.

Right thinking folks found such pessimism sickening. They knew that the world had been boiling in the great crucible of Fate and that from this would surely come far finer metal than we had ever known. Certainly, in the meantime there would be the scum of crime, vice and hate, but all those enemies of life would pass with the years.

Gradually, as the fires are smouldering and the great mass of molten humanity is simmering, we behold that more and more the finer virtues, the glad and noble ideals, the music of joy and of love, are being reclaimed and the baser elements eliminated.

Out of the Master Refiner's moulds come new Bells of Christmas, ringing more joyously than ever.

New Bells of Christmas everywhere! Can't you hear them pealing the same old glorious song of Bethlehem, with greater sweetness, greater richness, greater power, greater ecstasy than any music the world has ever heard?

"Peace on Earth Good Will to Men!"
Merry Christmas to Everyone!

*Courtesy of the Academy of Motion Picture Arts and Sciences.

A mite fancy maybe, but it come from the heart.

That was the Christmas Tom found out who held the mortgage to my house and gave it to me for a present.

"He was keen on credos," said Teddy, "and often became moralizing or ponderous. Pompous? Perhaps. He had a wonderful sense of humor, though, and adored comedians, especially Buster Keaton, but his humor, like Buster's, was visual. When he sat down to write, he could not help sounding like a parson. Listen to this. Just a minute, it's here somewhere."

Back she went to the rolltop and dug out a sheet of paper, which she read to me.

> "Many a man thinks he is buying pleasure,
> when he is really selling himself a slave to it.
> "He that can bear a reproof, and mend by it,
> if he is not wise, is on a fair road of being so.
> "If I can bear my own faults then why not
> bear the faults of others?
> "How few there are who have courage enough to
> own their faults, or resolution enough to mend them.
> "We will not be here forever. Soon death,
> the kind old nurse, will come along and rock us
> all to sleep, so we had better help one another
> while we may, we are going the same way.*

"So soon after he has died, what he said about death takes on new implications. It was an accident, Kid, wasn't it? A good cowboy just wouldn't do that sort of thing, would he?"

There's something about a direct question from a woman I never could handle. I let them slide by 'til they just kind of disappear.

His hero became Arthur Brisbane, a good shout from Buffalo Bill. Brisbane's column was on page one of the *Examiner*, the first thing read. Tom, though, somehow thought he enjoyed a private relationship and that Brisbane's writings was no more

*Courtesy of Vicky Midgley.

than what he wanted to say himself, if anybody would of asked him. So round the chuckwagon Tom would spout the daily Brisbane without giving due credit.

"What this world reminds me of is a crippled cat," he'd say.

It was Brisbane's thought for the day. We'd already read it.

"How's that, Tom?" asked Lynn Reynolds, who was directing.

"Well, I'll tell you, among classes of people there are misunderstandings that make a gulf as wide as that separatin' a cat from the man who might help it."

"Between friends, even. Husbands and wives, even," said Lynn.

"We got grain elevators full and still there are people starvin' in China."

"Send 'em my share, Tom, I never been fond of grain anyhow," said one of the boys.

"That's what I hated most of all," said Teddy, "the way they began to mock him whenever he attempted to enter the world of ideas. On the back of a galloping horse, however, it was an entirely different story. I wouldn't mind if they were just missing the point, but they were ridiculing him. Often they would look up a difficult word and conspire to drop it in conversation, all acting as though the word were a part of their common vocabulary, tricking Tom into pretending that he knew it too. Yes, we all knew that Tom was pretentious and vain, but none of us ever had the nerve to call him on it. Were they afraid of losing their jobs? Was I afraid of losing him? Is that why we supported any lie he cared to live? No, there was an element of fear there, to be sure, but it took the form of awe. We knew he was better than us, in spite of all his shortcomings. There wasn't a sarcastic, belittling cowboy in his unit who wouldn't shrink under his cold stare."

With maybe one exception, and my sarcastic times they are few and my belittling times none. Tom did have that quality, found in the best of big sugars, of being part of his boys and still

[161]

apart from them. He was traveling in some rarefied circles, still it warn't no surprise to have him show up at the house of one of his cowboys and sop his bread in common gravy, afterwards taking his turn at the bootjack and sitting back with his feet on the coffee table. And he didn't think it was socially daring to invite a cowboy and his missus to his fine house, though Vic warn't too enthusiastic about the practice and the studio was pressuring Tom to hang out with a better class of people. He was making himself look bad, they said. Maybe so, he told them, but he was making himself *feel* good.

He did put on some airs from time to time, not so much in a social way as when it come to the brainwork. Cowboys are just natural deflators, and I count myself among them. Tom warn't no slouch in it himself, as when he locked horns with Bill Hart. Only trouble was, Tom was growing to take himself serious.

Seems like in movies there's always been a few major cowboy stars, each with his own following, but there's room at the top for only one. I reckon it's 'cause cowboys as a group are so naturally competitive. There's got to be a champion.

Hart, like Tom, was born in the east, but he was raised in the west. He left it as a teen-ager and became a success on the stage as a Shakespearean actor. He took to the movies to portray the west as it really was. That was his fortune and his failure.

By 1920, Hart was fifty, Tom a youthful forty. Tom's films was everything Hart hated. He usually played a gambler or an outlaw who gets reformed by the love of a virtuous woman, sometimes his sister. Hart himself was uncommonly devoted to his sister, who lived with him all her life, even after he got married, which caused a lot of bad talk. His character was a hard-drinking scowler who was outside the law 'cause it seemed the only place for a true man to stand in the rat's nest caused by creeping civilization. His outfits and settings and stories was authentic. It was a craziness with him. And for a while it worked.

Then the country went moral and accepted Prohibition. His character no longer set well with the crowd. Tom gave them a character who enforced the law and never drank or smoked. He gave them a glorious west that never was. He gave them what they wanted: action, glamour, fantasy. Hart was out.

We went to a party, me and Teddy and Tom and Vic and a couple dozen of others, including Bill Hart. Hart was a gentleman, he never hung about with cowboys or wore cowboy costumes in public, as Tom almost always did. He was, in almost anything you want to talk about, the opposite of Tom. And they was at the turning point, where one would decline and the other step up to the top.

They screened one of Hart's films at the party. Tom fell asleep. When the lights come on, Tom straightened himself up and said, "Bill, you know what you are? You're an actor. I mean that."

Which was to say, actors put me to sleep.

"An accusation, I trust," said Hart, "that's never been made against you."

"No, and I never laid claim to it neither. I'm just a simple cowboy."

"Don't be ridiculous. Look at you, you belong in a circus."

"Hold on a damn minute. You was sippin' tea in New York salons whilst I was bulldoggin' steers in the Oklahoma Territory."

"I envy you your experience. It's a tragedy you're a traitor to it."

"Who're you callin' a traitor, old man?"

"You're a fine stuntman, I understand," said Hart coolly. "I hope you can keep it up."

I grabbed Tom's right arm and held it down. Tom slapped himself on the stomach and said, "Go ahead, hit me. Take a free one."

"Come along, Mary," said Hart to his sister and together they said good night to our host and left.

A bunch of us piled in cars and took the party to Tom's house

[163]

in Beverly Hills. Somebody said something about how sensitive Hart was getting in his old age. Whoever it was, Tom stopped him, knowing it would lead to sticking up for Tom's side of the argument. "Teddy," he said, "I want you to send Bill something in the morning and sign my name to it. I'd be happy if my pictures stayed around as long as his will. You can write that on the card."

I thought that was an above-average thing to say. No sooner said and he got in some petty fight with Vic. By the time I got around to reminiscing with Teddy, I couldn't even remember the beef. And she told me I had the whole thing wrong.

"First of all," said Teddy, "it wasn't the Beverly Hills house we went to, it was the Carlton Way house. The other hadn't been built yet. That's what they were arguing about."

It started coming back to me. Jack Ford was there, a cocky bantamweight who couldn't understand why I didn't want to fight him. I didn't want to 'cause he was drunk and he wasn't the sort that should be fighting one way or the other. Lynn Reynolds was there with Kathleen. Buster Keaton and Fatty Arbuckle was there.

The argument started over the tennis courts. Tom had bought fifteen acres near Chaplin's place and near Buster's place. He was going to build a mansion, if they could ever get together on what it should look like. Tennis was the hot game then and Vic was taking lessons. She wanted tennis courts at the house. She was designing them around a Grecian motive.

"Waste of good land, if you ask me," said Tom.

"You're only saying that because you're a sore loser," said Vic.

Tom was a natural athlete and a great gamesman, and once he landed solid in Hollywood he was introduced to games and sports he never seen nor heard of before. With every new one his first step was to call over his tailor and have him make up the proper togs in the brightest colors. He started out real keen on tennis, reckoning it was something he could share with Vic besides their bed.

But it warn't his game. Whenever that fuzzy white ball come at him and he managed to hit it he almost always sent it to parts unknown, confusing the game with baseball, I reckon, which was really his favorite. Vic beat him every time they played.

There was bottles of bourbon and bottles of gin on the table. A bit of the red, a bit of the white. Cowboys drink and turn into comedians, comedians drink and turn into cowboys. Now it was Buster wanted to fight me. I told him to fight Jack Ford, it was a better match, but each had his heart set on beating up a cowboy. Lynn didn't need a fight. He was barely conscious. Fatty was ready to take on the winner of any fight that could get promoted.

"The argument in the center of all of these challenges and counter-challenges," said Teddy, "was over the living room that should be in the house Tom would build. Tom wanted it to be western. He wanted heads and muskets and horns on the walls. He wanted Navajo rugs and mission furniture. That decorating proposal filled Vic with horror. She would be the laughingstock of Hollywood. She wanted a French drawing room with crystal chandeliers, an Aubusson rug, and Louis XVI furniture, something in which one could have a polite and elegant tea.

"The guests began supporting one side vociferously and as the night wore on would wind up wanting to fight for the other side, for there is no compromise between buffalo heads and crystal chandeliers.

"Jack and Buster finally teamed up and went out to find some cowboys who were tough enough to fight. Fatty went along with them to mediate in case they were unfortunate enough to find some. Kathleen took Lynn home. The others, if there were any, had gone, and you and I were saying our good nights."

That's the way it was. I was ready to take Teddy home, and Tom was dead set on leaving with us.

"You stay home," Vic told him.

"Well, no, I think I'm goin' out for a drink," said Tom.

"You've had enough to drink."

"Don't reckon I have."

He ordered his chauffeur-mechanic to bring around the new Isotta-Fraschini. This was an Italian car he'd just bought, long and open and worth a thousand acres anywhere in Oklahoma. It had his brand on both doors and brass trim around the headlights. A set of horns was on the radiator.

"You're too drunk to drive, you fool," said Vic. "You'll kill yourself."

"Well, I'm gonna drive."

Me and Teddy was stalled behind them and knew they'd have to settle it 'fore we could properly leave.

"You are *not* going to drive off in that condition," said Vic, and, partner, she meant it.

"I sure don't know who's gonna stop me."

He walked out the door and got in the car. Vic ran to the closet and come out with a pearl-handled .22.

"I was with her when she bought it," said Teddy, "and tried to talk her out of it. Tom had guns all over the place, but she wanted one of her own, a lady's gun."

She ran out in front of the car and Tom had to come down hard on the brakes to keep from running her down. Me and Teddy stood on the front steps. Vic aimed the gun at Tom and he dived to the floorboards. I pulled Teddy back to the doorway. Vic fired six times smack in the radiator. Water squirted out of the holes she made. There's a spooky silence always follows gunshots. We heard just the dripping of the water. Then we heard Tom's muffled laughing. His head come up slow as a turkey's. He started laughing, I wonder he didn't choke himself. Vicky was pouting, little-girl angry.

Tom got out of the car and took her in his arms. He thought it was the cutest thing he had seen. Her arms went around his neck, the gun still in her hand.

"Reckon we can go now," I whispered to Teddy.

They passed us, arms around each other, like we wasn't even there. They was both laughing now.

"Would you slow down if I put a bullet in *you?*" she asked.

"Depends on where you put it," he answered.

Staggering in each other's arms they found their way to the bedroom, or at least was headed in that general direction, and I took Teddy on home.

21

Looks like there was something about Tom that purely in-
spired certain ladies to take shots at him, and the fun ain't over
yet, oh, no. It would happen again, all in the easy-stepping
spirit of the times.

Mr. Wurtzel, though, and his colleagues at the other outfits,
was looking with real skitterish eyes at such antics in the houses
of their stars 'cause some of the fun it wasn't good and some
of it wasn't clean.

"Hollywood was certainly not Dubuque," said Teddy. "No
one wanted it to be. The pace was headlong, the people ex-
ceedingly beautiful, all temperamental, most immature and
hedonistic, some quite mad. Problems were bound to occur in
this bright new reckless factory town. No one expected or
demanded stability. The people drawn here had gladly for-
saken a normal existence to get here. Yet it was hoped by the
studios that a veil could be drawn across the stars at play.
Movies might reflect the changing patterns of morality, but as
private persons the stars were required to respect the public
attention their careers had brought them. The movie-going
public, and statistics show that in those days *every* single person in the country attended the movies at least once a week,

made no distinction between the character on the screen and the individual who played him. Mary Pickford, for one example, *was* America's sweetheart, and for her certain types of behavior off the screen were as unacceptable as on the screen. Tom had to be wary even about smoking a cigarette in public. Sure, he drank too much. For many it will be the final thing they remember about him, but he drank always at places he was known and only among friends. Should the newspapers report public drunkenness on his part, his fans might desert him and his career come to a sudden conclusion. In many ways he was in bondage to his public, as were the others, and no one in bondage has ever been entirely happy.

"Fortunately, the local police and D.A.'s office were very protective of the stars. The officials enjoyed the premieres and parties and presumably the favors of pretty young women. I sometimes wonder if that isn't what it's all about finally, Hollywood, and if someday the bedrock will rise to the surface. That will be the end of it."

Every Christmas Tom sent around a case of Canadian whiskey to his favorite local officials. He'd drive downtown handing twenty-dollar bills to the cops directing traffic. He wasn't necessarily buying them off, he was just a generous man. He liked to keep money in circulation. At Christmastime he'd fill up an upstairs room with gifts. Whenever anybody'd stop by to visit, which was more often than not, he'd say, "I think I got somethin' you might like," and up he'd go to find a present. If the person stayed long enough, Tom would remember a second or third gift and up he'd go, again and again. He liked to hand things out. 'Course, he took a fair share of pleasure in being able to pick up the phone and call a local judge to fix a traffic ticket for a friend, but this was giving too.

The D.A.'s office put the lid on many a blackmail attempt, many a paternity claim. Don't quote me on this, partner, if you do I'll deny it, but more than one Hollywood suicide was murder and more than one accident was manslaughter.

[169]

In 1921 Tom was one of the top ten box-office attractions. Single-handed, he took him an ailing studio and put them in the black. The adventures we filmed gave them a chance to experiment with artistic pictures that wouldn't earn a plugged dime. Tom was up to $3,000 per week, and for it they'd squeeze an extra picture out of him, nine for the year.

"He was worth more than three thousand a week," said Teddy, "and would get more, but he was always worth more than he got."

Hollywood in general was still flying straight up. There was no telling where it would go, if it could only keep all its beauties from going crazy.

"Tom and the others worked hard," said Teddy. "They were paid salaries far beyond those of other men who worked hard, but like those other men they felt they were entitled occasionally to blow a paycheck on a good time. There were nights when a phone call would bring Sol Wurtzel or Vic or me, or sometimes all three of us, to fetch Tom away from a club, a street, or a private residence. The potential for scandal seemed to us enormous and it was never a matter to be taken lightly. That September, however, a scandal broke that was to make Tom's peccadilloes seem like cowboy high jinx, which they were, really.

"Fatty Arbuckle was arrested in San Francisco. Drunk, and angry at the starlet and himself for his sexual failure, he put a Coke bottle where he couldn't be. The girl died."

The last time I seen Roscoe he was at the Vernon Country Club. Now, the Vernon Country Club wasn't in Vernon, and it wasn't a country club. It was only another stop on the Saturday-night circuit, between the Alexandria Hotel downtown and The Little Mill in Watts. He was out on the dance floor doing pratfalls with Buster Keaton. In those days no one gave a hoot for his own dignity. Stars was always out looking for fun, and when they met their public they was expected to entertain them, which they did happily. When Tom and me come in, him all dressed in a white western suit, the crowd cheered. He handed his great white sombrero to the hatcheck girl and announced, "I'll buy drinks for the house if I can't fall better'n those two birds." So Tom joined them and the drum beat whenever one of them landed.

Now we was told that Fatty went a little crazy in San Francisco.

Sober, he was the jovial fat man he portrayed on the screen. Drunk, he was a sweating, unattractive three-hundred-pound lump of flesh, kind of like a jellyfish, no direction but the current, hardly alive but beware the sting.

Roscoe swore he was never alone with the girl, that she was drunk and hysterical and finally had to be carted out of the party.

The going attitude in Hollywood was that he *could* of done it, and I reckon this judgment was as damning as the deed itself. He became untouchable.

I would put his pay at five, six thousand a week, and he lived well. It was a sobering thing for other stars to see how quick the public abandoned Fatty. His films were pulled. Chappie and Buster, who could of been elected first and second in any election in the land, gave him a character endorsement and begged the public to hold their water 'til after his trial, but even that did no good. The crowd who had loved him now wanted his ears.

The studios feed the crowd and feed off it, love the crowd and are afraid of it. They banded together and hired Postmaster General Will Hays as moral watchdog over the movies. The Hays Office was an honest effort towards self-censorship, in hopes of heading off the other kind. It was pretty widely respected.

After Roscoe went through three trials he was finally acquitted, but not by the only jury that matters to a movie star. Hays, who wouldn't say shit if he had a mouth full of it, asked the public, on Roscoe's behalf, to forgive and forget. Nothing doing. The crowd got a short memory for some and a long memory for others. To this day his pictures have stayed buried. In '33, in a New York hotel, he died in his sleep.

Roscoe's trial was still all over the headlines when William Desmond Taylor, the only director Teddy ever worked for, was murdered in a love nest on Alvarado Street, which he was supposed to be sharing with either Mary Miles Minter or Mabel Normand or both.

"Taylor was or was not a homosexual," said Teddy, "and his relationship with Mabel was or was not strictly spiritual. Mary Miles Minter, who was just a girl at the time, seventeen or so, was said to have been throwing herself at him but supposedly he brushed aside her attentions. When he turned up murdered and evidence in the apartment indicated a relationship with both women, speculation over who was the murderer ran from Mabel's drug supplier to Mack Sennett, who was rather fond of Mabel himself, to Mary's mother, to Mary herself. He was an Englishman, to judge from his accent. I learned after his death that he had once been a successful art dealer in New York who suddenly dropped out of sight, only to emerge years later as a Hollywood director. Drawn here, such characters, as surely as bears to honey."

His body wasn't hardly cold in the grave when Wally Reid, the original "boy next door," the feller every mother in the country wished for her daughter, and every daughter wished for herself, died at thirty of drug addiction.

No, it sure warn't no Dubuque, Hollywood, and ain't now though the new generation would be wise to learn from the one that went before, who had no examples to avoid.

"There was a whirlwind then," said Teddy, "when, to use the words of the immortal Poe, *unmerciful Disaster followed fast and followed faster.* But Tom remained unscathed. He lived his life a hero to children, an idol to women, a clean-cut All-American cowboy whose only failing was an earlier divorce, by now already becoming acceptable among movie folk. Others fell around him, their past mistakes and present indulgences overtaking them, but not Tom."

Which ain't to say it never got close.

It was at the time of the Arbuckle scandal when Tom decided to give up drinking forever. "I had my share, Kid, I leave it to you and the younger men. Though, frankly, a man is a damn fool to get mixed up with it."

He made his decision when temptation was its strongest. An Arizona cowboy name of Dick Crawford come to him for a job. Crawford was a darn good cowboy, but locked tight in the grip of drugs, and nobody in town wanted to give him a job. Tom's heart went out to him, he hated to see such hard-learned skills go to waste. Crawford use to read a newspaper on the back of a bucking bronc.

It ain't that he never tried to give up his stinking habit but the pains of leaving it was always too much to stand. He looked like a burnt-out case. By the time he come to Tom all his friends had turned him away.

"I'd like to use you, Dick, but can you promise me you won't use the stuff?"

"Well, Tom, I don't reckon I can."

That should of been the end of it. He was an honest man, but that brand of honesty would never get him a job. Tom offered him a drink, a bit of the red or a bit of the white, and Dick took a bit of both. Tom himself drunk root beer and pondered Dick's sorry situation. By evening tide Dick couldn't recollect his own name, and it occurred to Tom that if he could only keep him liquored up long enough he'd never notice the pains of kissing his habit good-bye. Maybe when he finally did sober up he'd be free of it. As thirsty as it made Tom to watch another man drink, he donned his missionary's robes and used one devil to fight another within that poor sinner's body. He kept him close at hand and he kept him drunk.

We was working on a picture, keeping Dick drunk setside,

and a man from the publicity department brought a critic over to watch and interview Tom. At Mixville it was and next we was to go on location to Victorville for a few months. We had our fair share of column-writing ladies visiting Tom, but a New York critic was something new.

"The more successful Tom became," said Teddy, "the less serious attention critics paid his movies. Some, including that one who called on us, had even said some rather unflattering things about the stories we did. The critics of those days had no theory for dealing with movies. They tried to use the same methods they had used with stage plays or books or paintings, and that sort of thing just doesn't work with movies. I don't know that they're any better off today than they were then. I've stopped reading them."

We watched the publicity man lead this critic bird towards us and Tom leaned over to me and whispered, "Looks like he sits down to pee, don't he?"

I stifled my laughter. Tom, with apologies to the genuine item, used to call critics cunts. I reckon it's a fair description of the lot of them, this one especially. He was cream of celery soup, about five degrees shy of room temperature. Gave you the feeling he was always about to spit out a lemon seed. Tall and blond, he wasn't out of his twenties yet. He wore this superior smirk on his face, disdainful of the scene behind the scenes, bored as hell. A ripe candidate for deflating.

The publicity man introduced them. Dwight Saunders of the New York something-something. I'd heard of him.

"The only function of a film critic is to make himself known," said Teddy. "That critic who can devise the cutest puns around the titles of films and the names of the stars will not only keep his post but prosper. The rest is all posturing."

Tom shook hands with him and so did I. I been more impressed with the grip of a raw veal cutlet. They called Tom untutored, the easterners, when what they meant was dumb, but as Tom always said, "Most of 'em don't know the proper way to peel an orange."

[174]

Untutored maybe, but Tom would never strangle on his own spit, a prediction I couldn't make for Dwight Saunders and others like him. They reminded you of animals that couldn't kill their own meat.

Tom pretended he couldn't figure out what a critic *does*. The feller knew Tom was playing the ignorant cowboy.

"What a critic does, Mr. Mix, is spend entirely too much time watching motion pictures that deserve nobody's time. Afterward, we caution the public not to waste theirs."

"Sounds like a thankless job."

"We all serve humanity in what ways we can."

"But you're the one has to stay cooped up in a dark room, watchin' adventures you didn't live and couldn't imagine. Can't be much fun for you."

"I have to admit, motion pictures being what they are, it's not often fun. It takes the form of an obligation."

"Ah, that's somethin' I know nothin' about. We might look like we're a-workin', but to us work is fun, and life is laughter, love, and work."

"But what is the work worth if it has no social significance?" asked our critical film gent.

"Well, hell, maybe it does. And maybe it don't, since I don't know what social significance means. I ain't sayin' you don't neither. Hell, you probably do, but more kids see one of my adventures on a Saturday afternoon than folks that'll read the sarcastic words you write about 'em in a lifetime. And during that time those kids'll have a hero to admire, if they don't have one at home or at school or in Washington, and they'll get a notion of the rewards of virtue and the punishments of evil, and I reckon there might be somethin' socially significant about that."

The critic smiled superior like. It's what they do when they got nothing to say. You wanted Buster to show up and smack him in the face with a fish, but Tom laughed, threw his arm around the feller's shoulders, and walked him round the place, introducing him to the leading lady and the folks in the unit.

When they got to Dick Crawford, drinking contented under a canvas lean-to, Tom said, "And this here is our writer and technical adviser."

"In no time that prissy fellow was actually enjoying himself," said Teddy. "He watched Tom make a hands-tied running mount with the wide-eyed wonder of any other urchin."

Tom asked him if he'd like to play a bit in the picture. He feigned polite reluctance, but once we got him in a cowboy outfit he dropped all his citified pretense. He played his part to the hilt and loved every second of it. We had one more day of shooting. By the end of it, Dwight Saunders quit his job on the New York something-something and joined the Mix unit as a supporting player. He left with us for Victorville. So much for social significance.

Victorville was the hot, dusty doorway to the Mojave Desert, a place so dull and gritty it could make Oklahoma look like those Elysian Fields you hear about. It was a drive of six or seven hours from Hollywood. Most of the cast and crew took the train, but whenever Tom could he drove one of his own cars. He purely loved to drive and many the evening he and DeMille and Fairbanks could be seen racing each other across the bean fields which now are the Wilshire District. He knew only two ways to drive, Tom, with his foot down hard on the gas or down hard on the brake. He'd drive alone if he had to, but liked to have others along. The way he drove, that wasn't always easy. I used to keep one eye on the speedometer and when that needle rose too high for my comfort I'd say, "Railroad crossing up ahead, Tom," and he'd automatically slow down for a while, usually so deep in telling one of his yarns that he'd never notice the absence of all those railroad crossings I used to see.

We left for Victorville with Vic and Teddy up front with Tom, Dwight Saunders, Dick Crawford, and me in the back. It was my job to keep Dick drunk, and I wasn't doing a bad job on myself neither. Saunders drank from the same bottle as us, like some English banker let loose in Havana.

Tom called the car his "Overland Express." I never did know the make of it, only that it was custom-made to resemble a stagecoach and the license number was all sixes. It was an open car, but it had a dark brown boxlike canvas over it, with roll-down flaps for the windows. Wooden slats was above our heads and they made a support for the luggage rack outside. The rear end was a trunklike affair, just like the old-time coaches. Appearances aside, that thing could really move. I used to imagine passing some old stagecoach driver of the '50s or '60s and picture the look on his face. Teddy had a drink or two, to calm her nerves, and I reckon Vic was as nervous as Teddy. By nightfall we was a fine high-speed spectacle, the driver the only one among us sober, if you can believe that.

He kept us entertained with the escapades of his past, as though there wasn't somebody in the car who wasn't with him for a good piece of it.

"I reckon I stared death in the face as often as any man," he said. "But each time I knew he was only makin' a social call. I believe a fella knows when it's his turn. I don't care if it's consumption or a bullet from behind, when the time comes you're gonna know about it and you're gonna know it's too late to do nothin' about it. Why, when I took them American horses across the water to South Africa for the English, I didn't even know there was a war on. Once I found out, I wanted a taste of it. Hell, I didn't give a damn which side. Unless you got a real stake in it, it don't matter who wins a war. So when the British asked me to do a little scoutin', I threw my gear in with them.

"When the Boers finally captured me, I didn't give it too much concern. I mean, I was an American and it wasn't our war. They told me I was a mercenary. Sounded kind of nice, like an angel of mercy, so I agreed that's the thing I was. I would have been slower to agree if I knew a mercenary was open game."

Dwight Saunders leaned forward to hand the bottle to Vic. "Does that really say sixty miles an hour?" he said, looking at the speedometer. Tom took a curve and Saunders was throwed back to his seat.

"Well, after I understood what a mercenary was, I put forth the argument that I couldn't be one of them, hell, I didn't even have a uniform. I felt pretty good about that point I had made 'til they told me that only proved I was a spy, which in their book was about three and a half times worse than your average mercenary.

"My little court-martial didn't last long. They asked me if I had anythin' to say before they wrapped it up, and since I figured I hadn't done too good with what I already said I passed.

"They sentenced me to be the target for their firing squad. It seemed fair enough. I couldn't work up any worry or fear. Just then a rider come up and said the British was advancin' fast and they should all pull back. Well, that made me think I was gettin' a reprieve and I started feelin' good about things. But the Colonel ordered them to make short work of me. Two soldiers tied my hands behind me, put a blindfold over my eyes, and hustled me out back somewheres for to send me up yonder. They pushed me up against a stone wall. I could feel it against my hands."

Besides Tom's, there wasn't a breath let go in that car.

"I was acquainted with the procedure, which is well nigh worldwide, and I waited for the order to get ready."

The headlights of an approaching car throwed a light on us. Right then we come up on a truck with no taillights. We was going too fast to stop and we couldn't move to the other lane. On our right was a deep dry wash. Tom cut the car to the left and passed across the path of the oncoming car. I heard it brush against a flying flap of canvas. We tore across the desert, slowed down some by the cactus we was mowing over. Our front right wheel hit a hole and we went over, like a flip off a diving board, and come crashing down on our wheels again. Our canvas and wood top was all but tore away. Me and

[178]

Dwight was throwed from the car. Vic was screaming. I felt blood on my forehead. I laid on the ground for a spell, watching the others crawl out of the car.

Tom calmed down Vic and called for us. Me and Dwight went crawling towards them on our hands and knees. Tom went back to the wrecked car to check Dick Crawford. Old Dick had slept through the whole thing. Tom woke him up and helped him towards us. We was all in a line, either sitting on the sand or lying down, each in his own way trying to get back his senses. Finally I just had to ask, "Well, what the hell did the Boers do to you?"

"The Boers?" said Tom. "Oh, they shot me dead."

For a minute I was ready to accept that explanation. But I said, "How could they do that? You're still living."

"You call this livin'?" said Tom.

To the coldly professional eye we must of looked hysterical, at the least, and I reckon that's why, though we wasn't keen on the idea, we was carted off to the nearest hospital. Tom was the only sober one amongst us and we blamed him for driving us to drink. The cut on my forehead took only four stitches, and Saunders only picked up some bruises. Tom ordered a car to be sent for us from the nearest town, and we sat down in the lobby and waited for it to arrive.

The word had spread through the hospital that Tom was there, and one of the doctors come up to him and asked if he'd mind visiting with a pretty sick little boy.

Tom went off with the doctor and didn't come back for half an hour. When he did, I noticed he had forgot his hat and I noticed his face had gone all white. He didn't say nothing to nobody, only went off by himself to where they had a spigot for a drink. I ambled over and offered him a tailor-made. We leaned back against the wall and smoked.

"That little boy I seen?" he said.

"Yeah."

"He's gonna die."

"Rough break," said I.

"When he seen me, he smiled, first time since he got here, they said."

I nodded.

"I held his hand, hell, I had nothin' to say. He told me he wasn't afraid. I only took off my hat and give it to him, said to be a good little cowboy."

Tom always knew he had some powerful effect upon his fans, but usually he seen them in mobs. It was near all he could handle, to think that the boy's death might be made a little easier just by his appearance at his bedside.

"It illustrates a unique responsibility that is almost impossible to bear," said Teddy, "even for the heroes who must. I remember he once received a letter from a lady who had been pregnant and miscarried while watching one of his movies, because of a scene in which he shot the head off a rattlesnake. The letter touched him so deeply he was all but immobilized."

Remember how it was when Tom first jumped Old Blue off a cliff and in the river? How he couldn't hardly ride by a body of water without wanting to jump in? Well, now that's the way he come to be about hospitals. We couldn't drive by one without stopping for Tom to visit the children's ward, and whenever he was on tour or location he'd go to the local hospital and pass out hats to the children, and they cost him $50 to $130 per hat.

We settled into our Victorville location, where we would shoot three pictures, each taking four to five weeks. The hotel we stayed in was the best in town, but it wasn't the Ritz. Vic hated it on first sight. The town itself wasn't nothing to wire home about.

The work we did was hard, the life we led dull, just like old times. The weather was either hot and still, or, worse, hot and windy, when the sandy soil took to the air. The only one who was enjoying himself, if you don't count Dick Crawford, was

Dwight Saunders, the critic turned screen actor. He loved the desert and waxed all poetic ever' time the sun went down. He loved being out of ties and jackets. He loved the horses, and greasy food we had from the chuckwagon. He loved the chuckwagon. He put behind him the city and all its attractions. "I'm through with concrete forever," he vowed.

"Did I ever tell you the time I was elected Mayor of a cement boom town?" asked Tom. "Well, I'd seen gold boom towns and silver boom towns . . ." and Tom was off and running, mixing truth and fiction no harder than bourbon and branch water. Nobody hardly cared whether these yarns was true or false. They welcomed the diversion.

Even Tony didn't like Victorville. He bit Tom once on his behind and swung his head against Tom's, knocking him out cold.

Over dinner one night they was lamenting the general state of things and the long weeks that faced us. "It's sure no way to treat a pregnant lady," said Vic.

"I don't know why she had been saving it," said Teddy. "Waiting for the right moment, I suppose. I knew when I saw his reaction to the news that I had lost him, but somehow I knew it was not forever. My God, now it is, isn't it?

"I could never fully accept how much he loved Vic. She was the love of his life. Strange words, coming from me, no? But true. I accepted it. Why should I try to explain? I don't feel the need to. What I did with my life is my business, no one else's. I chose to live the way I lived. I was the butt of cowboy jokes."

There's this here Indian chief and he got only one daughter left unmarried, the ugliest girl in the tribe. None of the Indian braves will have her. A cowboy wanders through their camp and the chief tries to trade her off on him. The chief offers him a fine pinto pony with her, but the cowboy can't get over her ugliness. The chief tells him what a hard worker she is and what good company she makes. "Wal', maybe she is, Chief, and no offense, but she's 'bout ugly enough to make a desert crab grow hair." The chief points out her fine breasts, her sturdy behind, and says what a good thing she'd be at night. "Got a right fine body, I don't deny her that," says the cowboy, "but what about that face?"

"Throw a gunny sack over her head," says the chief. He throws in a bearskin, and the cowboy agrees to marry his daughter. And things work out pretty good. She's a hard worker, she's good company, and at night the cowboy throws a gunny sack over her head.

The cowboy gets a piece of land and starts to build a cabin. His squaw is at his elbow in case he wants her to fetch something.

"Ladder," says the cowboy.

"Ladder, ladder, ladder . . . ," says the squaw, and she rushes off to find it.

When the ladder is set up, the cowboy says, "Box nails."

"Box nails, box nails, box nails," says the squaw, off like a shot to get them.

The cowboy gets on his ladder and says, "Hammer."

"Hammer, hammer, hammer," says the squaw, on her way to find it.

Finally the cowboy begins nailing his cabin together and hits his thumb with the hammer. "Fuck!" he yells.

"Gunny sack, gunny sack, gunny sack."

Just to give you an example.

"Vicky was packed off to the comforts of Los Angeles to rest and take care of herself and oversee the construction of their new home," said Teddy. "As soon as she had gone Tom came to me, the unpleasantness of what he had to say all over his face.

"Congratulations, I said, before he could say a word.

"Thanks. I'm so proud I could bust. I got to do my best now. I got to make my best effort to—

"I'd like to stay on as your secretary, I said quickly.

"Are all men so surprised that the women who love them know them so well?

"That would be all right with you? he asked.

"I love my job, I would be miserable without it.

"Well, gee, you're a crackerjack secretary, Teddy, if we could keep it strictly business.

"Whatever you say, Mr. Mix.

"And so it was the way it had been, but I knew that like before, someday, he would come to me."

With Vic gone he was a lonely old bird. He wrote her every day, sometimes twice a day. She didn't write that often, and when there was no mail for him he got testy. The picture became drudgery and his performance had no sparkle. I knew he'd start up drinking soon. Irony, he had just sobered up Dick Crawford, who never touched drugs *or* drink again and was never without a job.

We were sitting around our tables, having lunch from the chuckwagon. Tom set down with a bottle of beer in his hand. Nobody reminded him that he was taking his first step off the water wagon, but he knew what we was thinking.

"Sure is hot," he said.

A few of us said that it sure was.

"Cold beer sits well on a hot day, and then you get the healthy benefits of the hops and barley and whatnot."

After lunch he had a glass of wine and when he caught me looking at him, he said, "Somewhere in the Bible it talks about takin' a bit of wine for your digestion."

The last scene of the day was an above-average stunt. We always saved the dangerous ones for the end of the day, so's he'd have overnight to recuperate. They had built a long sluice running down past the villain's cabin. Tom got in it at the top, then they let out a rush of water and ore and he rode down the sluice. At the cabin he jumped off. It was the best scene he'd done since Vic left and he felt proud of it. He was limping pretty good when he walked away.

I saw him later, inspecting the damage, and he had a gin and tonic next to him.

"Englishmen drink gin," he informed me, "for the kidneys. You never seen a limey with bad kidneys. Oh, this ain't straight gin, Kid. I got some quinine water in here too. Best prevention for malaria you could use."

"Good," said I, "I seen how a lot of folks out here are coming down with it."

Evening come and he was drinking what he could get his hands on. Later, he took a jug up to his room and commenced entertaining himself by taking shots at the flies on the ceiling. It warn't what the drummer up above him would call a good night's sleep. The management said cease and desist. Teddy asked me to make him stop, but I politely declined the invitation.

In the midst of this, who should come in the lobby but Sol Wurtzel and two strangers. Teddy ran over to him and said, "Oh, Mr. Wurtzel, I'm glad you're here."

A shot rang out upstairs. The two men unbuttoned their jackets and I saw that they was wearing irons.

"Him?" asked Sol.

Teddy nodded.

"Meshuggah," he said.

"I led the three of them," said Teddy, "upstairs to Tom's room and knocked on the door, standing away from it in case he happened to shoot through. The two men drew their guns, but Sol asked that they put them away.

"Tom opened the door, a smoking gun in his hand. He broke into a big grin. *Why, Sol,* he said, *what brings you to this waterin' hole?*

"Tom, these two men are from the Bureau of Investigation."

"The color drained from his face. I was told to go to bed when Sol and the other two went into Tom's room, but you can be sure I didn't sleep. I couldn't imagine what they wanted with Tom, but I feared a scandal of the worst sort. My own room was just down the hall. The men were with him the

[184]

better part of an hour. When I heard the door open, I opened my own a crack so that I could hear. Only Tom's voice carried to me. *Good night, Sol,* he said. *Nice meetin' you, Harry and Frank, I'm gonna have Miss Eason mail them out to you in the morning.* My fears were abated. Whatever it was, it had been cordial. A couple of months later an honorable discharge certificate came in the mail from the Army Department. I gave it to Tom and he squirreled it away. When I asked him if it had anything to do with the visit from the government men, he changed the subject and gave me to believe it was a very personal matter."

Well, it settled one mystery for me. You see, I never told him I knew about his desertion from the army, but the question was always in my head: Tom's the king of the cowboys, everybody in the country knows who he is; how come the army ain't been by to fetch him back? What went on behind the hotel door in Victorville is going to stay a secret, but my guess is that for the good of the country, the studio, and Tom himself, a bargain was struck.

By the end of our stay in Victorville the reviews was in for the last picture we shot in Hollywood. Dwight Saunders' part was hardly a bit, and normally wouldn't get a mention in any review, but because he used to be one of them the other critics dumped on him bad.

He tried to laugh it off. Small-minded vindictiveness, he called it. Petty jealousy. But Tom studied each review carefully, stroking his chin.

"Dwight is wrong," Tom read. "What does that mean?"

"It doesn't mean anything, Major," said Dwight. "It's just a lame-brained snipe at me."

"But none of the rest of us was targets. We all did okay, the picture fared okay."

"Naturally. They're after me."

"Now, these men and women ain't dummies. They're the experts."

"Experts! Not a one of them knows cactus from canelloni."

"But what does he mean when he says, *The roles are well executed, with the notable exception of a new 'star' with the unlikely name of Dwight Saunders, who acts as though his gun belt were three notches too tight . . . ?*"

"Oh, they'll get over it, once they see I'm in this thing to stay."

"I'm afraid I can't keep you on," said Tom.

"What!"

"You'll only drag us down."

"But they'll never take me back on the paper."

"There's a train out tonight. Be on it."

"What about the picture? I've been building a characterization."

"Well, in the rest of the scenes your character just won't be there."

"You're crazy!" screamed Dwight, trying to laugh. "The audience won't know what to make of it."

"Let me give you your last lesson in movie-makin'. They won't even notice you're gone."

Talk about deflation.

That night Dwight boarded an eastbound train. No one's heard of him since.

To celebrate the end of shooting, and the end of a long, hard location, we held a dance at the local hall and invited a number of selected townies. Tom showed up an hour before it was over and started in playing the drums. He broke up the drums and come close to breaking up the dance. There was only one way to get him off that stage and out of the hall. I walked up to him and said, "I am the fastest man on feet."

He stopped his drumming in mid-stroke and looked at me for a spell, frozen-like. "But how can that be?" he said. "I am."

"Talk's cheap," said I.

There wasn't no way Tom could refuse a challenge, no matter what.

We laid out a course, once around the hall, then a circle of a mile through the streets of the town. Side by side, we bent over the starting line. Somebody had a gun (somebody always had a gun), and it was fired to start us on our way. Tom got off to an early lead. There was furious motion, but not much speed. Bear in mind we was racing in high-heeled cowboy boots. Around the back of the hall Tom lengthened his lead. I got closer by the time we come around front again and headed for town. The other cowboys all shouted encouragement to Tom. "Turn it on, Tom, he's gainin' on you!" And Tom gave it all he had.

I stopped out front, and after another yell to spur Tom on, we all went back inside to finish off the dance.

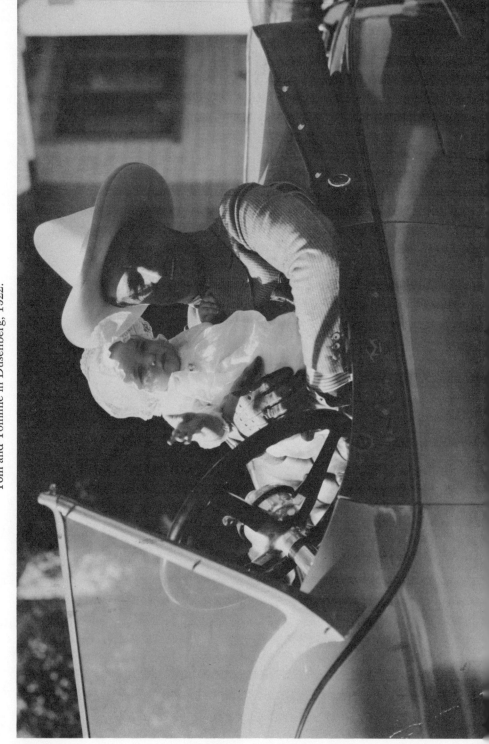

Tom and Tommie in Dusenberg, 1922.

Mother-in-law Eugenie Forde, wife Vic, and Tom on the Fox lot around 1923. (*Courtesy of Robert S. Birchard*)

Teresa "Teddy" Eason and "Pete" on the Fox lot with Tom around 1923. (*Courtesy of Robert S. Birchard*)

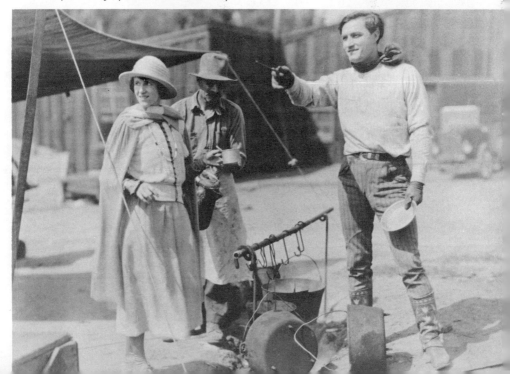

Tom and Vic, informal. 1923. (*Courtesy of Witzel Studios*)

Tom and Vic, formal. 1923. (*Courtesy of Witzel Studios*)

Tom Mix riding stunt horse *à la Comanche* in *Mile a Minute Romeo*, 1923.

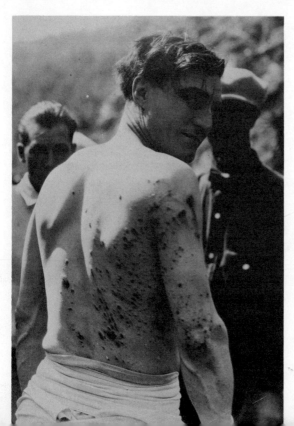

The result of coming too close to a dynamite blast in *Eyes of the Forest*, 1924. (*Courtesy of Tom Mix Museum*)

right:
During his first European tour, 1925. (*Courtesy of Tom Mix Museum*)

22

In 1922, the unit hit its production peak, ten pictures. It was the year they moved into their new mansion at 1010 Summit Drive, and little Thomasina was born.

Ten pictures a year didn't leave much time for nothing else. Wurtzel felt the unit had to work at that level of production to justify its own expenses. Tom had had all his cowboys classified as performers instead of extras, which put them on the payroll at $75.00 a week instead of the $7.50 a day extras pulled down. On top of that there was the stock and maintenance folks and Tom's salary.

In those days Fox had a system of "brand" pictures. From the bottom up they produced "Excel" pictures, "Victory" pictures, and "Standard" pictures. There was another category all to itself: "Mix" pictures. The budget for an Excel picture ran from $20,000 to $22,000. Victory pictures cost $25,000 to $27,000, and Standard pictures cost $30,000 to $32,000. A Mix picture averaged about $50,000. To bring the cost of his pictures in line with the others, Tom gave them only one selection: to squeeze as many pictures out of him as they could, 'cause he wasn't going to cut back on expenses. So as one picture was winding up, a director and writer was getting another script ready, and a leading lady and what support players was necessary was being lined up. As soon as the final scene was shot, these new folks would rush to the new set and we'd start all over again. He quit drinking again just to keep up the pace.

"A grind is a grind," said Teddy, "regardless of the glitter that surrounds it in the eye of an outsider. He had a new baby, who from the beginning was put into the care of hired people. He had a wife he adored but didn't see much. He had a new house whose luxuries he could hardly enjoy."

The house was near Chappie's and looked some like his, built like it was by the same feller. I reckon they wanted it that way. Hollywood's kingpin position kept trading back and forth 'twixt Chappie and Mary Pickford; Tom and Vic thought them the height of society.

The grounds covered fifteen acres, like I said, and had amongst them stables, a four-car garage, a swimming pool big enough to drown a couple elephants, with Tom's TM brand in mosaic tiles at the bottom, and Vic's Grecian tennis courts. She made one mistake with the courts. She had put some of her columns inside the fence and seemed like either you or your ball was always bouncing off one of them.

The house was fine indeed and had a cellar and a second story, with a roof of Spanish tiles, and ten thousand square feet of moving about room. The entrance hall was marble and in it a marble and oak table set there just for to take your calling card. On this table rested a pretty little gold-plated .25 automatic. Like all the other guns and rifles scattered about the house it was loaded. Tom's notion was that if his guests knew all the guns was loaded no one would pull the trigger of any one of them. It was his house and I reckon he was entitled to his notions. He was proved wrong.

Him and Vic never could come to terms on the living room so's there was two. Tom's was on the right as you come in. On the floor was Indian rugs and mountain lion skins; on the walls a clutter of heads, antlers, bows, rifles, sombreros, championship belt buckles, everything but Geronimo's right nut. Silver and tooled leather saddles set on stands. About the tables he put out silver spurs and bridles and a small arsenal of handguns. Leaded glass was in the arched windows. He had a great mechanical nickelodeon music maker and a set of drums he liked to play along on.

Vic's French drawing room was the next room beyond Tom's, hiding there like a poodle living next to an elkhound. She had her crystal chandeliers and amethyst sconces on the walls and Louis the something furniture and a few paintings by Frenchmen who was said to be red hot.

The dining room was off to the left. A huge mahogany table took up most all the room. In the center of the table was built a water fountain which spouted water in six or seven changing colors.

"I remember sitting among the celebrated diners at the first dinner party," said Teddy. "The fountain had a malfunction or a leak somewhere, and all during the seven courses of dinner a steady drop-drop-drop of water fell into my lap, but I was too embarrassed either to call attention to it or move away."

He hired him a first-class cook working in the latest word in kitchens, and he hired him a titled Austrian butler named Kai who went about in knee pants and a powdered wig. Downstairs there was a well-stocked butler's pantry and a small den where Tom worked on his writings, and a vault where Vic kept her jewels and Tom kept on hand a hundred thousand or so in cash.

There was eight marble bathrooms and eight fancy bedrooms. Gold-painted cane chairs disguised the pots in the bathrooms. The master bedroom had cupids dancing on the ceiling and the biggest bed I ever seen, covered over with a red velvet canopy and a bedspread to match. The furniture was all in gold.

On top of the house he set up his TM brand in blinking neon lights.

"There must have been a time, don't you think, Kid, when they stood with an arm around each other and looked at it, she remembering the seemingly infinite line of roominghouses and cheap vaudevillian hotels, he remembering a campfire and bedroll on the dusty plains of Oklahoma. All behind them now, like standing at an oasis so deep that one does not even consider the prospect of its ever running dry."

Well, I couldn't say for sure, but there was a time when I stood back and looked at it and had a few thoughts of my own.

"Tom indulged her every wish. She liked diamonds and emeralds and he routinely bought them for her. If he had no time, he sent me shopping, and always criticized me for buying too cheap a stone. His love for that woman was preposterous. I've never understood it. Her nose went straight out, and for some distance too. The operation she later had in France only made it worse. Do you remember that when she came back no one dared mention the word nose in her presence? She became a regular Cyrano on the subject. Well, maybe it was something she inherited from Fordie, but she had an undeniable allure for men. I listened as intently as she to all their stories. I was as attractive as she, more so I think, although the camera lied.

"I was riding with her once, in a new toy Tom had given her. I believe it was called a Royal Underslung, one of those sleek, low, sporty automobiles that you just know is hand-crafted and tremendously expensive. One sat almost on the road while riding in it. She made an elaborate hand signal for a right turn, and we were hit from behind. We were not injured and the damage to the car was slight, but Vic was furious. The man who had hit us apologized profusely. *Didn't you see me signal for a turn?* said Vic, peevishly. *I didn't see it,* said the man. *I went like this,* she said, and even more elaborately repeated it. *What can I say, lady, I didn't see your hand,* said the man. She looked at him and said, *If it had been my fucking leg you would have seen it!* Why, I could see the bulge rise in his pants. Can you explain to me the stimulation of anger, rudeness, and vulgarity?"

For a while, the attention and the riches had her floating in air, but finally her fear of poverty and her dread of losing her riches kept her from ever really enjoying them. Tom gave her cash and told her to toy with it, invest it in things she reckoned might give her a greater hold on security. She took it and bought certain stocks and bonds, following the advice of shrewd men she was in a position to invite to her home. Tom's cash? Hell, he spent it, figuring his wild spending no more than good cheap advertising.

He bought himself a boat and christened it the *Miss Mixit.* It was sixty feet long, but there was another down there in San Pedro, where he kept it, that was seventy feet. Vic wanted to make the boat longer. Tom ordered them to cut the boat in half and add a fifteen-foot piece in the middle, and damned if they didn't do it too. Be willing to pay the price and somebody will take care of you, whatever.

The *Miss Mixit* had a white hull, a mahogany cabin, and a canopy over the fantail where a meeting of eight could be held comfortable. It set him back $10,000. He hired a skipper at $100 a week and a crew of two, I called them Up 'n' Adam, at $150 a month a man, top wages for those days. He kept them on full time, even though there was times the boat wouldn't leave its berth for months on end.

He bought him a furnished house on Santa Catalina Island for nine thousand dollars, with cash he had on him. He put a neon brand on the roof there too. You could see it most all the way from the mainland. He told the skipper to help himself to the furniture and had new stuff sent out. I don't reckon he spent more than thirty nights at the place.

"Puritans will clack their tongues at such wanton spending," said Teddy. "They will never understand that what Tom bought were *necessities.* He *needed* these things to distract him from unceasing and dangerous work, to establish who he was in this bizarre community, to give him comfort from the crowd that owned him. Recently in a premiere mob a man had attacked him with a scissors, after a lock of his hair. He needed distractions from the distractions. That's why he came back to me. I wish I could have been enough for him. It is a foolish girl's wish, when in love with such a man."

There was a fair number of young cupcakes clinging to the studio's fences, but Tom preferred his leading ladies. They was close and they was quiet. They was all dark too, he wouldn't hire a blond. Vicky was fair, the only one who was.

The quality of our pictures didn't suffer much, but I could see the pace couldn't be kept. He started short periodicals. Vic would call the studio and tell them to get any close-ups and stunts they had left out of the way, 'cause he was off again. Usually when Tom finished a toot, the only stores still open was in Chinatown. Vic come in for a wide selection of Oriental pajamas, robes, jewelry, and objects of art.

"I have a few myself," said Teddy.

His boat made Ensenada easier. Whenever he went there four Mexican lawmen was detailed to walk with him on his rounds of the village fun spots, to keep the locals from pestering him, and vice versa. They was usually followed by at least seven mariachis.

Vic thought the place was filthy, so when he went there it was me or Frankie Dolan or Lynn Reynolds or Buster Keaton that went with him. John Gilbert made the rounds once, but he was so shook up by that remodeled boat and the clumsy way it cut through the water, like a caveman's club, he never went again.

"Remember that Saturday we gathered on the boat at San Pedro for a cruise to Ensenada?" asked Teddy. "That is, Vic, Kathleen, and I gathered on the boat. We were waiting for

[193]

Tom, Lynn, and you. You were all supposed to get away early from the set and join us. That was the day you were *alleged* to have been hit over the head with a bottle that *allegedly* turned out to be the real thing instead of a breakaway prop. You were sent home with stitches in your scalp, *allegedly*.. Tom and Lynn stopped at a few speaks before finally arriving at the boat. Tom was driving and Lynn was up front, in the Duesenberg. They had put the chauffeur in the back seat with a drink.

"During the drive from the studio to San Pedro, Tom and Lynn got into a discussion about the planned trip. Tom insisted that if time were a factor they would be better off driving to Ensenada than sailing. Lynn believed that a powerboat got there quicker than a car, because although the road to Tijuana was not bad, the road from there to Ensenada was treacherous. *But it all depends on the driver*, said Tom. While asserting such, he sideswiped another car, catching the other driver's spare tire against his own rear fender. There was a dull thud, but Tom kept right on driving and supporting his claim that a car could make it to Ensenada before the *Miss Mixit*.

"He was frequently bumping into cars without noticing it. Or if he did notice it, he ignored it. Yes, he could be called materialistic, but when you reach the level of materialism he did, the things you own start losing their value. You don't care about battered cars, your own or someone else's. Once in Santa Barbara he ran into a parked car. A crowd quickly gathered. Tom got out of his car and gave a courtly sweep of his hat to both the damaged car and the crowd and then drove off. When the girl who owned the other car returned to it and was told that Tom Mix was the culprit, she did nothing but lovingly stroke the dents in her fender."

When Tom and Lynn pulled into the marina they was still arguing the matter out. Tom got out of the car and saw the dent in the fender. "John," he said to the chauffeur, "how did this happen?"

"Gee, I don't know, Mr. Mix," said the chauffeur, probably reckoning it would save him some trouble.

"Well, have it repaired, and in the future be sure to drive more careful."

"Yes, sir."

"Drivin' an automobile is like handlin' a horse," he said to Lynn, "you can't just jump on it and ride away. It calls for some patience and practice."

They went aboard and tried to get everybody in the beef. The others couldn't care less, they only wanted to get going so's they could be there before dark.

"Well, if anyone should know," said Tom, "it'd be the skipper."

So he called down the skipper and put the question to him.

"Considering the delays and the bad road conditions, I'd bet on the *Mixit*," said the skipper.

That was all Tom had to hear. He bet the bunch of them dinner at the Montmartre that he could leave in the car at the same time they left in the boat and be there in time enough to have drinks and dinner before they ever arrived. They wouldn't have got there at all if they kept arguing about it, so they sealed the bet and took off, them in the boat, Tom in the car.

"As much as you might like to ignore such nonsensical challenges, once initiated they seek their own momentum," Teddy said. "Vicky ordered the skipper to keep it wide open and we locked ourselves in the cabin to avoid being swept off deck.

"We arrived in Ensenada just at dusk. We tied up and stepped off the boat. There, rounding the corner at a leisurely pace, was Tom, smoking a long cigar. Two beautiful dark señoritas sat next to him. Another sat in the back seat, between two *Federales,* each of whom was smoking one of Tom's Havanas. He wore a smile I've heard the cowboys describe as *shit-eating* as he chugged slowly before our astonished eyes.

[195]

"Vic reached into her bag and pulled out her gun, same .22, and began firing it in the direction of Tom's car. The señoritas screamed, the *Federales* threw themselves to the floor, and Tom hunched over the wheel and sped out of range.

"Vic slipped her empty pistol into her purse and said, *Well, we're here. Shall we find a decent place to dine?*

"Though the others drank and ate with hearty appetites, I can tell you the dinner was no pleasure for me. The madcap quality of our lives was escalating. I worried where it would end. I knew it would. People don't live madly ever after. Somewhere it comes to a head."

They looked at the opening door of the restaurant and saw, of all people, yours truly shuffling towards them. I took off my hat and said, "Ladies, Lynn, sorry to bother you whilst you're all eating, but Tom is feeling sure low and wants to tell you all it was nothing but a joke. See, I drove the car down right from Mixville. I had a good four-hour start on you."

In the confusion they didn't notice that the car in Ensenada warn't the car Tom drove away from San Pedro.

"Tom flew down here with some feller in an aeroplane. It was all a setup. Especially them gals you seen him with. They was only part of the joke. He wanted me to give you this here as a peace offering and beg your forgiveness."

I handed Vic a small box. It held a ring, platinum and diamonds. The large diamond was nine carats. There was twenty-some smaller diamonds clustered around it. Four to five thousand dollars was my guess, even in Mexico.

"I believe I sat there for most of five minutes before I realized my last sip of champagne was still in my mouth," said Teddy.

Vic slipped it on one of her bare fingers and admired it. "Tell Tom he may join us for dessert," she said.

"Ma'am, he was a-wondering if he might have a token in return."

"Well, let me see . . ."

[196]

"Your little gun, maybe?"

Vic reached in her handbag, brought it out between two fingers, and dropped it in my open hand.

In five minutes, me and Tom, a wicked smile belying his hangdog head, joined them. Dessert was salt, tequila, and wedges of lime.

23

Tom was no stranger in Tijuana neither. Because of Prohibition Tijuana became a favorite weekend spot for Southern Californians and the little border town grew like Topsy. Not that Tom was ever in short supply of booze. He had a regular bootlegger, a homely little man who had a wife even homelier than he was and a baby homelier than the two of them was. Every day they could be seen walking the baby through Beverly Hills, making deliveries. He kept his bottles in a secret compartment in the baby carriage.

"Tijuana," said Teddy, like you do of a place you want to forget. "I was awakened from a peaceful sleep. He was being 'detained' at the border, on the American side, and wanted me to get Sol Wurtzel and drive down there immediately without telling Vic about it. I roused Sol out of his bed and together we sped down to San Ysidro. These errands were so difficult for Sol. He considered Tom unreasonable and irresponsible, but he was a commodity in great demand, and as long as people paid to watch Tom, Sol would have to do his best to keep him contented and his image untarnished."

They found Tom in one of the small sheds at the international checkpoint, in the company of yours truly and a captain of the border guards.

" 'Bout time you got here," said Tom. He was sore, what I mean.

"What?" Teddy asked. She hadn't heard.

"I say, you took your sweet time gettin' here," he said, raising up his voice. "These birds mighta killed me."

Sol stepped forward and shook hands with the Captain. "I'm Sol Wurtzel, sir, superintendent of Fox Films, Hollywood. Mr. Mix and Kid Bandera are two of our leading contract actors, and men of very high character. What seems to be the trouble?"

See, in addition to more money than I could use, Hollywood gave me a very high character.

"Well, Mr. Wurtzel, Mr. Mix assaulted one of our border guards."

"It's the other way around, Sol. They assaulted me. I got a witness. They worked over Kid here too."

I corroborated his testimony. Perjury's a harder rap to prove than assault and battery.

Me and Tom had driven down two days before in the Rolls to see the races at Caliente. Tom, of course, had bedecked himself in a black cutaway suitable for the finest track in England. His britches was white and tucked in black patent-leather gentlemen's boots. His shirt had a lacy front and he wore a top hat. He bought the most expensive pair of binoculars he could find. There was a walking stick too, but that got lost pretty early on. Too bad too, there was a nice hunk of diamond in the head of it.

We opened up with breakfast in a tiny cantina. Me and Tom set down and he says, "Give us two bottles of *cerveza* and fifty dollars worth of *huevos rancheros.*" Now, *huevos rancheros* out of TJ are enough to burn off tattoos, so we had to keep the *cerveza* coming to wash it all down. How much is anybody's guess, but one thing I know: we never made it to the races that day.

We didn't make it the next day neither, but we came damn

close. Tom bought a racehorse from a gentleman we met in a bar.

Think of the biggest man you know. This bird was bigger, though that had nothing to do with Tom's buying his horse, except indirectly. Ever' head turned when he walked in that bar and set himself alone at a table. He was wearing a hat kind of like the one Tom had made famous, and he didn't remove it when he set down. Soon he became the subject of conjecture, and the attention of the patrons was took away from Tom and towards this giant, with a sense of fearful respect.

The situation finally become less than tolerable to Tom, so he walked up behind the feller and yanked his hat down over his eyes. The man jumped to his feet, struggling to remove it. Tom looked up at him and laughed.

Meet your maker, Tom, I reckoned.

He pulled the hat off his eyes and sized up Tom, who was laughing like a madman. "I'm Tom Mix, partner. Put 'er there."

Tom put out his hand. The big man looked at it for a minute, but his clear intention was still to break Tom in half.

"Aw, don't take yourself so serious," said Tom. "Put 'er there."

I reckon he'd reached his boiling point and begun to cool. He took the offered hand. "I have a ten-year-old at home, Mr. Mix," he said. "I don't know how I could ever explain away killing his hero."

"That's the stuff!" said Tom, and we all set down together.

The man bought a round of drinks and Tom bought his racehorse.

It was eleven that night before Tom had the idea, which he thought was original as hell, that we should go inspect the animal he had bought, just to make sure it was the bargain we'd been celebrating. We'd lost track of the feller who sold him.

We commenced on foot, and didn't do too bad neither. To

judge from the smell, we was near the stables. But just as we never got to the races, we never got to see Tom's racehorse neither, and by this time we even forgot its name, which was something in Spanish. A *Federale* blocked our way. *"Alto!"* he said, raising his hand.

"Just goin' to see my new hoss," explained Tom.

"Alto!" was all the lawman cared to say.

"Well, no, I got to go on over there."

This time he said nothing; he only raised his hand again.

"C'mon, Kid," said Tom, and together we walked toward the *Federale*.

"Alto!" he yelled again, this time leading me to believe he meant it.

"Look, I'm goin' to have a look at my new horse, and that's all there is to it."

"Alto, or I blow my whistle."

A whistle hung on a lanyard around his neck. The *Federale* seemed to think it was a mighty fine weapon, though maybe something was lost in his accent. To Tom and me it was only a whistle, a toy. If he'd drawn the gun he wore, then he probably would have had his way, but he threatened us with no more than the whistle.

"Blow that whistle and I'm apt to knock it down your throat," said Tom.

The *Federale* made good on his threat, and damned if Tom in turn didn't try to deliver on his.

Putting a law-enforcement officer in a state of unconsciousness is a grave act the world round. No nevermind what country you're in, you done a serious crime when you put a lawman to sleep. Tom and me made a mad rush for the border.

There was some worriful minutes when we forgot where we'd parked the Rolls. I took the keys and told Tom to try to make it on foot whilst I searched out the car.

On his way, as he later described it to me, Tom saw an American sailor nuzzling a señorita in a doorway. He stopped long enough to pull him away, pin him to the wall, and say, "Leave my sister alone or I will kill you!" Then he dashed on, the cutaway billowing behind him.

I couldn't find the Rolls and was having dark dreams about prison in Mexico. Luckily I run into the boy we hired to watch the car. He led me to it. I paid him off, and paid off the boy we'd hired to watch him. I overtook Tom less than a home run from the border. I slid over, gave Tom the wheel, and we made good our getaway when the Mexican guard waved us by.

Now, an ordinary person would have thanked his lucky stars and minded his manners, leastways 'til he had put a fair number of miles 'twixt him and the scene of the Mexican misadventure. Not Tom.

There was something about the attitude of the guard on the U.S. side that he couldn't abide.

"What was the purpose of your visit?" asked the guard.

"Horsin' around," said Tom.

"Are you bringing anything across with you?"

"Only what's inside us."

On the Mexican side a Rolls-Royce is an item of admiration. It shows the owner is a man of great cunning, good fortune, or rich heritage. They can experience a pleasure watching such a magnificent machine. But on the American side, there's a different feeling. Where's this bastard get off owning a Rolls? I've worked hard all my life, where's mine?

The guard broadcasted his resentment and lack of humor with a certain facial gesture. Then he reached in the car to frisk the driver. Tom never was the kind of bird anyone could get away with feeling up. He brushed away the hands, and when that official made to open the door, Tom leaned back and kicked the door at him, sending him sprawling on his post.

The official's miscalculation of the man in the fruity suit showed all over his face as Tom jumped on him. They keep extra men at the border for just such a disagreement. I took out one of them, but in short time we was subdued, as the descriptions of such things always end up.

Now, what happened after we was subdued is in dispute, and I can't recollect clearly myself. The guards claimed we was took to an anteroom and searched. Tom claimed they took us there to beat us, and it could have been that way, neither of us was feeling much pain. Sol tried to impress on them that Tom was practically an American ambassador of goodwill to Mexico, and all sides would be best served by third-person apologies and a speedy forgiving and forgetting, and that's how we finally got out of there.

"The press, however, got hold of the story," said Teddy, "and there followed a quick brushfire of accusations, denials, and counter-accusations. Fortunately, it burned itself out. It was a memorable night in another way, though to face the truth I must have known it earlier, when the quality of wind became more a touch and less a sound. On the ride back I had to interrupt Tom's story several times and ask him to speak louder. *What's the matter, Teddy,* he said, *you gon' deaf?* In fact, I was."

24

She told nobody she was losing her hearing, least of all Tom. She didn't want his pity, even if she could of had it. Pity, like fear, was an emotion out of Tom's acquaintance. He could feel sorry about another feller's bad luck, but only for the waste of it, like Dick Crawford's addiction.

"Sorrow without a means of correcting its cause was without meaning to him, and there was no cure. Use an ear trumpet, learn to read lips, I was told. Silence descending."

So she kept it to herself, walking on eggshells and faking it whenever she couldn't hear Tom. The important thing was that she stay by his side. She didn't want to be a reminder of declining power, failing sense. I don't know, though, maybe somebody worried about his own powers might be comforted to see their loss in another. Like it's only in the scheme of things.

Anybody who saw him then would figure he was going nowhere but up. He still had the body and energy of a man twenty years younger; his popularity and pay was rising steady as the sun; there warn't no visible signs of dissatisfaction. But I knew Tom Mix, for twenty years by then, and I knew that changes was coming over him. To give you a for instance, he had finally allowed himself to be talked out of a stunt—a horseback leap across the Newhall chasm, where a mistake meant sure death; when we gathered round the double to congratulate him on the jump, Tom had disappeared.

Then it come out that Vic was seen in the company of some young extra out of another studio.

Tom knew his name and I expected he'd go after him. When he didn't I credited his restraint to a momentary recognition of what's fair is fair. Either that or the fear that he might lose Vicky. Instead, he raised hell in Mexico, brawled on the Saturday-night circuit here, and took up some very dangerous stunts. Only this time instead of flirting with death he was courting it with serious intentions.

In *Eyes of the Forest*, done on location in Santa Cruz, he played a ranger after forest thieves. The scene called for him to ride along a mountain trail. Some dynamite behind a stump was to detonate, and him and Tony was to race down the side of the mountain, ahead of tumbling dirt and rocks. He wanted the dynamite planted somewhere besides behind a stump. He said the stump would take too much of the blast.

Lambert Hillyer, who was directing, argued that real outlaws would of planted the dynamite behind the stump, it was the only realistic place to put it. He promised Tom that the dynamite was enough to please the most skeptic audience. He cautioned him, in fact, to stay on the far side of the trail.

Our explosives expert set up his charge and lit his fuse. Tom and Tony was in position, and Lambert gave the signal to begin. I watched him as he rode the trail, angling Tony closer and closer to the stump.

"Get over! Get over!" Lambert yelled through his megaphone, and I yelled likewise, but Tom moved even closer to the stump, and the dynamite went off. They was wrapped round by the blast. We saw flashes of them rolling over each other down the mountainside, amidst falling rock.

As soon as we could we scrambled to the bottom to help

[205]

them. They was most all buried, but still conscious. Tom was more worried about Tony than himself. The horse had a gaping wound in his side. Tom and one of the trainers applied first aid, then loaded Tony in a trailer to take him to the nearest vet. Only when we heard Tony would be okay did Tom take off his shirt to examine his own wounds. It was a sight to behold. His back was scored, imbedded with different-sized pebbles. Reminded me of the day we checked out Chance Brothers. The pain seemed to give him a kind of release, and he was himself again. But shortly after, reports filtered back to Santa Cruz that Vic was seen with a few different cowboy actors.

"Vic has told me," said Teddy, "and I believe her, that at that time nothing had occurred between her and the men she was seeing. She had seen them only out of revenge because reports were getting back to her that Tom was carrying on with his leading ladies. Such reports, of course, were generally rampant in Hollywood. Lynn Reynolds lost his life because of one. But to my knowledge, at the time of which I speak, Vic was faithful, with one exception who will remain unnamed, since in the world of American sports he has become something of a beloved institution."

If she had really been unfaithful it would have given some sense to the mayhem that followed. We no sooner come back from location than Tom got into the first of two legendary fights with Hoot Gibson. Hoot was one of three leading cowboys at Universal. Harry Carey was another, and the third we'll discuss by and by. Hoot was a champion cowboy and had, like us, come out of the 101 Ranch, though that was after we left it. They hadn't met up 'til both was stars. They liked each other, in the way cowboys do, which lets them feel simultaneous both affection and malice towards one another. I'll give you an example. Once a cowboy I knew stabbed his partner with a broken billiards cue. The victim not only wouldn't press charges, he raised the other's bail. That's the kind of thing Tom and Hoot had, what most of us had.

Their first fight was in the Alexandria Hotel, where the women used to complain that when Tom danced with them his spurs tore their stockings. Tom always wore jangling spurs, the only star in town who seemed to get away with it.

They say the fight was caused by some remark Hoot had made about Vic's virtue, but I discount that. Cowboys never tire of discussing a lady's virtue, but it's usually done out of the hearing of her husband. My guess is the fight started out of what most cowboy fights start out of—nothing, mixed well with the white of an egg.

Hoot was twelve years younger than Tom. All right, so that's excuse 7B. What laid Tom low was Hoot was a southpaw and could deliver a powerful load in that left. It was the first Tom lost, and I seen him take four at once, including yours truly.

Tom could of slid his spirits under the door. Finally he come out of it and called up Frankie Dolan and put him on the payroll. Frankie was an ex-fighter from San Francisco, the bantamweight champion of the Pacific Coast.

He wasn't no bigger than your average paperboy, but he knew what to do with his mitts and he was strong. I remember one afternoon at Fordie's cabin in Topanga Canyon. That area was near a wilderness then. She had a simple twenty-by-twenty cabin where she'd retreat with friends for a weekend of partying. There was an outhouse in the back, where she had rigged up a pull-chain toilet. 'Course, there was no running water. Instead of water the tank hid a large brass bell. Whenever some proper lady guest excused herself from the cabin for "a breath of air" we would soon hear a loud clang in the outhouse. This would send us rolling on the floor in laughter. No, it sure didn't take much to tickle us.

The first afternoon Frankie visited the cabin he went out back to the outhouse and naturally he pulled the toilet chain. When the bell clanged this tiny hombre went right through the door, knocking it to pieces.

[207]

So Tom hired him and installed a ring at the studio and another at Mixville. Every day he and Frankie would train—for only one purpose: Tom wanted to knock Hoot's head off.

He stopped drinking, he did road work (on top of a schedule that was keeping me tuckered out), and he sparred daily.

"Am I ready for him yet, Frankie?"

"Pretty soon, Tom, pretty soon."

Long after the others went home Tom and Frankie would stay to work out.

"Now, Frankie, now?"

"Not yet, Tom."

Finally the day come when Dolan pronounced him ready. He and Tom got into Tom's Stutz Number Four and drove to Universal. They asked me to go with them, but I declined the invitation. They waited patiently near the gate for Hoot to leave the studio.

"How 'bout we warm up a little, Frankie?"

"Save it, Tom."

When Hoot did drive out, Tom forced him to the curb. He jumped out of the Stutz and said, "I'm callin' you out, bat hunter." (Hoot got his nickname because of his fondness for stalking bats.)

Hoot got out of his car and said, "Go home and sober up, Tom."

"I ain't had a drop for weeks, but, by God, I'm gonna catch up just as soon as I finish with you."

Hoot laid him out with one blow from that mighty left and I reckon it was the shortest rematch of record. Then Hoot took out after Frankie, who escaped on foot.

Now, Tom was willing to accept the fact that Will Rogers could beat him at roping, that Vic could beat him at tennis. He was even able to accept defeat from William Fox at golf, though Fox had one withered and useless arm. But to face the truth that he couldn't whup Hoot in a fair fight, a game that had always been his, took more effort than he could corral.

He gave the look of running hard just to move laterally. You ever try blowing up a balloon that has a pinhole leak that slowly gets bigger as you blow?

25

The other cowboy who shared star status over to Universal with Hoot Gibson and Harry Carey was Art Acord. Art was an authentic cowboy, and he had the character to enjoy his success with a level head. Too bad he lacked the character to survive the losing of it. Sound pictures put the finish to him. He took to drink. He drifted into rum running from Mexico, got involved with some hoods, and eventually served a year or two in prison. In '31 he was found dead of cyanide poisoning in a hotel room. Only the coroner wanted to call it suicide. Things don't ever get bad enough for a cowboy to kill himself.

Teddy wanted me to reassure her. I declined the invitation.

In 1924, Art was a star. Three years later he would be through, four years more and he would be dead. Now, he's unknown. There's no business like show business.

Vic and Teddy had been shopping, and they stopped by the Sunset Inn for dinner. I was there earlier and since I run into Art there we jawed a bit. We was about to eat some, and when Vic and Teddy walked in, we invited them to eat with us. Art sat next to Vic and that's how Tom found them when he come in later.

Vicky had a way of laughing brightly and listening earnestly and flirting to beat the band, giving the impression, especially to a husband, that she shares a secret or two with other men.

Tom was half in the bag, which struck me strange, only 'cause the Sunset Inn was the first stop on a long night's circuit and people at this hour usually was sober there. He worked his way towards our table, stopping at others along the way to say howdy and how's by you.

He stood over Vic and Art and said, "Well."

"A place to get water," said Art. "Have a seat."

"Vic?"

"We've just ordered dinner, darling. Have you eaten?"

He stood there looking at his wife sitting next to another cowboy and he couldn't find any words.

"Tom," I said, "it's all right."

Folks was starting to stare.

" 'Lo, Kid, you got a hand in this?"

"You got it wrong, Tom."

"Jesus Christ," said Vic, "either sit down or go away."

"Goddammit, don't start tellin' me what to do."

"Nobody's gonna tell anybody what to do," said Art. "I think our food's comin'."

"Care to wash your hands?" Tom asked Art.

This was an invitation to settle up in the men's room. Art leaned back in his seat and said, "Sounds like a good idea."

"Stop them, Kid," Teddy whispered to me, but I seen enough of these things to know you had to let them find their own conclusion.

I looked at Vicky. Again, two men going to fight over her. Off the record, in spite of what Teddy would say, I knew why. I guess you had to be there and be a man to know.

The waiter put our grub down as Art followed Tom to the men's room, both of them casually greeting folks about the room. Vicky speared a sliced carrot and put it in her mouth. We saw the door close behind them.

Thirty seconds later, Art come out, straightened up his tie, and walked away through the side exit. I got up to see to the damage. I went inside the men's room and there was Tom, out cold on the floor, and this scared colored porter backed up against the washstands holding a silver dollar.

"Mr. Mix grabbed Mr. Acord by the shirt," the porter told me, "and threw him against one of the stalls. But Mr. Acord come up with a punch out of nowheres and laid Mr. Mix out cold. Then Mr. Acord looks at him a minute, flips me this here silver dollar and says, 'When he comes to, brush this son-of-a-bitch off.' "

I splashed a little cold water on Tom's face and he came round. "You wasted one," I said and told him how Art come to be setting next to Vic. I helped him to his feet, and the porter started earning his buck. Tom shook away the porter's brush and shook away my helping hands. He left by the same exit Art took.

I can't honestly say he treated me any different after that incident, but I always had the feeling things was never quite the same.

I went back to the table and told them what happened. Teddy said to Vic, "You'd better go after him."

"Whatever for?" she said, slicing her steak.

"Because he's probably feeling very bad," said Teddy, peeved.

"Did I tell him to fight Art? Everyone knows Art is the toughest cowboy in town."

"Oh, I don't know," I said. "I saw Yak Canutt beat him twice in one afternoon."

"I didn't know that," she said, "why, I thought—"

"Stop it," yelled Teddy. Well, I sure did. I shut up and hunkered over my steak. Teddy turned on Vic, the first time ever I seen her riled. "He's your husband and he needs you," she said. "You should be with him. Can't you see what's happening to him? Do you want to—"

[212]

Well, Vic looked at her slow and easy, like for the first time. Maybe she was looking at a woman who loved her man, and better than she.

Vic laid down her knife and fork slowly and said, "Teddy, I believe I must remind you of your place. You are a person in my husband's and my employ. That we've known each other for some years does not give you the privilege to overstep your bounds."

True enough, but a little late.

"Are you going to find him or not?" Teddy asked. For the first time since I knowed her, she was standing up for something.

"My evening has already been arranged," said Vic.

"She said something after me as I rushed out of the Sunset Inn," Teddy told me, "but I could not distinguish what. I knew the places he might go, and in what sequence, but I just missed him at the first and at the second was told he hadn't arrived. I continued and backtracked, continued and backtracked. And when I found him, would he accept the comfort I had to offer him? I honestly doubted it, and yet I could not cease searching for him.

"I ran into Hoot at the Alexandria and he told me Tom had been there. He was on his way to the Superba Theatre downtown. Earlier in the week he had made a personal appearance there and was much distracted by the attentions of Georgia and Virginia, a sister song-and-dance act. I believe William Fox had an interest in the theater and used Tom to give the week's show a good opening. There were long lines outside and standing room only inside. I remember it was a frantic day and we were all late arriving. Usually the trainers walked Tony before a personal appearance, but on this night Tony arrived at the theater only seconds before Tom and there wasn't time for his customary exercise. Tom quickly mounted him and rode him onto the stage, Tony lifting his forelegs high and fancy. The applause was tumultuous. In the midst of it Tony raised his tail

[213]

and unloaded a great pile of manure. A deathly hush fell over the audience.

"Tom looked behind him, chuckled like an understanding father, and said, *Well, folks, he's only human.* The two sisters stood in the wings in their scanty outfits and tittered their little hearts away, as a trainer in a red jacket came out on stage with Tony's golden shovel.

"By the time I reached the Superba the last show had let out and the place was closed. I didn't realize how late it was. I don't know how much longer I pursued him. I know it was quite late by the time I went to the Beverly Hills house. I had a key for the place, since I spent as much time there as in the office or on the set. I'd just look inside to see if he had come home. I could have called, I suppose. Wish I had.

"Vic and I arrived almost simultaneously. I had already unlocked the door when she came up behind me. We could hear female laughter inside. I could not bring myself to open the door. Vic brushed past me, and stepped inside. Georgia and Virginia were descending the stairs. They stopped laughing when they saw us; one turned around twice, took a step back upstairs, then came down again as though she were lost in a maze. The other put her hand to her mouth. It was this one who recovered first. *Your house is just the berries, Mrs. Mix,* she said. We heard Tom's booming voice yell, *Where the hell is everybody,* and in a second he appeared at the top of the stairs holding a bottle of gin and wearing no more than his monogrammed shorts.

"The girls looked like two hamsters in a narrow cage. Vicky turned around and left the house. I stayed for only a second longer.

"He was ordered out of the house and must have moved in with Buster. At least we heard the sounds of shots and breaking glass coming from that direction. Rumors began to fly. Sol Wurtzel questioned Tom about them, but Tom was evasive. Vicky, however, related detail by detail and watched his eyes squint smaller and smaller, until they were tight little lines. She suggested that Tom might need a raise in salary. Sol wired William Fox, who wanted to know if Vicky could keep him in line. She made no promises except to try. Tom's salary was raised to four thousand dollars a week, and I was dispatched to Georgia and Virginia to deliver two identical checks. They told me what a fine human being Mr. Mix was."

Not what you'd call stingy either.

"Later a press luncheon for thirty-five guests was arranged at the Beverly Hills mansion. The occasion was Vic's birthday, though the real purpose was to calm the persistent rumors of scandal and divorce. The press people and guests had all arrived and still there was no sign of Tom. Sol Wurtzel was biting his nails for fear that Tom would either not show up or arrive in a state sufficient to cause even greater scandal.

"Vic had long before retrieved her pearl-handled .22 and she kept it hidden behind the mirror of her dressing table. Now she brought it out and tucked it away in her bosom.

"Vic, I asked, *what's that for?*

"I intend to be prepared, she said.

"For what?

"Whatever.

"She had already demonstrated her ability to use that thing. My nerves were almost shattered in anticipation of more gunfire. I stayed right next to her for the entire party as she moved among guests, chatting brightly, assuring all that Tom would be along any moment now.

"It got too late to wait any longer. Luncheon was served and we all gathered at the table. Vic sat at the foot of the table and I at her left hand. Vic and those sitting on my side of the table could, by leaning slightly, see the front door. We saw Tom come in wearing a magnificent purple suit. He had next to him a leather box, four feet high and on rollers. Best of all, he was sober and just looked wonderful. All eyes but mine were on him as he approached the table. Mine were on Vic, who was reaching for her gun. I quickly took it away from her and hid it in my skirts.

"Tom bid everyone a good afternoon, leaned over to kiss Vic, and said, *Happy birthday, dear.* He opened the leather box. Inside were two full length coats, one a mink, the other ermine with fox trim. Everyone expressed a proper admiration for them, and the press took notes. I gave him my seat next to Vic and went to dispose of the gun. I stopped when I heard him say, *Oh, I almost forgot. Here's a little extra present.* He handed her a check. She looked at it coolly and said in a flat voice, *How nice.* Then she called to me and said, *Teddy, take this down to the bank and have it certified.* The check was for one hundred thousand dollars.

"The press might have gone away convinced that rumors of strife in the Mix household were unfounded, but I knew that day that it was over, and even though their marriage endured for several more years, I believe Tom knew it too."

He moved back to the house, and they threw party after party, keeping themselves surrounded by other people. I reckon I was at most of them. One was like another, with too much of everything, especially other folks. Now, the only one I seem to recollect is the party for which Teddy had to mail just one single engraved invitation: to Louella Parsons. When Louella arrived, dressed in her finest, she discovered she was the only woman in a houseful of scruffy, dirty, half-drunk wranglers.

Tom led her inside saying, "Louella, I think it's time I put my brand on you . . . and I sure have enough area to choose where!"

There was those, most noticeably her leading colleague, who thought Louella exercised some poor taste in tying up at such a gathering, but she stayed 'til the cock crowed, dancing with all of us, drinking champagne from a split, helping Tom shoot out the bulbs in that infernal neon brand on the roof. Finally it was time to call it a wrap. Louella stood in the driveway, waiting for Tom to come take her home. Damned if he didn't come riding by on horseback. He leaned over to sweep her up and gallop away, as he was used to doing in so many pictures, but Louella went a mite heavier than Tom's leading ladies, and her weight pulled him off the horse. They both laid there dying in laughter on the driveway, whilst I stepped over and around them, yelling, "Cab!"

Tom grew sick of the constant crowd separating him and Vic, especially her new friends—young artists, actors, and writers—who loafed about the house at all hours, speaking French and running down America.

Tom called them her gigolos, a term he hung on all pretty, unmanly males with no visible means of support. They purely disgusted Tom and he said he had visions some day of a headline in the *Examiner:* TOM MIX REMOVES THE REVOLVING DOORS—THOUSANDS LEFT HOMELESS.

What I knew was bound to happen finally happened, on a clear warm Saturday afternoon in March, 1924. Hollywood is a town of many secrets, so it's no miracle that this one was kept for the next nine years. It could of been buried forever—if Tom and Vic had liked each other more and loved each other less. 'Course, if they had, it never would of happened in the first place.

A new building was under construction downtown. Earlier, me and Tom had stopped at the site, just watching. He knew there was a stunt in it. Finally he saw himself leaping out of the fifth-story window of the building alongside to grab one of the girders sticking out.

We took us a small crew down to get some footage of the stunt. He wanted to shoot it whilst the conditions was right, and save it for the time he would have a good story to fit it in.

It was a method of his. Once he took a crew to film an auto race in Santa Monica. During the race there was a spectacular

TOM MIX DIED FOR YOUR SINS

crash and the driver was killed. It was an impossible stunt to stage, and the footage was so good a whole feature, *The Speed Maniac*, was filmed around it.

Tom spent some pleasant hours flying out of that window and we come away with many good feet of film and some hairy stills. We took the stills to the Beverly Hills house to show them to Vic. She was surrounded by six of her "gigolos" and a few anemic girls, sipping sherry.

Vic glanced at the stills and handed them over to one of her gigolos without saying so much as howdy. Disappointed, Tom turned to pour a drink. The gigolo laughed and said, "Mrs. Mix, have you ever thought about having your husband's head examined?"

It's a good thing for that young feller that it was unseasonably warm that day and the French windows in Vic's sitting room was open. Tom would of throwed him through a closed one as easy. His friends was put in a thorny situation; they was called upon to do something, but having no experience in the world of throwing folks out of windows, they hadn't the notion what. Two of them awkwardly grabbed Tom's arms, not to deal out any misery, but as a kind of restraining gesture they hoped would be acceptable to both sides and would put an end to any more rough stuff.

Tom threw them off like a dog shaking off water, and out they went the same French window.

The two or three fellers left over looked to the terrified girls and ushered them away.

Through it all, Vic was screaming at Tom to unhand her friends. He was crude, insensitive, she yelled, a brute and a bore, and if he continued like that she would never have any decent friends of culture.

"It's this *brute*," Tom yelled back, "that gave you this palace to invite your friends *to*. This *bore*," he said, grabbing one of the stills and shaking it in the air, "who needs to have his head examined, that's given you every jewel, every car, every fur, every advantage you ever wanted. What the hell am I risking my life for?"

"Because you *like* it," she hissed. "Because you're nothing but a stupid cowboy!"

She began to take off the rings and bracelets and throw them at him, one by one.

"What good are they?" she said. "You might as well keep me in bare feet and a gingham dress."

He blocked them with his arm, and when she'd stripped herself of jewelry she threw a silver ash tray. It hit and shattered an antique vase she prized highly, one which Tom always considered ugly and useless, since she would never risk putting water and flowers in the thing. He laughed and walked back to his own sitting room.

"Reckon I'll be going now," I said. "Can I have the driver—?"

"I'll go with you," Tom yelled back at me.

Vic raced after him. I ambled on to the front door, but turned to see them one more time before leaving. Tom was at the mantel. He took a cigarette from a hand-carved ivory box. Vic grabbed the nickel-plated .38 that always sat on top of the nickelodeon. When he turned toward her she aimed it at him.

Somehow I knowed that this time it was for real. She fired and the bullet tore through the chair next to Tom.

Tom had the cigarette in his mouth, the unlit match in his hand. He turned his head calmly to see the damage the bullet had done to his stuffed leather chair, almost like it was only a rowdy child had throwed a toy against it. Then he turned back to Vic to see what she would do next. What she did was shoot him.

He looked at the bleeding wound in his arm much the same way he looked at the chair. Both of us had in our day been shot and shot at, you'd think we'd know something better to do than stand around. Partner, for those few seconds we was at Vic's mercy and she knew it too.

She squeezed off four more rounds. Things broke, bullets ricocheted. Tom seemed to follow the courses of the bullets, befuddled. I was rooted to my spot.

The hammer clicked on empty chambers. My brain finally cut through the busy signals and I had power to run to Vic and twist the gun out of her hand. She was wide-eyed and breathless. Tom moved to his chair like a very old man, and eased himself down to it. A bottle of Scotch was on the table next to him. He took it and drank from the bottle.

"One out of six, Vic," he said. "You're improvin'."

Vic was almost choking for air. Her back was curved forward.

"Only your aim was high, wasn't it? Kid, I reckon a doctor is in order," he said, putting a hand over the bloody wound.

"I reckon," said I and put the gun in my belt as I went to the telephone.

"No, wait a minute, I don't want him comin' here. C'mere, Kid."

I went to him and helped him to his feet. He put his good arm around my shoulders and I walked him to the car, past Vic who still stood where she had fired, staring at nothing.

26

"Guns are mysterious creatures, doc. Just about the time you broke one in and think you know it pretty good, why, *bang*, off it goes in your face."

The explanation to the doctor, and then to the press, was that he'd been practicing twirling a gun on his finger and it shot off at him. The press bought it, but the doctor, he wasn't so easy.

For years Tom didn't trust doctors much. Oh, he'd use them if he had to, but he kept his own well-equipped medical kit and preferred to do his own doctoring. Once I caught him in his tent fixing to pull out an aching tooth with a pliers. I told him, "Tom, you oughtn't be yanking your own tooth like that. It ain't sanitary."

"You're right, Kid, here." He handed me the pliers. Well, it wasn't half as hard as I expected, and, by God, I always knowed it wouldn't be.

"As his injuries became more complex," said Teddy, "he yielded gladly to the ministrations of the best doctors money could buy. Later, on those exhausting personal tours, he would have one nearly always in attendance."

The bullet, it went through his left arm, creased his back and found a home near the spine. The doctor removed it and kept his questions to himself. Tom appreciated his close mouth and would in the future appreciate it again, the times his body couldn't handle the great rivers of booze he took in. The official diagnosis was always pneumonia. Tom had pneumonia and lived more times than any man you know.

Still, he managed to finish seven pictures that year, and for each of the next few years. His popularity kept rising, his salary rose with it. In 1925 he was up to $6,500 per week. There was extra money, too, from endorsing products. Suddenly nothing would do but that kids had to have toys approved by Tom Mix himself.

Along with the usual run of Napoleons and Jesus Christs, asylums was noticing a new identity amongst their patients: Tom Mix.

Some uncommitted borderline loonies about town was claiming to be Tom's brother, trying to make their way with the cupcakes, I reckon.

An actor named George Kesterson formed his own company and took to acting under the name of Art Mix, hoping to trick enough people with his cheap imitation to reap a windfall. Sol had to take him to court to make him cease and desist.

In the meantime, Tom finally got his ranch, 11,000 acres in Arizona. I think he hoped it would lure him to tuck his success in a saddlebag and run off with his family to desert peace. But since he hardly traveled the twenty-six miles to the peace and quiet of his Santa Catalina home, it wasn't likely he'd ever spend much time in Arizona, and he didn't.

"He spent more time in the old Carlton Way house," said Teddy, "which they had retained, visiting with himself, wondering why, as he wrote in a letter, . . . *there don't seem to be anything you can just keep nailed down . . . the flowers that you admired by the roadside wither overnight.**

*From the Tom Mix letters, courtesy Victoria Midgley.

"Though his career could not have been going better, it was a period of uneasy limbo in his personal life. Vic showed no remorse over the shooting incident. *It's your fault!* she cried. *You can't stand anywhere in this house where you're not within reach of a pistol or rifle.*

"Tom didn't want any remorse from her and he brushed aside her rationalization. All he hoped for was that the pain and injury she had inflicted on him would act as a purge for both of them. Their life together, as it passed day by day, grew more and more impossible. If one of them could have honestly declared not to love the other, things would have become easier, simple, really. But that's at the end of the game, and when the game is over, of course everything becomes simple. There is the simplicity of no love—what could be simpler than that? But does a game, so intently played, ever really end? I know theirs didn't, until now. And it was a game, just a foolish game. Wait a minute, let me read you something he wrote to her."

She went to the rolltop and fetched it and read it at me out loud:

"Let's play it out as if it were sport,
Wherein the game is better than the goal.
And never mind the detailed 'scores' report
Of errors made, if each with dauntless soul
But stick it out until the day is done,
Not wasting fairness for success or fame
So when the battle has been lost or won,
The world at least can say *We played the game.*"*

She tucked it back in the desk drawer and mumbled to herself, "Oh, world, leave me alone, and I will be as nice to you."

*   *   *

*From the Tom Mix letters, courtesy Victoria Midgley.

Tom and Vic decided to steal away for a quiet tour of Europe, to set back and reflect during an ocean cruise, to enjoy each other's company and try to pull themselves together. He went with Sol's blessing. Tom's pictures was hot over there and it was time he showed his face.

He could never believe the tales of his popularity in Europe. Europeans, in Tom's view, didn't take to Americans and they was either very cultured and quietly wealthy or impoverished worker-slaves wanting to bail out of Europe for to overcrowd America. He reckoned they didn't know the difference betwixt a cowboy and a hamburger, or could care.

He packed up twenty-five white sombreros, six pairs of patent-leather boots, twenty-two western suits, some burgundy-colored dinner clothes, and a diamond-crowned walking stick. He put on his diamond-studded watch and his belt with the buckle that spelled his name in diamonds, and he was ready to go. As an afterthought he tossed four or five loaded pistols in his bag, and, partner, I wish you could of seen the look on the customs inspector's face in England when he come upon *those.*

He had a printer make him up some cards with a red, white, and blue border that showed a breakfast of ham steak, gravy, and eggs, with coffee and toast on the side, so that he could order breakfast in any country, in any language.

A story circulated that sometimes Europeans would tear up an American's calling card and throw the pieces in his face, so Tom had his cards made of leather, with Tony's head stamped in one corner, a buffalo's head in another.

That taken care of, Tom and Vicky and Thomasina and Teddy and Fordie and me and Tony and Pat Chrisman our foreman and Dan Clark our cameraman and Frankie Dolan our trainer and a publicity man whose name escapes me, and maybe one other feller whose face even escapes me, all boarded the Twentieth Century Limited for New York, where, behind Tom and his jangling spurs, we come down on the Biltmore like some desk clerk's bad dream.

After all the interviews and the picture-taking and the outdoor rally on Fifth Avenue with the Mayor and a crowd yelling, we boarded the *Aquitania*. Tony walked up the gangplank with the rest of us, and we set sail.

"We occupied some six staterooms," Teddy remembered, like a nice dream, "a parlor, a veranda, and three baths. It was quite the grandest thing I'd ever experienced. And to think I could have wound up typing threatening letters for some suspenders-wearing lawyer downtown, or, worse, walked through my days as a film extra going from one studio to another, as monotonous as an ice wagon."

In London and the other capitals of Europe, Tom's welcome was beyond which you could of predicted. On the streets he was mobbed, by kids and adults alike. Even where English wasn't the tongue the crowd would chant, "King cowboy! King cowboy!" Later, Tom made a picture using that as the title.

One man was trampled in England. Another was killed under the wheels of our train in Belgium. They went for him with a devotion that scared me a little, made Vicky self-conscious, and rendered Tom humble. Our reception was that overwhelming.

Not only titled people was inviting Tom to their mansions; invitations was coming in from *heads of state*. Under it all, Tom became subdued. He wasn't invited by such fancy people for to entertain them, they just wanted to meet him, to shake his hand, to express their admiration. The mob over there didn't demand him to put Tony through his paces; it was enough just to see him astride the Wonder Horse.

"What *was* this fascination Europeans held for him?" Teddy wondered. "In his own country, in the circles he traveled, in New York and Hollywood, he was considered a phenomenon, but to be brutally frank, not to be taken seriously. He was never invited to the parties at the Hearst castle. He was never given an acting award. Jack Ford, one of his best friends, did not want him for *The Iron Horse*. But in Europe he was revered, and in Europe things last, not like here."

We stayed there for most all of ten weeks and the good feeling lasted through the coming year. I recollect the year as one of quiet understanding and peace, the little stillness in the storm.

Nothing much happened. He organized his own baseball team from boys in the unit and played first base. The idea appealed to other stars, who formed teams of their own, and in no time the movie industry had its own baseball league. Many an assistant director in town owes his job to his powerful bat or unhittable knuckle ball.

Will Rogers became the Mayor of Beverly Hills.

Tom bought and trained a double for Tony and named him Buster, after Keaton.

His salary reached its peak, $7,500 a week, though the publicity always put it at $17,500, wed to the notion that bigger is better.

I left the unit.

I was making a hundred, hundred and a half a week, and me and the lady I had just gotten around to marrying was living comfortable within it. I had no ambitions in this business, it was never my line of work. I took the easy money, kept a fine edge on my roping, riding, and shooting, and felt satisfied with myself. I knew all those boys, knew them well, Tom and Hoot and Ken and Art and Harry, and I don't deny I envied them what they had, but I also seen what they paid for it, and foxy old Kid Bandera was going to escape the net. Ain't it easy to when nobody ever tried to slip one over you?

Then along comes Sol Wurtzel, puts his arm around my shoulders, and says, "Kid, how'd you like your own unit? How would you like to be a star?"

Well, like any other man I got a hard time drinking the water I spit in, but don't they flavor it up for you?

Tom knew what Sol was up to, even if I didn't, but he gave me his blessing and nary a word of advice. Next thing I know I got me a promising director, an up-and-coming cameraman, a journeyman crew, and a scruffy company of cowboys right off of the sands of Santa Monica. All my life a good hand, and now overnight a big sugar.

I read over the script as they measured me up for my costumes. "This hombre I play," I said, "ain't he a lot like Tom?"

"There are some points of similarity," I was told, "but you will bring to the character a fresh approach."

I stepped into the costume they made for me and looked at myself in the glass. My old friend Kid Bandera was disappearing and looking back at me was just another third-rate imitation of my old friend Tom Mix. I went ahead and did the picture and when I finished it up started on a new one. I was forty-three and had just fallen victim to dreams of stardom.

Tom was forty-seven and he started to give some thought to making that one picture, the one that would outlast him and say something permanent about the era, the Old West, the art of motion pictures, and himself.

What was going to blow it up for both of us was all this talk about adding sound to pictures.

27

Most exhibitors fought the coming of sound. It would mean costly refitting of their theaters and might finally be no more or less than a passing fancy. The ailing industry was horsing around with other novelties as well as sound, like pictures in three dimensions and pictures projected against a wide screen; no one wanted to jump on any one bandwagon 'til he had some guess at where it was heading.

"Tom was unable to believe that audiences would buy the intrusion of noise with their pictures," said Teddy. "It seemed contrary to the nature of the art. We were in the business of making pictures that move, after all, not pictures that talk. If one wanted to listen to actors speak, one could attend his choice of many live stage plays. Movie acting was pantomime. That was its strength and its charm. Such acting was fast, expressive, and full of action, unlike the slow, heavy plodding along that the confines of a stage always dictate."

"If pictures with sound," said Tom, "takes hold, you might as well kiss the western good-bye. Where are you gonna hide your microphone on a gallopin' horse? And what about comedy? Can you see Chappie or Buster talkin'? What the hell would they have to talk about? It'd only slow them down."

A world without western movies, or Chappie and Buster, seemed real unlikely to me, and I agreed that laying sound on the sort of thing we did could not come to pass. Our movies would only get better by means of better stories, faster action, and more thrilling stunts. All the rest, sound and such, was just cheap gimmicks.

But some film makers was going ahead with the idea, sold on it and determined to shove it down the throats of theater operators across the country. Their early success caught us up short. We watched theaters, slow at first, one by one, convert to sound, fearing that in the near future the others would fall all over each other not to be the last into this unknown.

"Tom thought he knew audiences better than they," said Teddy. "Audiences, like seamen ashore, go for the quick nip in the kip with whatever new and exciting thing falls their way, but the long and loving embrace comes only after repeated satisfaction and is reserved for those, like Tom, who have brought it to them and can be counted on to bring it again."

This sound thing, though, it couldn't be ignored. So far, Tom had made sixty-four pictures at Fox, and not one of them lost any money, but he had still not made that one picture he hoped for, the one that would last. *The Iron Horse* would last. It would outlast Jack Ford and its star, George O'Brien. Both of them worked for Tom. Why, George used to be a crew member with our unit, behind the camera. And only a year before doing *Horse* Jack had directed Tom in *Three Jumps Ahead* and *North of Hudson Bay*. Why didn't the talent jell on them pictures?

Now, if sound became a fixture, he might never have another chance. And my own future wasn't shaping up too rosy neither.

"Tom took to the bottle again; he took to me again," said Teddy. "There was another estrangement from Vic, this one after another press party at their house. The press had assembled for refreshments, which were to be followed by an exhibition of shooting by Tom on the front lawn. Spinning targets and assorted paraphernalia had been set up under large outdoor lights. Only Tom did not show up for his own party, not until the guests were departing, and then he showed up drunk on Tony, who, ham that he was, started to do his routine as soon as he noticed a crowd at the front door. Tom fell off him and lay flat on his back. The press, embarrassed, tried to drift quietly and inconspicuously to their cars. *Don't go yet, folks, the show is just beginning,* he said. He drew a Colt .45 he was wearing and started shooting at the various targets from his supine position on the ground. He didn't miss a shot. For a man in his condition, the feat was nothing less than astounding. Every balloon, every glass ball, was broken in order, and when he ran out of bullets he reloaded and shot some more. No one ever realized he was so good a shot."

Least of all yours truly.

"The press was so disarmed by his incredible display of marksmanship they forgave him certain other failings. Vic was not as charitable. She moved into the Carlton Way house and lived there alone with little Tommie."

Tom begged her to come home, he worried about her eating her own cooking. No one could ever convince him it wasn't just that which caused her to have the inflamed appendix which sent her rushing to the hospital in March. The operation was a close one and for a time she was a mighty sick gal. Tom claimed, and I believe him, that it was the first time in his life he ever experienced fear.

"I'd often heard fellas talk about being afraid, Kid, and I never really knew what they meant," he said. "Like tryin' to understand what a toothache feels like if you never had one yourself. Well, now I know what fear feels like. I wonder if I haven't been a coward all along."

Tom would go to the hospital every day but Vic wasn't seeing him. He'd sit outside her room, just to hear her voice as she took visits from friends. He wrote her notes daily, and Teddy carried them for him, often with a diamond ring or some other trinket. She never answered his notes or returned the trinkets.

"As I recall," Teddy told me, "it was during Vic's hospitalization that Kathleen and Lynn Reynolds had a few people over for drinks. I was one of them. You can imagine how many times I wish I had been excluded from that particular guest list.

"It was a small party, and started out quietly, but as it went on and more liquor was consumed a tension between Kathleen and Lynn became obvious. There had been rumors from the set of Lynn's current picture that he had been carrying on with the leading lady. Innuendoes led to accusations, accusations led to anger, and anger, as it does, led to violence.

"Lynn went to his study and, detectives later determined, took one bullet out of his loaded gun and replaced it with a blank from the prop department. He intended to give Kathleen the fright of her life. When he returned to the party and the argument resumed, Lynn leveled his gun at Kathleen and fired. She fainted and fell to the floor. We were horrified, believing he had killed her. The true horror was that he believed it too. He thought he had made a mistake and had fired a live bullet. He turned the gun to his own head and fired again.

"Would you be a dear and get me a glass of water?"

Tom wanted Vic to move back to the Beverly Hills house after getting out of the hospital, so that she could have her comforts. He promised her that if she did, she wouldn't have to see him. He would stay out 'til after she went to bed and leave again after breakfast. He only wanted to be able to see Tommie and to know that Vic was well cared for.

She accepted his terms. The arrangement sapped his confidence and cheer and all but unmanned him, something he wouldn't stand for before. They was under the same roof and still he communicated strictly by letter. He compared himself to Gladstone, some gent he heard about who slept on Queen Victoria's doormat.

In May, she went off to France with Kathleen Reynolds, for to recuperate was the story. Truth was, she wanted a divorce. It was the last thing Tom wanted, but finally he said he'd cooperate. He was hoping that once she got there she would miss him and their home and think twice about leaving him. But I think she met a feller there. More than ever she wanted to divorce Tom. But he reneged on his promise and told the French courts to go whistle round the bend.

Someone else was making the crossing to Europe at the same time as Vicky, but in a mite less time and unlike any man had ever crossed before: alone and in the air.

Talk about heroes and the people who need them, meaning all of us. That young feller went up in the air and changed everything. He quietly put his life on the line to hurry us out of one era smack into another. He was another Columbus and next to him us cowboy heroes seemed tame and more and more out of date. The children would stop looking for the dust of cattle and horses on the horizon and start looking for the speck in the sky, thanks to Charles Lindbergh.

Things was sure stacking up against the kind of picture Tom had made famous and profitable. Together we set in Tom's room and spent our evenings getting peaceably drunk. One night we was setting there thus, and Tom heard woodpeckers on the roof. We went outside with his Winchester and took some shots at them, and then went back inside. The noise of them peckers kept up, though, according to Tom. I never heard it, but I humored him.

We went out again this time each with a shotgun, and even Teddy and the others hard of hearing would of thought the late world war had started all over again.

Two Beverly Hills lawmen arrived, thanks to some neighbor's complaint. Tom invited them in for a drink. They had their drink and assured Tom and me that every woodpecker in Beverly Hills was now either dead or shell-shocked. They went away and Tom and me took to passing a six-gun betwixt us, taking turns shooting out the panes of leaded glass in Tom's sitting room.

"I answered a knocking at the door," said Teddy, "afraid it was the police back again. But this time the caller was a little old colored cowboy with white nappy hair and a face like a section of oak bark. He stood on bowed legs in worn and tattered clothes and held in his hand a slip of paper. Our conversation was punctuated by the gunfire from the other room. At each shot the little man reacted with a quick implosive jerk, but he went on, as though we were talking outside a factory and had to speak in snatches between the litany of industry.

"He had come for a job. This was a very common occurrence, people coming to see Tom about a job. A week before, in exchange for some football tickets the coach at USC had given him the previous season, Tom got a job in the prop department for one of the team members, a boy named . . . what was his name? Marion Morrison. John Wayne now.

"I told the man at the door that the time was not right, and he would stand a better chance if he came to the studio the next day. He seemed willing to accept this. He put his hat back on and was ready to leave when Tom yelled out, *Who's at the door, Teddy?*

"*A gentleman inquiring about a job, Mr. Mix.*

"*Well, show the gentleman in,* he yelled, *this room could use one.*

"*This way, Mr. . . . ?*

"*Stubbs, ma'am. Willie Stubbs.*"

Teddy led him to the sitting room. Tom and me was on two armchairs. A table containing the refreshments, a bit of the white, a bit of the red, was in arm's reach. Tom held a smoking gun.

"This is Mr. Stubbs, Mr. Mix," said Teddy.

"You got another name, Mr. Stubbs?" asked Tom.

"Stumpy," he said. He was five foot four, no heavier than a sack of spuds.

The man who had recommended him was old Bulldog Pickett. Bulldog, it seemed, had lost his taste for steer lip and was now doing a bit of farming.

"You look like you can ride," said Tom. He took aim and knocked out another piece of glass. He handed the gun to me.

"Broke 'em once, was a jockey once. Once you could grease 'em and I'd still ride 'em," said Stumpy. He sure didn't feel the need of any confidence.

"You ever do any actin'?"

"Actin'? I never done nothin' else."

"You want to be in the movies?"

I fired off a shot and handed the gun back to Tom.

"No, sir, I want a job."

"Can you shoot?" asked Tom, handing him the gun.

"I shot them that crawls and them that flies. I shot them that walks on four legs and them that walks upon two. I shot what slithers through the water in the dark of night."

He turned and fired, missing the window and damn near missing the wall. A hunk of plaster fell to the floor. Tom and me fell out of our chairs laughing.

He handed the gun back to Tom, saying, "The eyes go."

"Can you cook, Stumpy?"

"Whatever you can eat, I can cook it up. I can cook it all in one pot or separate-like. I can cook it so's you'll feel it one end to the other, or I can cook it so's you'd hardly know it was there."

Tom poured a glass of bourbon for him, laughed once more and handed him the drink. "Welcome to the Tom Mix unit," he said.

Stumpy became the assistant chuckwagon cook and when Dried Apple Pete left to open a restaurant, Stumpy became head cook, and hell on boots.

His hands was calloused to elephant hide and God only knows how deep the skin went. When he made doughnuts he turned them in the hot grease with his fingers.

"Once the leading lady tried to steal one of those doughnuts as they sat cooling," said Teddy. "Stumpy's rule was that no one got a doughnut until lunchtime. He stopped her hand with a fork. She went screaming to Tom, demanding that that vile man be fired immediately. Tom laughed at her and said, *Nobody tells a chuckwagon cook what to do. What the hell do you think he is, a director?*"

That was the summer Vilma Banky and Rod LaRocque got spliced. It was right out of the storybooks and in this case everybody reckoned they would live happily ever after, and they have. Near everybody was invited to the wedding, including yours truly, and this was one invite I did not decline. Me and Tom went together, and since the rest of them had rented Rolls-Royces for the occasion we showed up in a carriage pulled by a fine team of horses.

Just two days before, a temporary ten to fifteen percent salary cut was laid down industry-wide for to get the studios over some current rough spots. Folks was glum about the cuts and wasn't in much of a festive mood, but Tom and me thought it was more fun than mud wallowing and Tom wrote up his observations of it in a long letter to *Variety.*

The wedding cost $25,000 and Sam Goldwyn, who was Vilma's boss, picked up the tab. Cecil B. DeMille was the best man, even though he was suing La Rocque at the time. It's that kind of business, I reckon. Personal and business gets so sifted together you never know what the hell will roll out.

Vilma Banky, whose real name is Banky Vilma, which is about as good an example as I know of Hollywood genius, was Hungarian and like most foreign-born actors her career was on the firing line because of sound coming on so strong. She had a heavy accent, which was out of line with the image the public had of her. Goldwyn hired a voice teacher to help her beat the accent, at $50 a week. Sam wanted Vilma to pay for the lessons. Nothing doing, she said, it was a legitimate expense of the producer. Sam argued that it wasn't his accent that needed getting rid of but hers, and long after he was cold in the ground she would still have the benefits of her voice lessons. She had a moral obligation to pay. Vilma didn't see it that way. Goldwyn fired the voice teacher, and Vilma never made another picture. Sam had to keep paying her $5,000 a week, like her contract said, 'til over half a million had gone down the hole.

The *Variety* piece was near the funniest thing I ever read. Tom said as how it was the only wedding he ever attended where he wasn't one of the principals. Sam Goldwyn gave the bride away, and Tom wrote that as far as he remembered it was the only thing Sam ever gave away. When the wedding was late starting, Tom reckoned as how it was 'cause Sam was out in front counting up the house and waiting for all the seats to fill up. He said it was nice that DeMille knew right where the rings was and didn't have to send no grip to the prop room. Stuff like that. He even had the brass to claim that Adolphe Menjou called him up to ask him what he ought to wear and if he could lend him an extra silk hat. "I was mighty sorry that I couldn't oblige him," wrote Tom, "as my butler had gone somewhere in my extra suit."

"This was not his first published piece of writing," Teddy reminded me. "He had already written some articles for *Ladies Home Journal* and *Photoplay*, but those were pieces on how he got into movies, that sort of thing. This was the first time he had written humorous social commentary, and the comparison to Will Rogers was obvious. Everyone urged him to do more. *Variety* asked him to do another piece, a full-page article assessing the current state of Hollywood. Would you like to read it?"

Well, I had read it when it first come out. Who didn't? But back again she went to that rolltop. I wouldn't of been much surprised to see Tom's head peeking out of one of those drawers.

Dear *Variety:*

Prompted, I suppose, by recent events, a lot of people including the Editor of *Variety*, have asked me what I thought was the matter with the picture industry. The answer is easy, and can be told in one, short sentence.

The industry has quit work!

The moment Standard Oil, Ford, National Cash Register outfit and the steel makers quit work and turn their industries into a self-perpetuating, seven-day-a-week rodeo with country fair trimmings, people will be asking what's the matter with them.

More attempts have been made by those running it to kill the picture industry than politicians have put in trying to make Calvin Coolidge talk. But through it all, the aforesaid industry has survived—survived in spite of them.

I'm not a business man. Cowpunching is my trade. But I'm not afraid to gamble any part of $100,000, and I say this seriously, that I can take any studio in Los Angeles and reduce its overhead 25 per cent from the day they make me top sergeant of the outfit.

Other industries have efficiency men who can fish and catch something. We don't. We have the other kind. We have a lot of birds sitting around on high salaries whose chief ambition seems to be to see how much money they can waste. . . .

Let some director go out and spend $500,000 making a picture that should cost somewhere around $175,000 and every other producer will promptly offer him a job, thinking he's great.

I've been making pictures for quite some time and I'm making no better pictures today than I turned out seven years ago, yet their cost has increased 200 per cent and that don't include the fancy salary the press agents credit me with. When I want my salary raised, I don't go to Mr. Fox. I go to the studio press agent. I like to do business with him; that bird will raise it to any price I mention and then add a little on his own hook.

[237]

Only a few years ago, my cowboys got up at five in the morning—the usual ranch getting up time—and rode their horses 15 or 20 miles to location and thought nothing of it. Will they do it today? I hope to tell you they won't. Things have changed. Today the horses must be shipped out by truck and the cowhands sent out in automobiles, ridin' around in more style than the owner of the ranch, where they started, ever dreamed of.

Will my horse "Tony" walk any more? He's a horse and ought to be fond of walking. But they've spoiled "Tony" until today he makes a fuss if they put more'n two horses in the truck with him.

We used to start shooting scenes the moment the sun was high enough to make shadows. I ask you confidentially, do we do it today? The only way to get a director or a bunch of actors up in the morning is to invite 'em to one of those before-breakfast golf tournaments. That'll get 'em out.

The pictures I made five or six years ago, so far as story, thrills, cast and scenic values are concerned, are as good if not better than I'm turning out today. *The Untamed, Unnamed, The Texan, Mr. Logan, U.S.A., Three Gold Coins,* or *The Deadwood Stagecoach* will compare equally with anything I've made in the last few years and they cost 50 per cent of the present production prices.

Today, because of trifles that the old time director would laugh at, we will hold up a picture for hours. We are ready to shoot a scene; the director discovers the carpenters have put the wrong kind of a doorknob on the set and the company waits until some one hustles up a requisition, goes over to the prop room or carpenter mill and brings back the right kind of a knob, providing they have one. If not, they go to town after it.

Meanwhile at an expense of over $500 an hour, the company waits. The doorknob in no way advances the story or action, but the director's artistic soul feels better when the right one is in place.

Five years ago we'd have knocked the doorknob off and gone on without it.

Today, the picture producer, director and actor, have great ideas about luxury, and yet not one of 'em out of 10 know what real luxury means. To get a lot of this luxury a

[238]

lot of money is needed and salaries are forced high as a result. You don't hear of anything like that being encouraged in the other big industries.

Every one in pictures now must have an "estate," high, high in the Hollywood Hills or in the Beverly district. Mansions with mosaic swimming pools, marble tennis courts, butlers, second men, fourth and fifth assistant door slammers and a reasonable equity in a flock of high powered and high priced automobiles. Some bird started this and the rest, like a bunch of Mexican sheep, trailed along.

I plead guilty right here and now to owning and possessing one of those high powered Beverly Hills estates, differing only from most of 'em in that everything I got is paid for.

But when you get down to cases, have I any business living in a house with a butler and a $100 a week chef frying my morning bacon and eggs? I have not. I don't belong there any more than the rest of 'em belong where they are. In my own home, I can't get over the idea I'm visitin'.

The other night I watched a young miss, not yet much past 20, have her butler call her maid from upstairs to come and open a pocketbook about three feet from where the young woman was sitting to pay a messenger boy for a telegram. Less than three years ago this same young female was selling tickets and making change at a beach concession near New York. I know the real inclination of that same young woman, except that she was showin' off, was to have handled the money herself and short changed the kid —he looked easy—and a knack at which she was very deft.

I'm not mentioning these things to say anything against persons who came from humble walks of life and today occupy important places in the picture industry. I'm just trying to show that a lot of us are living at a pace and doing things we're not used to and the pictures have to pay for it. Producers are encouraging all of this and themselves living in the same foolish way.

You don't hear of Judge Gary, of the U.S. Steel Corporation; or Mr. Ford, or the Standard Oil, who seem to be running their outfits with more or less success, encouraging any such doin's or goin' ons, among their hired help.

It's surprising how terribly picture making "saps one's

vitality"—sap, bein' the correct word in such cases. This applies to both a lot of picture directors and actors. They make a picture, which consists of about eight weeks of six hours a day, sitting around in studio chairs and playing occasional scenes or suffering the terrible discomforts or being away on location and living in a hotel with better accommodations than they've originally been used to, and everything paid. Once the picture is finished these birds have to seek the mountains or sea shore to "recuperate," they're so utterly exhausted and run down.

The exalted opinion some of these birds get of their own opinions is astounding. Directors think nothing of taking a book the producer paid a lot of money for, the author being a recognized master of fiction, and changing it all around, substituting scenes for those in the book. And this because the director or scenario writer think they are smarter and know more about "drama" than the man who wrote the book.

Directors whose knowledge of the west is confined to twice having seen Buffalo Bill's Wild West show in Madison Square Garden, argue with me for hours about how western sets and scenes should be built and played. The only thing some of these birds haven't told me about the west where I was born and raised, is how to get on a horse. It may sound funny, but I had a slick director once who spent more than an hour trying to tell me how "Tony" should play a scene so he would act like a horse. I was ashamed to even tell "Tony."

If all the money golf has cost the motion picture industry could be put into one pile, our friend Secretary Mellon could retire all outstanding Liberty bonds, paying a substantial bonus. In several instances, golf has added more to the cost of one of my pictures than horse feed for my 75 head of stock would come to in a couple of years.

You don't notice any of Mr. Ford's foremen out playing golf two afternoons a week, laying off a whole unit of his plant because the steam was "a little weak," as some of our directors often do when the sunlight "isn't quite right." They send the company home for the rest of the day and beat it to their favorite golf course.

Picture theatres are charging too high an admission. There isn't a picture made that's worth more than 50 cents as an admission price. Pictures started out as an entertainment for the masses and they should have remained there. Prices have been advanced until today the average working man can't take his family to see a film until it's six months or a year old and is found in some near neighborhood house. It isn't the picture that has shot up the admission price—it's what they offer with it. Elaborate prologs and 50-piece orchestras have advanced the price until so far as the moderate salaried man is concerned the first run houses are on a par with grand opera.

Any time I can't make a picture that the public and boys can't understand without a prolog, it's time for "Tony" and me to go back to my ranch over on the Hassayampia River in Arizona and commence punching cows again.

Recently I saw a prolog to a Mix picture—an atmosphere prolog. It showed the inside of a livery stable, a corral full of yearlings and wound up with a blacksmith shoeing a horse while he sang a song.

I've never known a singing blacksmith. I've known quite a few singing waiters in my time and a few drinking blacksmiths, but you have to get a blacksmith stewed before he'll sing, and I contend there's nothing especially edifyin' or educational in havin' a small boy or the public in general seeing a half crocked blacksmith pretend he's singing a song and shoeing a horse that's already shod.

A lot of smart birds laughed when Secretary Mellon argued he could increase government revenues by reducing the income tax 25 per cent. And what happened—he made millions for us. The same howl went up when they cut the letter postage from three to two cents, but the stamp receipts jumped 30 per cent over the previous year. Put the admission prices down to a fair sum and the bad business exhibitors complain of today will end.

All this providing the producer gives the exhibitor real pictures at a fair price, which can be done if the producer will run his affairs in a business-like manner and in some such way as the fifth and sixth industries of the world—smaller than ours—are operated.

The first thing our producers know, a group of smart, wide-seeing, wide-understanding and widely efficient business men will find out there is money to be made in pictures, and these gentlemen will step in and take over the industry with the same ease that a certain gent named Grant rode his horse into Richmond.

It may be that the picture industry is going to follow the Romans. Those old birds, clever and tough, thought they were great. They started in with a continual procession of round-ups, rodeos and county fairs, with a barbecue thrown in now and then. The result was that all became soft through too much luxury. A horde of seasoned birds came in from the north and made the Romans look like a bunch of ham and egg preliminary fighters. Then the invaders started in with the same kind of living and a new outfit showed up from the south and took Rome and its 7 hills away from them.

As soon as we cut out a lot of our foolish business methods, still more foolish ideas of living and extravagance, eliminate a lot of unnecessary "put-on" and "show-off," get down to common sense, be ourselves and become picture men in the morning, noon and night, with no other business, not even golf, we will rightfully take our proper place in the commercial world, not only as the fourth industry we are today, but probably rating along on even terms with even the second and perhaps the first.

TOM MIX*

It wasn't any one thing that finished Tom in this town. Sound had a lot to do with it. The crowd's changing tastes moved another way. Maybe growing older didn't help. But, partner, don't you ever underestimate the damage done by the article you just read. It was the boot that kicked him through the studio gate.

Exhibitors jumped on it for sales resistance. Committees of them marched to branch offices and demanded that Tom's

*"Tom Mix Digs Way In and Tells Just What's the Matter with the Industry." *Variety*, July 20, 1927. Reprinted with permission from *Variety*.

pictures be reduced to the price they'd paid for them three years before. Others sent wires right to the studio or New York with the same demands.

"Pantages wouldn't play Tom except in Los Angeles, Memphis, and Minneapolis," said Teddy, "and there only at greatly reduced prices. Why they lumped those three cities together is a question I avoid, since I live in Los Angeles. San Francisco wouldn't buy him any more. Nor would Seattle, Portland, or San Diego. Baltimore paid fifteen hundred dollars a picture the year before, now they wanted Tom for seven hundred. Cleveland had paid twelve hundred, now they would go no higher than eight hundred. Providence would play them at six hundred. The Stanley Company of Philadelphia, who had paid a thousand before, notified New York that the current price would be five hundred. Fred Thompson and Ken Maynard pictures, they claimed, sold for a third of the price, yet grossed as much as the Mix pictures."

A doctor can look through one of them microscopes and see the stirrings that mean a slow but sure death. Anyone in Hollywood can look at the figures Teddy rattled off and see just as clear the same thing, with the same sinking gut.

The studio began to ride him. They took away his free hand. They put a ceiling of $100,000 on the cost of making a Mix picture. The memory of the days when Tom's pictures was the mainstay of the whole studio was wiped away. He was turning rancid to them. They wanted to spit him out.

"At the same time," said Teddy, "he was besieged by offers from *Life* and *Cosmopolitan* and *Liberty* to write articles for them. He wrote to Vic in Nice, telling her he might leave films and become a writer. Such a change, he promised, would make him a new man. He begged for one more chance.

"*I used up about all my physical ability,* he wrote her, *in making money and failed to be returned with any too much happiness as a reward and I am now trying to harness up what mentality I have and see what results it can bring. It looks as* *if I can make around a hundred thousand a year from it, and the beautiful part is I can work in any country or climate without the help of horses—not that I am going back on my horses, but I would like to substitute them for a few lead pencils as a change and give the old body a chance to recondition itself."**

I don't want you to miss that note of guilt about giving up on his horses, partner. It'll mean something later. He loved his horses, loved horses all his days, but lately they come to be a ball and chain around his ankle, holding him to a life that asked for a strong body and a simple mind. And now he was bucking fifty, with some of his own ideas to tell. He wasn't stealing from Brisbane no more, he was thinking on his own, and he was sure he had a way with words, just like he had a way with horses. Maybe it was time to be carried by words instead of horses?

"Vicky said she would come home and try for one more reconciliation," said Teddy. "She admitted she had no great optimism for its success, but for the sake of Tommie she would give it another try—on one condition. Would you like to know the condition, Kid, under which she would come home? Teddy would have to go. Can you believe that? After all those years, to pin their doomed marriage on me. Everyone who heard about it thought it the greatest joke imaginable. My sense of humor does not extend that far. But for me, their marriage would not have lasted as long. Suddenly the blame was Teddy, instead of years of selfish superficial excesses, it was Teddy. Once again I was convenient.

"Teddy would have to go, not only out of his arms, but out of the house and office as well, cut adrift. Naturally, he agreed; he would have agreed to anything.

"Ah, but don't you see, Teddy had become indispensable. When Vic came home, I was gone all right, and a new girl was sitting at the phone taking messages, but that was all she did.

*From the Tom Mix letters, courtesy of Victoria Midgley.

The files and records had been moved to my house, and I was still very much his secretary, and his mistress."

Things got worse at the studio. After expressing the high regard in which he held him, Sol Wurtzel told Tom that since he was able, by his own words in *Variety*, to cut the overhead of any studio by twenty-five percent, he should do it for his own unit, cut it by twenty-five percent.

"Can't you take a joke, Sol?" said Tom.

"Tom, whoever wrote that article for you was not doing you any favor."

"What are you talkin' about?"

"The writer you got to do that thing for you. For what? What useful purpose to stir things up like that?"

"What writer? I wrote that *myself*, you son-of-a-bitch."

"Sure, sure, Tom. What difference does it make, right?"

Tom picked up the telephone on Sol's desk and throwed it through his window. Then he walked out.

"He also walked through his next two pictures," said Teddy. "He became adamant again about doing his own stunts, no matter how simple or difficult. If a director told him the stunt did not look good and suggested using a double, Tom would just assure him that it would cut perfectly. Then the director would have to wait until Tom drove off the set before calling in a double and reshooting the stunt. When the scene was finally seen on film, Tom would say, *See, I told you that stunt would edit out okay.* It became hard on the unit morale. Our people were seasoned in show business and could sense when the loaf was gnawed to the heel. Some of the less loyal began bailing out, trying to land jobs in Jones' unit or with Hoot or Thompson."

Forget about my unit. I was waiting for my own ax to fall.

When it got right down to talking figures, Tom saw that his original guess at what he could pull down as a writer, $100,000 a year, was a mite high. He couldn't earn nothing near what it would take just to cover his expenses, even if he cut back on the way they lived. Tom called up Will and asked him how writers managed to live on what they wrote. They don't, Will told him.

"He began showing up on the set under the influence," said Teddy. "We spent all of one morning shooting him trying to rope a branch so that he could swing down among the heavies. It was a rear shot and a simple stunt. There were young cowboys standing around who could have done it on the first try, but Tom would not listen to the pleas of the director. When we broke for lunch and Tom drove away—he seldom ate at the chuckwagon anymore—the director had one of the cowboys costumed correctly and shot him roping the branch. Tom found out about it when he returned, was humiliated and infuriated, and fired the director."

Near the end of the year Sol Wurtzel called him to his office. Winnie Sheehan was there, along with a gent from the New York office and two smaller potatoes from the studio. That was the second trail marker. The first was that he'd been kept waiting in the outer office.

He looked them over when he stepped in the inner office, and said, "Greetings, gents."

"Have a seat, Tom. You're looking well today."

Tom sat down and everybody asked after the families of everybody else. All was well and happy.

"I believe I speak for everyone in this room," said Mr. Sheehan, "when I say I've always admired your work."

"You have an eye for the finer things in life, Winnie," said Tom.

They laughed it up, and Sheehan said, "We have had a fine association for several years now."

"Since 1917," said Tom.

"Profitable for both," said Sol.

"May it always be so," said Tom, and that seemed to make them uncomfortable.

[246]

"The studio's in trouble now," said Sol. "You know that as well as I do. The whole industry is in trouble."

"Did you know I was the one who told Mr. Fox to buy the piece of property we're on right now?" asked Tom.

"I did know that," said the gent from the New York office. "Mr. Fox told me about that. It was a very wise move."

"Wise indeed," said Sol. "And now we're at a crossroads where other wise decisions must be made. Tom, we're going to go deep into debt to get into sound pictures."

"That's a mistake. It ain't gonna stay."

"You're wrong there, Tom."

"Well, it ain't like I never was wrong before. There was the time back in Nineteen, when I had to drive a coach and six through that narrow pass. Remember? The horses got through all right, but there was me and the wagon, stuck between a rock and a hard place."

They laughed some more, remembering the failed stunt.

"Those were the days, huh, Tom?" said one of the small potatoes.

"We're all still learning about this business," said Sol Wurtzel. "It is going to be constantly changing. Not to change will be to die. That's what we're learning."

"Are we?"

"Believe me."

"Well, I'll tell you what's not changin', 'cause it can't. The Old West ain't changin'."

"Tom, you changed it yourself. Others will continue to change it."

"You know, you fellas are soundin' like they're about to nail the lid down on me."

"Tom," said Sheehan, "I want to go on record as saying you're the hardest-working actor I've ever known."

"We can't renew your contract for next year," said Sol.

Like a baseball bat right across the stomach, was the way Tom pictured it to me.

[247]

"That's not to say we don't want you to continue to make pictures for us," said Sheehan. "We all love you, as does the public. You're tops in our book, but the plain truth is we can't afford you."

"Why, goddamn," said Tom, "I took cuts in the past, I'm ready to take them again."

"I knew we could count on you," said Sheehan.

"We have to cut your entire outfit," said Sol.

"What!"

"Nobody feels worse about this than Mr. Fox," said the gent from New York. "He adores your pictures."

"But we're entering into a new era and sacrifices have to be made or we'll simply go under," said Sheehan.

"We would still like to use you," said Sol, "in two pictures a year, at a flat fee per picture, which we can negotiate later."

He was near tempted to take the crumbs they was feeding him, just to hang around the place that had become home. The thought of breaking up the unit brought him 'way low. He knew he wouldn't be able to take it whole to another studio, like when he left Selig and joined up with Fox. It was a different business then.

"I can't operate that way," he said finally, in a steady voice.

"As you wish," said Sol.

"Maybe you'll change your mind after you think about it for a while," said Sheehan.

The meeting was over. Still Tom couldn't get himself out of the chair.

"Tell me, fellas," he said, treating it light, "what's your pick as the best picture made here this year?"

"The best of your pictures, Tom?"

"No, no, the best of *all* the pictures."

"I'd have to say *Sunrise,*" said the gent from the New York office, "I think it's the best picture we've ever done."

The others went along with that. "George O'Brien," said Sheehan, "proved himself an actor to be reckoned with in that

[248]

one. You can take a good deal of pride in that, Tom. He was your discovery."

"What do you figure it'll make, in rough figures?" asked Tom.

"It's too soon to say," said one of the small potatoes.

"Could be a big surprise," said the other.

"The truth is," said Sol, "that it will lose money."

"That's all right," said Tom rising, "my profits will cover its losses."

He walked to the door and had it opened up, feeling pretty good about the point he drove home. Then he heard the voice of one of those small potatoes. He wasn't supposed to, it was for the benefit of the others. "Rin Tin Tin is serving the same function over at Warner Brothers."

Tom shut the door behind him and pretended he hadn't heard. He got in his car and drove off the lot, and that was the end of it.

On December 12, they asked him to put his prints in cement at Grauman's Chinese. Remember that, Jack Nicholson, now, before your own prints are dry.

28

Teddy took him home, just after dusk. She couldn't tell me what they talked about, if they talked at all. She didn't have to take him home, he could of drove himself. Reckon he had no heart for it.

"He did not speak," she said, "not until we turned into the driveway and noticed a small fire in front of the house. When it came within range of the headlights we saw that it was a campfire."

Tommie was in her Brownie uniform and setting beside the fire, on a little Persian rug. Kai, the butler, stood at her side. The fire was made in the middle of the driveway, so's not to set up the hills around.

"Oh, shit," said Tom. Looked like with all else that was turning sour, he hadn't been such a hot father neither. Teddy and him set a long time, seemed like, and watched the expressionless faces of Tommie and the butler staring at the glare of the headlights. Teddy had in mind dropping Tom off and going home—she wasn't supposed to be seeing him—but when he struggled out of the car, she followed.

"Hi, Daddy," said Tommie. "Good evening, Miss Teddy."

"Hi, baby," said Tom tenderly, "whatcha up to?"

"We're having a cookout," she said. "Kai showed me how to build a fire."

"When I was a boy, sir," said Kai, "I spent very much time out in the woods."

"Well, it's a right fine fire you built, Kai. I built a few myself once." He sat down beside Tommie and asked Kai, "What's on the menu?"

"Hot dogs, sir."

"And marshmallows!" said Tommie.

"Bring 'em on!" said Tom.

"Very good, sir."

"Stay for supper, Teddy."

"I knew I shouldn't," she told me, "but I sensed some sort of end coming. I sat down on the other side of Tommie. Kai brought us hot dogs on a gold serving platter and supplied us with long barbecue forks on which to roast them. Later we had marshmallows, Tom told a yarn or two, and he taught us a few of the cowboy songs he had learned on the range. It turned out to be, I could see, one of the nicest nights of Tommie's young life, and of mine. There were tears in Tom's eyes, revealed whenever the fire would rise.

"Eventually Vic came home and saw that we had shared some precious moments together. Had she sat down and been quiet we could have had some more. I think I would have liked to stop being his lover and start being their friend. But she took Tommie and said it was far beyond her bedtime.

"Within a week she and Tommie had gone to France, not to visit, but to live."

Tom's brand of living didn't permit him the real luxury of hanging around for the best offer. He took the first—a nation-wide vaudeville tour at $2,500 a week, a two-thirds cut in pay. He was the headliner of a Publix Unit, a review on the Paramount Theatre Circuit.

The tour reminded of that European tour in '25 when he was

always mobbed by fans. Every show was a sellout, at $1.10 to $1.65, a hard ticket for the time. Times was he had to do four shows a day to handle the overflow. No arguing, he was still popular with the crowd. Everywheres he went he was met by the Governor and interviewed by the press and gave the key to the city. He come to be convinced that once Fox heard of the SRO business he was doing he would get a wire begging him to return.

"He hired a voice teacher to travel with us," said Teddy, "a very theatrical man with a bushy moustache and a bald head. When he first removed his hat, Tom laughed at his shiny head. The teacher said, in perfect diction, *You were expecting feathers?*

"They got along well, but nothing the teacher could do would force Tom to open his mouth and move his lips when he spoke. *Mr. Mix*, he protested, *your voice is an unwavering, expressionless monotone which will make the eyelids of the audience grow very heavy. I doubt a microphone would be able to pick it up even if they hid it under your hat.*

"*Hell, you can hear me okay. You can hear me when I talk, can't you, Teddy?*"

By this time Teddy was reading lips, and nobody knew.

The wire from Fox never come. What did was the separation papers from Vic, whilst Tom was playing Omaha. He told her that she could have all he had, and to prove it he ordered Teddy to put everything in her name. He wanted her to be a real partner, he said.

"I was deliberately slow in executing the order," Teddy told me.

His act was a mite short of high adventure. Eight girl dancers in cowgirl outfits would dance out on stage and sing a chorus of "Pony Boy," with all the gestures used those days to "sell" a song. At the end of the chorus, they'd cry out, "Whoa! And now, ladies and gentlemen, the one and only, himself in person, *Tom Mix* and his Wonder Horse *Tony!*"

As they'd dance off the stage, Tom and Tony would prance on it. He'd do a few passes with a rope, take a couple shots at a target, and then put Tony through his paces. All in all, it was about twenty minutes stage center. But it was three or four times a day, seven days a week, and then there was the interviews, the banquets, the civic occasions, and his regular visits to the children in hospitals.

He finally got around to taking all eight chorus girls for a ride in his open yellow Rolls. According to Teddy, all eight was deep in love with him. When he took them back to his hotel room, he had a waiter come up and take their order. They was all young, pretty, and empty-headed; all from small towns somewheres; all nervous of Tom. No one of them was bold enough to order first. Finally Tom had to order for himself: a bowl of milk toast. One by one they shyly ordered the same thing.

"He contracted a cold that would not go away," said Teddy, "and he was riding the edge of exhaustion. By Chicago a physician was in constant attendance. It was there he met with Joseph Kennedy, to discuss a deal with Film Booking Office. FBO was the last of the holdouts against sound and were trying to corner the market for westerns."

Two ship-building executives was put in charge of the outfit, and they wanted to build films like they built ships. "First, we must lay the keel." Well, it can't be done. Anybody tries to run a movie business like some other business is going to land on their ass, I don't care what Tom wrote for *Variety.* The business don't have place for the usual corporate policies and boards of directors and all the other riggings of legitimate businesses. It wants madmen with visions, this business. Outsiders do a cluck in pure wonder to see that the bird who used to deliver ice to the studio now runs the place. But if you lived through the opening hand of this industry you wouldn't see nothing unusual about that. You'd know that every winner here was a loser somewheres else.

[253]

Tom knew there wasn't much future with FBO, but they offered him $1,000 a day for every day before the camera, and that's still a notch over digging postholes in the Oklahoma mud.

It wasn't near as good as Fox, but it had to be better than touring, which made him lonely, sick, and unhappy, and cost as much as it paid. He shook their hand.

Like it always seems to happen, he had a flash flood of other offers. George M. Cohan wanted to write a Broadway play for him. Ziegfeld wanted him for the Follies. Nearly every circus in the country wanted him. Europe wanted him to come to their shores. 'Course it never cost nobody nothing just to want him. He was happy with his decision. It was movies again, a chance to prove that he was right and they was wrong.

"Without the ministrations of the bright young doctor who traveled with us," said Teddy, "we might not have made it through the tour, but by the end of it, when he was to start directly with FBO, he had found his second wind. He felt comfortable at FBO. No one there was giving sound a second thought. They went happily ahead turning out pictures like the kind Tom had made a tradition. Only Tom was noticing that *he* had changed. The uncanny reflexes and split-second timing that had made his stunts of ten years ago so spectacular were failing him."

Well, why should he be any different? I was showed the door myself, both by Fox and the missus. All that saved me from walking the days away along Sunset Boulevard was Buck Jones took me in his unit, where damned if the other wranglers didn't start calling me "the old boy." What do you reckon they meant by that?

On Tom's third picture at FBO he whacked up his leg bad. He was trying to make a flying mount with his hands tied, and Tony took off before he had him well in hand. He slid over Tony's side, grabbing at the saddle horn, and up comes his leg which hit the branch of a tree. The leg wasn't broke, though it had been in the past and was giving him a fair share of misery since then. They put it up in a brace and he took pain-killers to get through the next two pictures.

He made only those five at FBO, none of them much worth dwelling over. He wouldn't have a chance to improve the product neither, like he did at Selig and Fox. FBO shut down production and reorganized to become R.K.O. Radio. Then like most all the others they got into sound pictures and out of westerns.

So, let's see, partner, reckon that brings us to 1929. *That* year. Tom had already sold off his boat, the Catalina house, and the Carlton Way house. He put the Beverly Hills place up for sale, leaving Minnie the squaw and Teddy in charge of it.

"I spent as little time there as possible," said Teddy, "leaving it to Minnie, who didn't seem to mind its emptiness."

The only other employee Tom held onto was Stumpy, who went out on the road with him for another personal tour. Stumpy's only job was to look after Tony.

"Off they went," she said, "cutting up the country into weeks that were cities, cities that were weeks. Time and place had turned back on each other and had rendered themselves meaningless. Detroit, Buffalo, Rochester, Boston, Brooklyn, Jersey City, Philly. How lonely he must have been."

Some say Tom lost a million in cash in bank closings. I don't reckon he had a million to lose. But he lost most all he had. Vic, now, she managed her own money, got out of the market in time, and wound up making money on the depression.

Whilst he was in Minnesota he was indicted by the IRS folks on three counts of tax fraud and conspiracy to defraud, along with his past tax expert and publicity manager. The good years come back to bite the bad ones.

"Mr. Mix will be heartbroken," his lawyer told the press, "and so will the millions of kids who have always idolized him and considered him as their hero. I want to assure them all that

Tom's only crime was in putting himself in the hands of so-called tax experts."

That and leaving the wide open spaces of Oklahoma.

"When my letter finally arrived it came as no surprise," said Teddy. "Not any easier to accept, but at least not a bolt from the blue. He enclosed a check for one year's wages. My life with Tom, like his with Vic, had drained me emotionally and I was ready to accept the end of it, but never would I stop loving him. I worried so about the end of his letter, in which he spoke of . . . *the pass into the valley beyond, where the pastures are always green, the streams always blue, and shade always soft and cool—that's the valley from which no one ever returns.**

"He wanted to die. I do believe that finally he looked away. But don't call that suicide. That's a mistake, an accident. What's that, Kid? What? Move closer to the light. Speak slowly."

*From the Tom Mix letters. Courtesy of Victoria Midgley.

29

When I read in the papers they was going to cash in old Tony, I wanted to go pay one last visit. Two years after Tom's death it was, almost to the day. Next to my own Toby, long cold in the ground, he was my favorite. A smarter horse never kicked up dust. He was being kept at Tom's old place in San Fernando, which had, like Tony himself, gone to the lawyers.

He was looking out of the stall, through eyes near gone blind, when I come up on him. Old critter had some grizzled gray whiskers on his chin. I brought him a carrot. Tom never let him taste sugar, but he was real partial to apples and carrots. Time was you could feed him a carrot with your finger running alongside it, and he would nibble down to your nail and not a bite farther. But mind yourself when a camera was turning. I tried to give him his carrot in the old way, but he didn't have the teeth for it.

"Don't eat nothin' but ground alfalfa and molasses no more." The voice come from inside the stall.

It was Stumpy. He struggled himself up from his sitting position on the ground and come to the door. "I got the rheumatism, he got the rheumatism. I ain't got but half a dozen teeth, neither do he. We're both goin' blind. What I got, this hoss got. What he got, I got. They might as well do me when they do him. Why, it's Mr. Bandera. Nice to see you again, sir. Nice of you to come by."

He was dressed, like usual, in Tom's retailored castoffs, like some glitter-lost miniature of Tom himself, left too long in the sun.

"Howdy, Stumpy. I didn't know you was still on."

"If'n he lays down on his left side, he got trouble risin' to his feet again. I help him."

"He had a good life," I said.

"This hoss once carried a three-thousand-dollar saddle, hand-wrought silver and leather."

"Well, I reckon he earned it."

"There's talk of stuffin' him," he said. "Like some bobcat or a fish. Put 'im in the ground, I say. Let 'im rest." He ran his hand over Tony's neck. "He ain't been right since the Major went. Let 'em both rest. Now's the time for quiet, we had our excitement, din't we, Tony? Ah, yeah . . ."

We waited on opposite sides of the stall door, stroking Tony, waiting for the vet and the lawyer.

"I been through every state of the forty-eight, and women I seen them all, from the world's smallest to the world's tallest. I shared my grub with the fattest and took the night air with a human skeleton; I seen an albino gal and one blacker'n me. I was *Stumpy dear* to Koo-Koo the bird girl, Wanda the frog, and Annabelle the snake charmer; I knew some women would take money for it and some would give money for it; I seen one could swallow swords, another who et of human flesh; knew one could turn her head and lay her chin upon her back, knew another who could tie herself up like a knot; I knew a girl who could fry chicken. Oh, I have observed my share of the ladies, but Lupe Velez won't never have to worry about gettin' lost in the crowd.

"*The Mexican Spitfire,* they called her. *Hot Cha,* they called her. *The Hot Tamale,* they called her. I din't call her nothin', I stayed away from her, and wished the Major would of done likewise, but that was like barkin' at a knot.

"She became a star when she made a picture called *The Gaucho,* with Mr. Fairbanks. No more'n twenty years old, but already the hottest pants in Hollywood. No taller than five foot, she wasn't, and din't weigh more'n one hundred pounds, but what she did with what she had!

"The Major took her to the fights. She loved the fights, havin'
so much of it in herself. A lot of women'll say they love the
fights. She'd go herself if there wasn't nobody around to take
her. Then one thing led to another, as it usually does, especially
with Miss Lupe. She once got a hold of Mr. Cooper, the story
goes, and wore him down to skin and bones. The studio had to
send him on a safari to Africa just to get him away from her.

"With the Major it was like a feller who's been workin' hard
and behavin' for so long he decides he deserves a little wild
stuff, but never knowin' how wild is wild, he wonders how the
hell he ever got himself into this.

"You could see all that on the Major's face as he ran round
and round the house, with Miss Lupe after him blastin' a .38
in his direction and screamin' a lot of stuff in Spanish. 'Scuse
me for laughin', Mr. Bandera, but it sure was a funny sight. See
the Major on hossback and you want to sing a hymn, but tryin'
to escape on those high heels and bowed legs he was another
Keaton.

"Which is where he escaped to, by the way, to Mr. Buster's
house and holed up there, 'til the Mexican Spitfire had a
chance to kick a few things, shoot a few more, cool off, and go
on to somebody new.

"He was only holdin' on to that palace in Beverly Hills
wishin' Miss Vic and the girl would come home again. He loved
that woman like they did in the old days, and no wonder,
pretty young thing she was. Little bit bossy maybe, but she'd
grow out of that once she got to feelin' comfortable with all she
had. But it was never the money with the Major. *They don't
put pockets in shrouds.* That's the why he gave folks who
fussed 'bout the money he spent. Out of work and with the
Internal Revenuers jumpin' up his ass, he still din't give money
a damn or a half. Makin' a hoss mind was lots harder'n makin'
money, and as long as he could do the one he could do t'other."

After Tom went out on personal tours, we kind of lost touch
for a spell. I was still with the Buck Jones unit, but it was

starting to lose its flavor. I was ready for something new. I never reckoned it would take the shape of something so familiar as our old big sugar off of the 101, Colonel Zack Miller.

He asked Tom to go out again with him, and once he heard I was still alive, included me in the invite. They finished their dickering at $7,700 a week and then we all had us a good laugh remembering the day we used to draw but eighteen dollars a week from the Colonel.

"I ain't sure I wasn't richer then," said Tom.

Well, that settled it, I thought. I told Buck I was going on down the road, back to where I come from. Out of the perfume-covered stink of Hollywood and heading back to the honest smell of horseshit and straw, where we belonged and knowed what was expected of us. Hollywood, it'll kill you. It'll boost you higher than you ever thought you could go, but don't get to liking the atmosphere up there 'cause when you take the time to look down you're going to find out there's nothing holding you up.

I packed my bag and set fire to my raft. They wouldn't know I was gone. For the first time in years I had the feeling of having aholt of myself. Then when I went over to Tom's place to celebrate, he told me, "Kid, I got some good news for you."

"I don't know as I can handle any more," I said, a big smile all over me.

"We ain't goin' out with the 101."

I don't recollect that I could say nothing. The heart just fell out of me.

"Don't look so glum, 'til you hear me out," said Tom. "Mr. Ballard, of the Sells Floto Circus, has come across with a better offer. Two hundred thousand on the barrelhead, with a percentage of the profits come season's end. It'll make me the highest-paid circus performer in the history of the world!"

"Well, Tom," I said, "if that's what you want, then I'm happy you got it."

"You're gonna be with me, Kid, just like always."

"No, I ain't."

"C'mon, don't be that way. A travelin' show is a travelin' show. What's the difference who we link up with?"

"The difference is the 101 don't have freaks and lions and sharpsters trying to do little kids out of their nickels."

He argued the finer points at me some, and Tom was never nothing if not persuasive, but I had just made the decision to get out of one uncomfortable situation, I wasn't going to land smack in another. I stood quiet.

I tried to sign on the 101 myself, but Zack was so riled at Tom for reneging on him, he just kind of transferred his beef to me. Tom went off with the circus and I found myself deep in my forties and a day-worker chore boy on the meanest spread of them all.

"One way or another," said Stumpy, "I've been in and out of all kinds of entertainment, and that includes the illegal kind, but my absolute favorite is still the circus. Every man's got the one thing that washes him through with joy every time he partakes in it. For me, that's raisin' the big top.

"First of May is what they call a tenderfoot just joinin' up with the circus. Well, the smell of lions was a new one on us, but me and the Major sure wasn't no first of May's. We'd seen a travelin' show or two in our day. We kind of fit right in.

"The season went like a fish through water, with no more trouble than a fall in Dallas which busted up the Major's shoulder. They wired it together for him, and 'part from that, everything went smart. At the end of that first season, for the first time ever, Sells Floto showed a bigger gate than Ringling-Barnum, *The Big One* to circus folk. God, warn't it wonderful to be down and then back on top again!

"Then seein' what was happenin', John Ringling started buyin' up all the competition. He bought all five of the shows in the American Circus Corporation. Ours was one of them. He did right by us, though. He gave the Major a private car to travel in, furnished by Gimbels 'n' fancier than a New Orleans whorehouse, but it wasn't any too easy for him to get sleep in it. In every town, early in the mornin', the kids would wait for the circus to roll in and then start in crawlin' all over the Major's private car. What with punchin' cows and makin' movies, he was used to risin' early, so it din't bother him none. Besides, he loved kids, they made him what he was. He'd see a poor kid hangin' around the circus and he'd find a way to sneak him under the big top.

"Depression? What depression? Even with the new seats Ringling gave us, straw days was routine."

A straw day is when the crowds are so big you got to spread out straw so folks can sit on the ground.

"In all the paper that was posted and all the newspaper ads," said Stumpy, "the billin' was *Sells Floto Circus presents The Star of Stars, Tom Mix [Himself] and Tony, the Wonder Horse.* Wherever you saw the name Tom Mix, next to it was *Himself,* in whaddayacallums—brackets. That's when you're a legend in your own time, when you have to convince folks that they're really goin' to see you, in the flesh. Tom Mix [Himself]. That's what they come to see.

"And now, ladies and gentlemen and children of all ages, the one and only, the star of stars, direct from Hollywood, California, Tom Mix!

"The Major'd come in on Tony Jr. full tilt. He'd ride 'round the hippodrome and step off that gallopin' hoss like a man takin' a step off of his porch to fetch the mornin' paper. As soon as his boots hit the ground, he'd draw his gun and twirl it on his finger and walk big as you please to the center ring. You used to ride good, Mr. Bandera, and so did I, but did we ever ride *that* good?

"In the center ring he'd do a trick shootin' act. I used to make the rosin balls myself, heat 'em up in molds and fix 'em to a spinnin' wheel and such. The Major'd shoot 'em 'tween his legs, over his shoulder, ever' which way from Sunday. Never missed a one. 'Course, he'd have to be a poor shot indeed to miss any, 'cause his shells they was loaded with pellet shot, a stunt he first used in Hollywood at a press party, when he come in all liquored up."

Good old Tom, he knew how to fill in a short suit.

"After the shootin' part, he'd do some trick riding with Tony Jr. and then a liberty number with some of John Agee's trained hosses. It's called a liberty act 'cause the hosses are trained so good they know what to do at liberty, and all the trainer has to do is kind of stand in the middle and crack a whip once in a while and give the look of bein' in control.

"Always leave 'em wantin' a little more was his motto. The afternoon was our meat. For two-bits more the folks could come back after the main show to see the Major star in a Wild West Exhibition, and I don't reckon there was one person in the audience who wouldn't come up with the extra quarter, and there were times, I swear, when the aftershow was more crowded than the regular performance. The Major'd lead the other cowboys round the hippodrome so's the folks could have a good look at 'em, and then they did a pony express routine, showin' how it was in the old days. Then there was a lariat and ropin' number. The Major would start out ropin' one hoss, then two at a time, and finally he'd put a rope round three at a time.

"The crowd loved him. He was still the number-one cowboy in the land. When we pulled into winter quarters we had profits even higher than the season before.

"Only his spirits was lower. The busted shoulder was hurtin' him and his back started to go bad, because of a movie accident when he got too close to a dynamite blast. He checked into the hospital to have the wire took out of his shoulder. He still hurted. They commenced to X-rayin' him and runnin' all their tests tryin' to figure out what was wrong with him. Well, he had the arthritis.

"The Major promoted a smile and said, *Maybe if I don't bother it too much it won't bother me.* He made up his mind to live with it as cheerful as he could. Just the same, it's a old

man's disease and gettin' it can only remind you you're be-
comin' a old man yourself, and that ain't hardly ever a laughin'
matter."

Old friend Zack Miller took him to court for backing out of
his deal to go out with the 101, suing him for $432,000, which
is what he figured he lost when Tom decided not to go with
him. Hell, he probably lost more. But that was harder to take
than the arthritis or the IRS 'cause he counted Colonel Zack
as a friend. He always figured a friend would understand the
way you'd take the better offer, no hard feelings. Nowadays
everybody knows there ain't a friend living in Hollywood—for
nobody, but the sad truth is that when it comes to large sums
of money, no matter where it's found, friendship gets lost in all
the zeroes.

"I do this with great reluctance," was Colonel Zack's story,
"for Tom and I go back many years and I have nothing but the
highest respect and admiration for him."

"I wish certain fellas would stop havin' so much respect and
admiration for me," said Tom. "It's puttin' me out of business."

The government had just that in mind, and I don't know that
all that much respect and admiration went along with it. They
had set their sights on him, fixing to make him an example to
the others. They figured they was losing a million a year from
movie folk alone and wanted to start picking them off like
ducks at a gallery. I reckon they went for Tom first 'cause he
was never too shy about throwing around his money.

Nobody pulling in the kind of money he was ever messed
around with working over their own tax returns. He hired an
expert to do that, a young girl whose best qualification for the
job might of been her friendship with the lady who was Assistant Treasurer of these United States.

Well, she made a couple mistakes. The biggest one was hiring two of her other clients onto Tom's staff in jobs they never
worked at, for high salaries they was never paid. Now, I never

had more money than I could fit in a tobacco can, and I got a small head for figures, but it only takes a short lesson to learn that what she done is called conspiracy, and when it's done against the U.S. government, you're in real big trouble.

"I reckoned the Major had seen the inside of a jail before," said Stumpy. "A youngster knockin' around the west when he was, before it had a real chance to get used to civilization, might pass a night or two playin' checkers with a jailer. It was nothin' to be ashamed of and never lasted too long. But, Lordy, now he was facin' a civilized federal prison, just for makin' too much damn money. Don't you think I never thought about what would happen to this country if Tom Mix went to jail. We'd wind up with a generation of sour 'n' silent kids, not carin' about being their best, not seein' the best in others. Can you picture it?"

He had one fancy lawyer fighting Zack Miller, he hired another to fight the government. But when Vic sued for divorce in December of that year, well, there was no fight in him for that.

31

If Tom had set out to be the top circus attraction in the country, he would of had to be satisfied, at least in his work. But he could never get over the feeling that the circus was some kind of exile.

"He watched Buck Jones moving into talkies without a scratch," said Stumpy. "He couldn't understand how a guy like Buck could edge past him and leave him behind, just like the Major himself done with Bill Hart. If there hadn't been a Tom Mix there never woulda been a Buck Jones, but the Major, he was an original. *He came out of a circus,* said the Major, talkin' about Buck, *and I went into one.* There wasn't no joy in observin' the way things work out. *Well, what do you think, Stumpy?* he put to me one afternoon, half in the bag. *Are they here to stay?*

"What's that, Major?

"These talkies. You figure they're here to stay?

"I had to tell him the truth. *I reckon they are, sir. They're doin' a real good business.* He nodded his head and said, *Looks like I'll have to get into them.*"

At the end of the '31 season Ringling pulled the Sells Floto off the road for good. Tom could of gone with his pick of the other circuses, but he wanted to shoot for a comeback in what he always figured he knew best: the movies. He hired a voice teacher and set himself to work.

Like I said, I was only shuffling around anyways, and when Universal took him on and he was back in business, I shuffled on over there. He was about to make his first talking picture, not like anything he'd ever done before. The old formula was dropped down the toilet and there was going to be a story with some meat below the sauce. It was from a good book and there was no way it wouldn't be a good movie. It was called *Destry Rides Again.* His bet was it would put him back on top again.

"A few days before shootin' was to start," said Stumpy, "he started feelin' poorly. His stomach was botherin' him. He figured maybe it was on account of he was tryin' to stop drinkin', so he had a drink but it only got worse. There was just me and Minnie at the place with him and when he started to throw up so bad she called me and I called his doctor, who got there it was about ten that night."

They hurried him to the hospital and by the time they opened him up his appendix had already gone bust and the poison was in him. His doctor warn't none too optimistic about his chances. But other doctors wrote him off before. Tom always had the idea that a feller's life is pretty well laid out for him right from the time he's born, and death always comes at the best time. The idea don't appeal much to me, but there might be something to it. Leastways he claimed he would know when his time was up, and this wasn't it.

But I reckon it was close enough. There was a little airplane in San Francisco that made runs between the Frisco *Call-Bulletin* and the L.A. *Evening Herald,* and they got the pilot to pick up a supply of poison-eating serum at the University in Berkeley and high-tail it to L.A.

I waited in the corridor with some others for that plane to arrive, and you couldn't help getting the notion of what Tom Mix meant to this country. The hospital was flooded with wires

and letters. Surgeons from Chicago and New York was calling
to help out his doctor with advice. The radio was broadcasting
regular reports on his condition. A crowd collected out front
of the hospital. Movie stars walked the hallway with plain old
cowpokes. Teddy was there, poor deaf girl, trying to handle
the reporters, just like she used to when we was all together.
Vic was in Washington, D.C., and though she was divorcing
him she kept in close touch on the telephone. Women had a
hard time letting loose of Tom.

It dragged on like that for two days, looking like he wasn't
going to make it, but then all of a sudden he turned the bend.
Once he was out of danger, the crowd drifted away, and the
radio and newspapers went back to the news of the day. He
rested up for about a month to get his strength back, and then
he went over to Universal to take his shot.

He reckoned he really had something in that story, and went
along with whatever Ben Stoloff, the director, said. Stoloff
helped him keep a lid on the broad gestures he used in silents
and tried to teach him how you can get mileage out of the
things you say and the way you say them instead of just by the
things you do, which was what he was used to.

Everybody on that show gathered together to watch whenever Tom had some riding or fighting to do. "Ain't he something," they all said. "There'll never be another like him," said
they. "He hasn't changed a bit in the past ten years," they said.
"I hope I look as good as him when I'm that age," was the going
opinion.

Only, damn it to hell, it was all wrong. The picture'd be
going along swell and then all of a sudden they'd put him next
to the leading lady and have them talk over things. There
they'd be, out on some dusty field, nobody going no place,
nothing happening nowhere. Tom would kick some dirt up
with his toe, she'd kind of fold her hands and look at them; he'd
tug on his chin, she'd brush some dust off of her sleeve. All
whilst talking about what they did so far in the picture and

what they figured on doing in the rest of it. It was like a wet blanket on a horse for him to make a scene like that; it wasn't much better for folks watching it.

"There was some," said Stumpy, "that'd look at it and say, *Uh-oh, the man can't act.* Call that actin', standin' around jawin' and doin' nothin'? That ain't actin', that's discussin'. Actin' is when you pretend you're someone else, and you pull it off so's folks really believe you and want to be like you. *That's* actin'. And that's what makes Tom Mix one of a handful of the best actors ever come through this town, I don't give a damn what nobody says.

"He did it in silents, he coulda done it in talkies, if only he coulda got used to microphones. He'd see a microphone loomin' over his head and he couldn't hardly keep his eyes off of it, for fear it was gonna jump on him or somethin'. Nothin' anybody could do could get him over it. It's my belief that time woulda done it, but in the movie business time is somethin' you give to a twenty-year-old kid, not a fifty-two-year-old man."

His age started working against him. He could still ride off a cliff and into a river, up stairs, through a window, and over a balcony, but there was something missing. The fire was gone out of it.

"The stunt wasn't convincing, Tom," says the director.

"Sure felt convincin'," says him, rubbing the bruised parts.

"I wonder if an audience is going to accept a man your age doing a feat like that."

"Well, I just did it," says Tom, like a bumblebee to a scientist who just declared his body's too big and his wings're too small to ever get him off the ground.

But there was something in what that director said. Like for instance, they was beginning to worry about him playing opposite girls thirty years younger than him. They didn't think the audience would accept that neither. At the same time, ever'-one knew that he could have his pick of girls any age he wanted, and not just because of what he was neither. Still, there was something in what they said, I don't know. I've looked inside a camera more than once. It ain't all that complicated. Where's it get the power to turn foul to fair, fair to foul?

One week after she got the final divorce papers, Vic married an Argentinjun, attached to the Argentina embassy in Washington, and commenced cutting a fine swath through Washington society, going to diplomatic parties and speaking French and such.

"She's a girl been a long ways under the bed for her boots," said Tom.

Next month he married one of the aerialists off of the Sells Floto Circus.

right:
At the races, almost 60 years old. 1939 or 1940. (*Courtesy of Tom Mix Museum*)

In a serious vein, circa 1930. (*Courtesy of Ostland*)

On Tony, Jr., in *Destry Rides Again* (*Universal*), 1932. (*Courtesy of Ed Jahnke*)

32

We spent the rest of the year making talkies out at Universal. They were pretty good movies too, but, Lord, they come so hard. On Christmas he retired Tony and announced that he himself was also through with pictures.

"It's over, Kid," he said. "Who'm I kiddin'?"

Over for him maybe, I had to get back scratching.

Colonel Zack had won a judgment of $90,000 against him, but Tom come right back at him and won a new trial. He had to get up on the stand and deny what his own posters said: that he was the champion horseman of the world. "There are better riders in the world than me," he had to say, "and better horses than Tony."

"Maybe so," said Stumpy, "but I didn't know who the hell they were. We had to get witnesses who would say he wasn't that good a draw, that Clyde Beatty was a better draw than him. You ever heard of such foolishness?"

The new trial lasted over two weeks and at the end of it Tom got bit for $66,000. It probably would of been cheaper to pay Zack the $90,000 two years before. With this trial and the hassles with IRS and Vic over visitation rights, most of his time and money was spent on lawyers.

He had to make more money or he'd sink, so he looked me up (I wasn't hard to find) and we put together seven cowboys, two aerialists, and a six-piece band and called it "The Tom Mix Roundup." We took to the road.

It wasn't exactly ragtag, but it wasn't exactly class neither. It paid the bills, like the big one that got the IRS off his back once and for all. He walked into the courtroom and paid up $173,000 in cash, with a smile on his face. Anyway, it was a mite better than what the young lady who was his tax expert got: five years breaking rock.

His court appearances, they was lessening and some of those problems was behind him, but him and Vic was still spending a lot of time there. If it warn't over the youngun, it was over money. It was like they wanted to keep seeing each other and it was the only safe place they could meet. He was suing her to pay her share of the tax bite, and she was suing him to collect on $50,000 worth of promise notes he gave her to buy little Tommie a home.

"Kid," he told me, "I wouldn't mind making good on them, for a home for Tommie, but I never had no intention when I signed them of providin' a home for some goddamn Argentin-jun."

Anyway, there must of been some real hard feelings during that one 'cause he let go after keeping it a secret for nine years how Vic had plugged him one day and would of shot him dead but for her poor aim. You could say it set the courtroom on its ear. Maybe it warn't the gentlemanly thing to do, after all those years, but gentlemen are found where ladies abound, and when folks are after each other's money in a court of law, well. . . .

The judge went along with him on the matter of the $50,000, and by the end of '33 things was starting to brighten up a mite.

He come out of retirement to make one more picture for Universal. I declined the invitation. He warn't the first star to come out of retirement at the drop of a reasonable offer. He ain't going to be the last. Sure, he was kidding himself. They all do.

The picture was called *Terror Trail*. He made it, he drew his pay, and he went home, dog-tired. They didn't ask him to do another. In a couple months he'd be fifty-five.

His radio show went on the air that year. Well, it wasn't really his radio show, it was a show about him. Well, it wasn't really about him neither, it was about the escapades of Tom Mix, not the real ones 'cause the airways ain't allowed to carry such. What the Ralston Purina people, who sponsored the show, had in mind was to tell stories about Tom fighting to stop crime. What they really had in mind was selling cereal and a lot of crap like secret whistling sheriff's badges. I listened to it once, and then since I could hardly believe it I listened to it again. Once would of been enough.

I reckon a whole generation of kids grew up thinking that Tom Mix was a radio hero, never realizing that once there was a man. Well, in the long run that's likely better. Men come along ever' second of the day, but heroes are spaced further apart. Reckon that's how come we invent them, and when the truth be known about them, ignore it.

No big money came for the rights to use his name for the radio series. Some say he gave it to them for $100 and a bowl of cereal. Well, he never touched cereal, and he'd spend $100 before he even had any breakfast, but I believe he did sell cheap on that one, because he didn't want the kids forgetting him.

I lived me a long life, and now I find it wasn't no more than accidents, not the bone-breaking kind, though I got my share of them too. Just like I didn't want to get in the movies and wound up there, so I didn't want no parts of the circus and still I got in one.

Our Tom Mix Roundup joined up with the Sam B. Dill Circus. I wasn't keen on it, but there honestly wasn't another open door nowhere. You know what? It wasn't half bad. Had things gone one way and not the other, I might of been with the circus yet.

We gypsied 'cross half the states in the forty-eight, covering 13,000 miles the first season and then wintered out in Compton, California.

Wonder of it all, we made money that year. Instead of hurting us, the depression was playing along with us. Folks had to forget their troubles some way, didn't they?

"To my way of thinkin'," said Stumpy, "things couldn't have been better. Sam Dill was a top manager, the Major was a star attraction. I saw a long and profitable association before us and then a soft retirement on the Major's ranch in Arizona. I do believe the Major was seein' it the same way. He had made his mark on Hollywood and 'specially on western movies and had to be content with the signature as it stood. He only hoped it wouldn't fade too fast."

Well, things warn't looking too bad at that.

Then early on in '35, Sam Dill, clever as he was, was dumb enough to die on us. It left us kind of at loose ends. Thanks to Tom's example, other circuses had signed on Hollywood cowboys too, hoping to corner some of the trade we'd been getting. Harry Carey, Monte Montana, Tim McCoy, Jack Hoxie, all had plans to go on the road. Which meant that the good circuses already had their star attractions. So what Tom did was, he up and bought the Sam B. Dill Circus and renamed it the Tom Mix Circus.

It warn't the wrong thing to do, he was just the wrong bird to do it. He was a star and a fair roper and a helluva horseman and a couple of dozen other valuable things he was. Only he warn't no circus manager. Give him credit, though, he sure was a showman.

Up to this time circuses had traveled by rail. But Tom's favorite method of transportation, next to the horse, was the automobile. Oh, he liked trains right enough and featured them in lots of the movies. He'd ridden them a good bit too, but usually when he did he took a car along with him. Problem with a train is when you get on you got to go where the tracks go, no matter what change of mind comes over you. Such ain't the case when you're behind the wheel. And that's why he put the first motorized circus on the road in America. He wanted to come and go as he pleased.

'Course, there was some drawbacks, like breakdowns, accidents, and the fact that it takes one truck to transport one elephant, when you can get three of them in a single railroad car. His answer to that was that we'd carry only one elephant, a gentle old cow named Babe, since one is pretty much like all the others.

He bought the trucks and painted them red, white, and blue. He bought new canvas with his brand all over it. He bought the best of equipment. No expense was spared. He wanted a class operation. What he did for western movies, he'd do for the circus.

He had General Motors make him a special kind of vehicle for his personal use. It wasn't exactly a truck and it wasn't exactly a bus, though it was kind of shaped like a bus and was as big. He called it his "motor home" and it was for him to live in on the road, with all the comforts. Now, of course, you can't step outside without being run down by one of the monsters, but I reckon Tom had the first.

It cost him $3,400, but that was only for the chassis. The rest was extra. He had a bathroom in the thing, with a stained-glass window. All the fittings was either silver or chromium. There was a bedroom and a kitchen and a den, with bookcases where he kept his books: O. Henry, *Death in the Afternoon*, Max Brand, a couple Bibles. He had horns on the walls and a holstered gun hanging from a peg. Damned if it didn't remind me of his setting room in the Beverly Hills mansion!

Whenever we come into a town to set up, and we always paraded through town first, they'd put a canvas canopy over his "motor home" so's he'd have something separating the metal roof and the hot sun. Then they'd put up a fence that went round the side of his vehicle. This was called his back yard and often when he wasn't needed somewhere we'd set out there together in a couple of director's chairs. We'd play a hand of gin or maybe just sit quiet and look.

"I din't have it so bad myself," said Stumpy. "I lived and slept with Tony, which was as much as I needed, and I found a way to keep myself in all the gin I could handle.

"By this time Tony was not expected to do a thing, 'cept stand around in that little roped-off area where folks could look at him and take his picture, which he purely loved. The Major had been usin' Tony Jr. and Tony II and now was ridin' the white Arab, the one named Warrior. I stayed with Tony and answered questions folks put to me about him. Well, a few times every day there'd be some boy and his father who couldn't get over what they was actually lookin' at—Tony the Wonder Hoss. They'd go on and on about all the Saturday matinees they had seen him in and the one movie that was made for him special, called *Just Tony,* and on and on and on. You know how I mean. I'd kind of shuffle up and say, *You sure sound like a real fan of Tony's. Like to have one of his shoes? I saw he threw one here someplace this morning.* Well, the kid'd have to twist his legs to keep from peein' his pants. I'd go root through the straw and come up with a hoss shoe, brush it off agin my pants and hand it over to the brat. The old man was always good for a half a buck, a buck. Mr. Bandera, all across the country there's hoss shoes hangin' in boys' rooms, hoss shoes of ever' description off of ever'thing from Shetlands to Clydesdales, all of 'em once wore by Tony the Wonder Hoss. Like I say, it kept me in gin."

33

Put it up, bring it down, pack it in, move it on down the road, put it up again . . . 12,000 miles a season. It was the life we was in now.

The first season out with our own show we got hit with most ever'thing in the book. We started in California in cold weather that finally turned to rain. For hundreds of miles we was in a running paper war with the Barnes show. We'd be a couple days ahead of them and their advance man would paper over our posters, WAIT FOR THE BARNES CIRCUS. Or they'd get a day ahead of us and our boys would paper over their posters, 'til the locals would know the circus was coming by the fistfights in front of vacant storefronts.

By the time we got east and away from the Barnes show, we run into heat waves so bad nobody wanted to be within smelling distance of canvas. Mud would follow heat, seemed like. If it wasn't heat or mud it was the scare of infantile paralysis. And in Kentucky the law ordered Tom to install rear-view mirrors on all the trucks. Instead we raced for the border, leaving behind us a string of unplayed dates.

It finally come time to face Butte, Montana. If the circus route is one long desert, Butte, Montana, is a poisoned water-hole. No performer in any circus ever wanted to step foot inside the Treasure State. We went there 'cause there was such good business, but it was strictly hit the clowns, three balls for a quarter. Montanans figure that included in the price of their ticket is the right to stone you after the show.

We was just raising the big top when two local "officials" cornered Tom and tried to shake him down for a "surety bond."

Well, we'd had some experience with these small-town punks, and hadn't gave in yet. Tom's feelings was a circus owes something to any town that welcomes it inside. We'd give them a free parade, hire some local kids for day work, or Tom would speak to some of the local clubs. If they was struggling to add a new wing to the hospital, we'd dedicate one show to the cause and kick in a percentage of the gate. But never a shakedown.

"Would two o'clock be all right?" said Tom. "In your office? I'll post my bond then and there."

"No, we'd ruther do it here, in cash," they says.

"Well, I'd like to oblige you, gents, but I always like to include the Mayor and Chief of Police in a transaction like this."

"Goddamn, you got more money than you know what to do with," they grumbled.

In their bone heads they had him for an easy mark 'cause they reckoned he was rich.

"See that lion in the cage over yonder?" said Tom.

The punks allowed that they did.

"Well, I don't like him, don't like any kind of cat, so's with the money I got no use for, I stuff it up that lion's ass. Help yourself."

"You been warned, Mr. Tom Mix. This ain't Hollywood here."

They grumbled some more and sulked away. You seen the kind. A real low form of life.

Tom put the word out to watch for a "Hey, Rube!" that

night. We'd been watching for one since we crossed the state line, but to hear it from Tom didn't make for very relaxed performances that night.

There was a hill up behind the lot and suddenly during the last performance beer bottles and stones started raining down on the trailers and big top. It sure played hell with the aerialists to hear the popping above their heads.

Tom ordered the concessions closed up and ever'thing outside the big top loaded up.

"I got Tony," said Stumpy, "and was goin' to put him in his trailer, but somethin' told me to put him in with the common stock instead. By now the roustabouts was dodgin' stones to get everythin' off of the ground and in the trucks and the farm boys started to come down off of the hill."

The minute the show was over some townie started cutting guy lines. On Warrior, Tom rode up to him and gave him a boot in the head. I picked up his knife and the "Hey, Rube!" commenced in earnest. The gang come after us with rocks and clubs. You ever try to load up a big top, a 120 with three 40s, whilst holding off a gang of toughs throwing rocks? Try it sometime.

"First thing they did," said Stumpy, "was topple over Tony's trailer, hopin' to maim the Wonder Hoss. Collect all their hearts together and you couldn't sink half a walnut shell."

We was going at it hand to hand. As I fought them off, I couldn't help recollecting all the other crowds Tom had waded through. Now he was riding through this one on Warrior, bashing heads with a four-foot pole. When three of them looked close to pulling him off the horse, I put a knife in one of their thigh parts. He screamed and the others saw the shiv sticking out of him. It slackened their fight considerable and they backed off for a time. It gave us breathing room and everybody fell to wrapping up gear and getting it on the trucks so's we could get the hell out of Montana.

They made one more charge at us. This time we put a long

TOM MIX DIED FOR YOUR SINS

length of chain in Babe's trunk and she went through them swinging that chain. It gave us the time we needed to load, and we was able to send the shitheels in a bona fide retreat.

We loaded up Babe, put the women and children on the floorboards, and made our getaway through town, under a hail of rocks. Good-bye, Butte, see you next year, assholes.

That August Will was killed in a plane crash. Our trails used to cross a lot, since he was on the road so much. He'd come visit us and the three of us'd spend a day or two getting drunk. When we got the news, Tom lowered the flag to half-mast and kept it there for the rest of the season. We left the circus on its own for a few days and went back to California for the funeral.

"Somethin' fine was knocked out of him with the death of Mr. Will, and whatever it was I din't see it come back," said Stumpy.

Well, I reckon they shared something, those two, besides their trip from rags to riches, something I warn't along for. And in that trip they shared the loss of something too. The thing wrong with success is the way it undercuts what made you a success in the first place. You take a lawyer, he gets to the top because he loves justice. Then once he's there he finds he can finagle justice to his own wants and he winds up despising the law and himself. A writer, he writes his stories out of loneliness and fear of dying. Then he becomes successful and all of a sudden he's surrounded by folks and they're all telling him how he's going to live forever.

All that really counts, though, is character. Take it before money, power, or love. Anyone would, if he'd think about it for a minute. Problem is, you never have to think about it 'til it's already slipped away from you, and, partner, ain't it hard to recover something that came with your raising and was lost with your rising?

We wintered in Compton again. After all our troubles the

circus was just about breaking even. Tom took an offer from Mascot Pictures to do fifteen chapters of a serial called *The Miracle Rider.*

He wasn't thinking about another comeback this time. Mascot was a shoestring operation and the stories was bad. I reckon they wanted to see how many easy bucks they could pick up from what popularity Tom Mix still might have at the box office. I reckon that's all he had in mind himself.

It was the worst he ever done. He knew it, and he knew it would be his last. He was a man of few regrets, but after doing two hundred sixty pretty decent moving pictures, why'd he have to go and do a dog like *The Miracle Rider?*

34

He started out the '36 season with a fair imitation of the drive and energy I was used to from him, using the money he got for *The Miracle Rider* to put on the road the best damn circus anybody ever seen. New trucks, new acts, and he even took on two more elephants, maybe remembering from Montana what a useful critter an elephant can be. He hired a lot of new people, old friends. It might of been the loss of Will that made him want to surround himself with old friends. Nothing wrong with that. Long as your friends are also good workers. Some of them wasn't even friends, just old rummies who showed up saying they served with Tom in China or Africa or some god-damn place. Sign 'em on, says Tom.

By this time other shows had gone to wheels, but ours was still the biggest. We raced each other across the land, trying to be the first circus of the season in town, and there was many paper wars.

Floods in the east, winds in the west, drought on the plains. In Colorado a truck full of fine horses went off the road, killing the stock and driver and destroying the truck. We buried the driver in the next town, and Tom had to go in debt to replace the stock and truck.

"Well, he started in drinkin' real heavy again," said Stumpy, "and got to be pretty moody, as Injuns do when they drink. The circus children was warned to stay away from the big top and the motor home when he was goin' that way. He began missin' shows and one of the younger cowboys would have to doll up in his clothes and pretend he was the Major. Tom Mix, Himself, wasn't himself no more. He took to leavin' the show for days at a time, joinin' up with us again down the road. He was goin' to hell in a handcart."

His dream of a comeback in movies was over, and his dream of becoming a writer he gave up and just settled instead for giving out political opinions to the press: "My vote or that of any other American whose father or grandfather broke and tilled the soil should equal three votes by a foreign-born citizen."

"Go along with that," said Stumpy, "and you'd have to give us darkies about five votes apiece."

We wintered in Alabama that year, in the red, and during the winter had a fire that wiped out five grand worth of equipment. Then in the spring there was great floods all over the south and Tom sent the Red Cross canvas and equipment to help out in them places the hardest hit.

Money was tight and we couldn't replace our lost or damaged equipment. When we finally was able to get on the road, starting the season late, we saw that business had dropped off something fierce and we just didn't know why. Tom's guess was that we was finally coming out of the depression and circuses was associated with hard times. They wanted to put it all behind them and go on to some prosperity for a change.

We still had the heat and mud in the east, the polio scares, the truck accidents. In Kansas an epidemic struck the animals and wiped out some horses and good old Babe. One of our aerialists took a nosedive. The geek lost his appetite.

Well, there was circuses folding all around us, but somehow we managed to hobble out for the '38 season. What '29 was to bankers, that's what '38 was to circuses. And like the other, nobody wanted to believe it. Most thought that circuses was a permanent part of this country. Just like a lot of folks thought about silent movies and Prohibition.

He cut the ticket prices and he reduced the salaries. When that wasn't enough, he had to lay off fifty people. Some of those folks went a long way back with him. I stopped drawing any pay, but I reckon I knew the way the snow was drifting.

He did his shows drunk now, and in one of them when he bent over to shoot between his legs, he fell over on his face. He took off by himself, didn't come back for over a week, 'til Wisconsin.

In Wisconsin we got caught in the path of a twister. I was sitting in the donniker and all of a sudden I could hear folks yelling outside. I come out hitching up my pants to see this big old ugly dark funnel in the sky swooping towards us. Everyone scattered. I seen old Stumpy running to Tony. No one in the big top had any hint of what was to land on them. They was right in its path, and Tom performing in the center ring.

One mid-pole cracked, the others and the side poles was pulled free of the ground, and the big top come down on four thousand people. The twister, quick as it arrived, just went on its way.

Those of us outside tried to pull up the bottom of the canvas, and we was able to get out some folks that way, but for the others trapped inside it was pure Katie-bar-the-door. Tom's was the first knife to rent an opening. He ordered all inside with knives to use them to cut free of the canvas. Soon blades stuck through all over the tent, slashing long lines which the people then pulled apart and crawled out of.

No one was kilt, though a few was hurt bad. There was lawsuits, naturally, and without a big top we was out of business, and nobody was extending credit to a circus. Tom had already sold the Beverly Hills mansion and the Arizona ranch, trading real estate for circus dreams. All he had left was one Cord automobile and ten acres in San Fernando he called home.

He left us in Wisconsin and went off to try to raise the money for a new big top. Like good troupers the performers rehearsed while he was gone, hoping they'd have something to rehearse for. Damned if he didn't come back with $50,000, and the morale shot up again.

We sat in his motor home, on opposite sides of that big pile of greenbacks. We was giggling like kids, not really giving much thought to its being the last chance to keep the circus afloat.

"How in the hell did you do it, Tom?" I asked. Tom had a mighty bright smile, but for the life of me I couldn't calculate how he could of raised fifty grand off of it.

"I reckon my credit ain't all that bad in certain centers of commerce," he said. He cracked off a cap and poured us a drink.

"Who even *got* that much to lend these days?"

He laughed, the smile come down in steps, then he was quiet. I looked and waited.

"Vic," he said.

That's the same lady he fought tooth and nail with just a few years earlier, over the same amount.

"I got it from Minnie," said Stumpy, "that he'd been meetin' with Miss Victoria in little hotels round L.A. You can figure it out for yourself, Mr. Bandera."

We got a new big top, but business only got worse, and the natural obstacles got no softer. Nobody was getting paid now, but they couldn't leave for another show 'cause the few shows that was doing any better was already overmanned from taking on those that had been let go from the shows folding up. Tom himself had to take to embroidering his monogram on his drawers, with eyesight that were no longer up to such fine attention.

In August, the creditors put a hold on his circus. It's the kind of hold so tight you can't hardly wiggle an extremity.

"We been under fire before, Kid," he said.

"Sure, Tom, and will be again."

"Got any ideas?"

"Well, we never robbed a bank before."

I ain't sure I wasn't half serious. He wasn't neither.

"It ain't my style, Kid." He put his feet up and said, "I hear tell I'm still a big name over in Europe. Hell, lots of the little burgs are just about now getting my old Fox films. I'm likely the latest thing over there. What's to stop me from arranging a personal tour, raising the money, and bailing us out?"

"Not a damn thing, Tom."

"Then it's settled. You comin' along?"

"I better hang around here, look after things."

"You don't have to, Kid."

"It's all right."

He walked to the door and looked out over what was left of his circus. "Better not, Kid."

Well, maybe I talk slow but I don't think slow. "Okay, Tom, I'll look for something else."

"He had to sell his motor home to finance the tour," said Stumpy. "Most of our people just had to leave and look for somethin' else. You can live on nothin' for only so long. The show was cut to one ring, not hardly a reminder of the classy outfit we used to be.

"We never heard from the Major.

"Just one week into September, we limped onto a patch of

cactus in Pecos, Texas. The elephants satisfied one creditor, another took a truck. Something for this one, something for that one. What was left went to our own people for back pay. Finally there was only me and old Tony and a truck to drive home in."

35

"He played every big house in England and Scotland and din't come back til the spring of '39," Stumpy told me. "Comin' back across the water, his ship was stopped in mid-Atlantic by one of them German U-boats. The Captain of the boat came aboard just 'cause he knew the Major was on her and he wanted to be presented to him. The Major come out on deck to look at the commotion, and this Nazi skipper all in black and brass was led over to him by the skipper of the cruise ship. He clicked his heels and snapped off a salute and said in German, *To meet the cowboy king is a great honor. Should God give me to see my children again, I shall share it with them.* Then he was lowered back down to his U-boat and the ship was let to pass on safely.

"The Major came back to San Fernando and for the first time in his life he had nothin' to do, and din't seem to want nothin' to do. The circus business in America was dyin' anyway, a sure death. Vaudeville warn't far behind. Western movies was fixin' to share the same grave. The hottest item in the field was a young feller named Autry, who strummed a guitar and sung, for crissake. How'd we ever get to that?

"Well, he'd made his mark on the movies, on vaudeville, on

[289]

the circus. He had the key to every major city in the country, and foreign big shots had all made a fuss over him. On the radio he was as big as Superman. And you want to know somethin'? It had come to be near as dreary as the lone prairie.

"For over a year he did nothin' but tinker under the car, train the dozen hosses he kept, and sit in his slippers on the sun porch and read. 'Bout the most excitin' thing ever happened was once a week a few old boys would drop over for penny ante poker. Usually they was just wranglers or fellers that was with the circus, but once in a while old Hollywood friends who didn't fare much better than the Major would come over. Fellers like Buster Keaton, Jack Gilbert, Hoot Gibson. Oh, they'd talk a bit about old times. How could you help it? But mostly it was just penny ante, from after dinner to eleven o'clock, when they'd have some coffee and hot biscuits and go to bed.

"If the Major ever reckoned on havin' an old age, he mighta put a few dimes away for it, but come as close to death as many times as he did and you don't never get around to thinkin' about evenin' tide. He lived high when he had it, how could he figure the horn would ever run dry? How could any of 'em? What he had left, and it warn't inconsiderable, got pissed away on the circus and his lawyers, who still held some IOUs on him.

"Truth was, by the middle of the '40s, he was pretty well tapped out. He had to go someplace. There warn't no 101 to go back to, no circus neither. He couldn't go back to Europe 'cause of the war. He went back to the only place he could. He went to the Fox Studios, the place he helped build.

"I don't care to guess what happened there. Let's just say the welcome mat wasn't out. I had a little room built to the one end of the barn. With the years I'd come to sleep kind of heavy. The first shot was mine in a dream. I'd just blown the head off of a rattler. The second one told me it warn't no dream, but my head was still all fuzzed up from the gin I always took at bedtime. I rolled out of bed and grabbed my pants. The third shot rang out as I pulled on my boots. They was comin' from inside the barn, spaced regular, and I din't have the notion what they was.

"The lights were on in the barn. I had no weapon myself, but I flung open the doors anyway. Just in time to see the Major put a bullet in the head of one of the hosses. He already kilt three. *Major!* I yelled. *What you do that for, Major!*

"He din't answer me. He din't even know I was there. He just staggered up to the next stall, this crazed look in his glarin' black eyes, and he leveled his gun and kilt another hoss. *Please don't do that, Major!* I yelled. *They's good stock!* Only he crossed to the next stall in line and kilt that hoss too. I was half crazy myself. Tony was in the last stall. If I wasn't so crazy I woulda opened his stall and slapped him to runnin'. Instead I rushed the Major.

"Well, he swat me 'longside my head with the gun like I was a mosquito. It din't cool me out completely, but I was awful fogged over. I brought my hand away from my head, full of blood. He was reloadin'. I got to one knee. I wanted to find a fork or an ax or somethin', but I couldn't get off the ground. I watched him reload, plug another hoss, and go on to the next in line, gettin' closer to Tony. I crawled towards him on all fours, tryin' to keep from passin' out. I kept cryin' to him, *Major, please!* but I don't think he could hear me. I could hardly hear myself, like it is in a dream. But the shots were real, and so was the hosses fallin' dead in their stalls.

"Well, he kilt them all and now stood before Tony, his gun at his side. Tony ain't only the smartest hoss there ever was, he must be the bravest. The others had seen what was happenin' and their nostrils widened in terror and they kicked about in their stalls waitin' on their turn. But old Tony, he din't even flinch. He looked at his master like the Major's own soul starin' him down.

"I crawled closer. I was hopin' to get the Major's feet and maybe trip him up. I got close enough to see that when he raised his gun and aimed it at Tony's head, his face was runnin' with tears. Why shouldn't it be? He had just kilt himself eleven times over. I reckon he realized that when he couldn't pull the trigger on Tony. His hand fell back to his side, and he walked out of the barn into the dark.

"Good old Tony, good boy. Now it's time for you, but you don't mind. Good old Tony."

36

Died rich, died broke; died old, died young; died loved, died alone. This story ends like all the others, partner, when the Big Sugar calls trail's end.

The main reason I never became a star, I was told, was my lack of humor. I never smiled and always looked woebegone. The words was hardly out of their mouth when along comes a feller named Gary Cooper, and you'll remember what a life of the party *he* was.

All water under the bridge now. I got out of the business and never had no regrets. Hollywood was never my home nor movies my trade.

In the fall of '40 I found myself working a Hilton dude ranch in Tucson. I'd greet the guests at the dining room, tell them some yarns at the lodge, nothing harder than that. In exchange, I got a cottage and chuck and a couple bucks. Was all I needed.

October 11, it was, and I was in the midst of glad-handing a couple dudes when the desk clerk runs up to me and says a friend of mine just checked in. I follied him to the desk and there leaning his back against it, smiling like the width of Texas, was Tom, all dressed in white. I had heard he was up against it, but he didn't lack no prosperity in his appearance. And though I knew he was sixty, he could easy pass for forty.

"Well, I'll be damned," I said.

"Just ridin' around," he said, knowing what I was going to ask.

The dining room was closed, but I told him I could rustle up something for him in the kitchen. He said he wasn't hungry, so we sent a boy to his cottage with his bags and we went out to the porch for a smoke.

"They told me in El Paso you were workin' here," he said.

"Yep, same kind of job you first had at the 101."

He laughed and said, "I hope they're payin' you better."

There was a bright yellow Cord convertible parked out front. "Yours?" I asked.

He nodded.

"Looks new," I said.

"It ain't used much."

"Well, what brings you out here?"

"Just ridin' around. Really."

"Where you headed?"

"Reckon I'll go back to Hollywood."

"You got something lined up there?"

"I'm workin' over an idea. I believe western stuff has just about lost its thrill for folks. Hell, they'd rather sit around and listen to Autry sing. So what I'm thinkin' of is puttin' together a wild animal act and takin' it on the road. Not a circus, mind you, but just all kinds of wild animals. It'll be an educational thing for kids who wouldn't get to look at such critters except in books."

"You ain't thinking of becoming another Clyde Beatty, are you?" I asked. I was only making a joke, but I reckon I stepped on something tender.

"You don't think it's such a hot idea, huh?"

"Hell, I don't know."

"I was thinkin' of askin' you to join up with me."

[294]

I thought back to us becoming the law in LeHunt, Kansas. Now, like then, I had the impulse to say, hell, why not? Only this time I beat the impulse.

"No, Tom, I think I'll stick to what I got here. I ain't in the mood to tangle with no wild animals. Remember the wolves in Chicago!" I yelled, and we fell to slapping each other on the knee and could hardly stop from laughing.

Finally we come back to ourselves and Tom slowly nodded his head in agreement, as if with something I had said.

"Every wound," he said, "every stitch and broken bone used to give me a feelin' of pride . . . my own little dance with death . . . it intensified my life. Now, to tell you the truth, they just *hurt.*"

He offered to take me for a spin in the Cord. I wasn't too enthusiastic about the idea, remembering what kind of driver he was, but I went along anyway. Maybe he'd learned caution. No such luck.

"Open the glove compartment," he said.

There was a silver flask inside. I took a drink and passed it to him.

"I used to have a gold one," he said, "but I always thought it spoilt the taste."

We went tearing along some back-country dirt road. Coming down a hill he sent stones flying over the edge of the drop.

"They don't put up guardrails around here, Tom," I said.

"They're no good anyway, unless you're gonna go off the road."

We got back on the flatland and he opened it up. "You ever hear from Wilma?" he asked. Wilma was the girl I married once.

I looked at the speedometer. It was nearing ninety.

"Railroad crossing up ahead, Tom."

It always worked. He slowed down and in a few miles stopped to look at the saguaro cactus. We lit up cigarettes and passed the flask back and forth.

"She got the house," I said. "Wilma did."

"Sure a few women in this world did well on us," he said.

"Depends on what rock you're looking over. We done well on a few ourselves."

For a long time we didn't say a word. The desert has a way of making conversation worth less than silence.

Finally Tom said, "God, I love this country. You picked a good place, Kid."

He started the car and drove back to the ranch. We stopped in my cottage for a nightcap.

Once we was young together, when the years still lay before us like a cool rolling river. The Tom Mix I was drinking bourbon with only looked like the Tom Mix of before, minus about a pound of glitter. Going back even further, minus a pound of dust. But inside he had become somebody else and we was having a mite of difficulty conversing. For no reason he stood up and emptied his pockets on the table. He had a big roll of bills that he started to count.

"Six thousand dollars," he said, "and another fifteen hundred in traveler's checks."

"Hell, and I thought you was broke."

"This is it, Kid. It's all I got."

"Tom, we both know a lot of people worked hard all their lives and don't have that much to show for it." To prove it I emptied my own pockets. I had a hundred dollars and some change.

He pushed his pile of money towards me and said, "I want you to have it."

I figured the booze was getting to him.

"I don't want your money," I said.

"Go ahead. Why, when I was at Fox this was only one week's pay. I'm sure there was a time you gave me a week's pay. Now it's my turn."

We almost came to fighting over it, until I convinced him I had just enough money. Any more would only cause me problems. He accepted that explanation and stuffed the money back in his pockets.

I opened up two cans of sardines and put them in front of us, their lids curled back, next to our shots of bourbon. We had worked up an appetite arguing and took to eating the sardines. Halfway through we both kind of stopped and looked at each other. He was remembering, I could tell, but he said nothing and neither did I. But for one small second we was two cowpokes again, satisfied with ourselves.

I saw him off the next morning. The trunk of the Cord was too small for all his luggage, so one small metal suitcase had to go on the space above his seat. I shut the door after him and shook his hand.

"Tell me," he said, "do they still remember the Bandera Kid, these dudes that come here?"

"A few of 'em. But they all remember Tom Mix."

"Well, we had us a few good years out of it, didn't we?"

"More than anybody could hope for," I said.

About eighteen miles south of Florence, on Highway 89, a work crew was about to repair some damage to a dry wash. Quarter mile down the road they had set up a barrier and a detour sign. They saw the speeding trail of dust and followed it with idle curiosity, waiting for the yellow Cord that was causing it to slow down. It never did. It crashed through the barrier and hit the dry wash, flipping over. When they ran over to the wreckage, the workmen found Tom Mix, his neck broken by the metal suitcase thrown against it. There wasn't a mark on him.

ACKNOWLEDGMENTS

This kind of storytelling involves more than libraries and old newspapers and experts on the subject. It requires finding the people who were there and having them open up. Most helpful in this respect was Gene Forde, Tom's brother-in-law and friend. Others were Thomasina Mix Gunn, Yakima Canutt, Paul Wurtzel, Lilian Wurtzel Semenov, R. L. Hough, Duke Lee, Ollie Carey, George Marshall, Herold Goodwin, J. B. Avian, Ernestine Clark Baer, Millie Ward, Colleen Moore, Louis Breslow, Richard Arlen, Dorothy Dwan, Marion Levin, F. B. Kelley, and correspondents across the country too numerous to mention.

In addition, I am obliged to Robert S. Birchard, a young expert on silent films in general and the career of Tom Mix in particular. Grateful acknowledgment is also extended to Vicky and Jay Midgley, Jerry Zeitman, Bernadette Benson, Judy Christensen, Alleen Nellman, William Halter, Ed Howe, Alex Gordon, William Self, Mr. and Mrs. Gerald Oppenheimer, Charles Higham, Buff Brady, Sam Garrett, Sid Kellner and the George Matthews Great London Circus, Circus World Museum, *Amusement Business, Ladies Home Journal, Photoplay, The Life and Legend of Tom Mix* by Paul Mix, *The Fabulous*

Tom Mix by Olive Stokes Mix, *The Western* by Fenin and Everson, the New York Museum of Modern Art, the Academy of Motion Picture Arts and Sciences, *Variety*, the Tom Mix Museum in Dewey, Oklahoma, and Twentieth Century-Fox Film Corporation.

Today, a Thriftymart stands at the heart of Mixville. Old Blue, Tom's first movie horse, lies buried somewhere below the asphalt of its parking lot. Tony's gravesite has been kept a secret. That of Tom Mix, in Forest Lawn Cemetery, is marked by a simple stone. The site of his fatal crash is marked by the statue of a riderless horse.

Teresa "Teddy" Eason committed suicide shortly after Tom was killed. Stumpy died peacefully shortly after Tony was put to sleep. Kid Bandera never existed.

Victoria died in 1964, a victim of alcoholism.

Tom's first daughter and last wife are alive, but chose not to be interviewed by the author.

His second daughter, Thomasina, now lives in New Zealand.

Relatively few of the two hundred sixty films made by Mix have survived. Decomposing nitrate ignited in a storage area and destroyed a good number of his Fox films. Others were routinely destroyed to clear out old stock. Most of what remains can be found in the Czechoslovakian Film Museum, Prague.

D.P.